MW01520344

DRIVEN TO KILL
VEHICLES AS WEAPONS

J. PETER ROTHE

THE UNIVERSITY
of ALBERTA PRESS

Published by
The University of Alberta Press
Ring House 2
Edmonton, Alberta, Canada T6G 2E1

LIBRARY AND ARCHIVES CANADA
CATALOGUING IN PUBLICATION

Rothe, J. Peter (John Peter), 1948–
Driven to kill : vehicles as weapons /
J. Peter Rothe.

Includes index.
ISBN 978-0-88864-487-9

 1. Automobiles—Social aspects.
 2. Violent crimes.
 3. Traffic violations.
 4. Road rage.
 I. Title.

HV6493.R68 2008 364.15 C2008-900627-5

The University of Alberta Press is committed
to protecting our natural environment.
As part of our efforts, this book is printed
on Enviro Paper: it contains 100% post-
consumer recycled fibres and is acid- and
chlorine-free.

The University of Alberta Press gratefully
acknowledges the support received for
its publishing program from The Canada
Council for the Arts. The University of
Alberta Press also gratefully acknowledges
the financial support of the Government
of Canada through the Book Publishing
Industry Development Program (BPIDP) and
from the Alberta Foundation for the Arts for
its publishing activities.

In memory of my son, Nicco, whose spirit will always reside within me—my eternal flame!

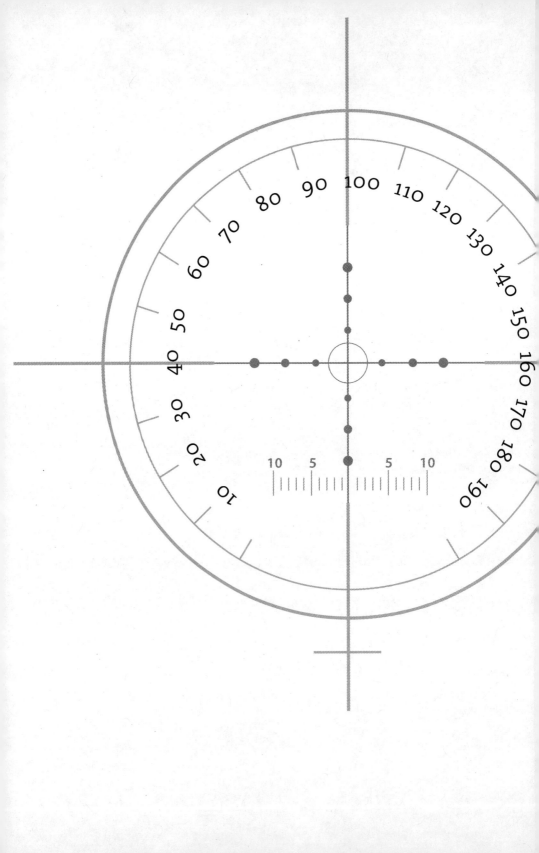

CONTENTS

SECTION III:
THE IMMEDIATE ZONE

15: SUICIDE 175

16: CAR BOMBS 187

17: HOMICIDE 195

CONCLUSION 205

POSTSCRIPT 209

APPENDIX:
THE INQUIRY PROCESS 213

FOREWORD

Peter Rothe systematically documents the variety of ways in which violence in society is perpetrated through automobiles. This specific theme runs throughout the chapters and is brought out clearly and forcefully, often in a relentless shocking manner that may disturb as well as inform readers. The author's recognized expertise in the sociology of traffic enables him to present the evidence in the context of social norms, laws, and widespread practices associated with automobiles, transportation, and drivers. The descriptions rely on empirical data and statistics from traffic safety sources, including newspaper reports.

Rothe speaks with authority and knowledge in an effective journalistic writing style. Unlike some of his prior authoritative works, this book avoids the technical style that is common in scientific volumes, and instead provides students and researchers with extensive research and scholarship. *Driven to Kill* contains a rich trove of information collected and organized around the theme of vehicular violence. It is a fascinating read that will evoke discussion among professionals, educators, journalists, and the general public. Traffic safety experts and law enforcement officials will find it eye-opening to read the many horrifying details of how people use motor vehicles as deadly attack weapons or as aids in committing criminal behaviour. Some readers may find the thorough coverage of vehicular violence in a wide range of social contexts disturbing. *Driven to Kill* is a wake-up call to society to engage the topic of vehicular violence and begin to work on solutions and mitigations.

Rothe stays close to the subject, but shows how each different type of vehicular violence is related to social practices in a community. Readers interested in social issues related to automobiles and transportation will find here information that is easily comprehended and assimilated. Other books on road rage and aggressive driving are relevant, but do not cover the systematic range of social areas found in this book.

During the first century of car society, the use of automobiles has steadily diffused into every layer of industrialized living. The daily round of urban and farming activity relies on the wheels of vehicles that are driven on streets, roads, highways, docks, and parking lots. This is all useful and good, but these same instruments of good have also been abused, as is evidenced by the anti-social behaviour of some drivers. To quote Peter Rothe's opening paragraph:

> Homicide, road rage, carjacking, drive-by shootings, smash and grabs, hit and runs, police chases, auto theft, auto break-ins: the list goes on. Thousands of North American drivers have become victims of such pernicious daily acts.

Rothe argues that in order to rescue "our deeply troubled traffic safety system" we need to understand how motor vehicles have been integrated into both normal and criminal behaviour. People not only drive to work in their cars, but along the way they also use cars to settle relationship battles when they are angry or feel provoked and justified to retaliate with violence. The author's research on how vehicles hurt people has uncovered evidence everywhere, justifying the serious announcement in the Introduction: "Vehicular terror is ubiquitous." More than one hundred million motorists and passengers in North America are exposed to the potential of roadway violence daily. Rothe observes that "auto-centred violence" is seen as a "common subset of an increasingly violent society." It is a wake-up call to read that "automobiles kill more people than do all weapons combined" that are used in homicides.

Realizing the seriousness of violence engendered by cars and trucks, we want to know how vehicles lead to violence. How does "automobility generate violent intentions and actions"? What kinds of people do these things? How is it justified and normalized in their group or community? These questions receive concrete answers in the careful way in which Rothe has collected and presented the evidence. He finds data that support his basic assumptions of the causes of roadway violence, and weaves them into a comprehensive, rational account that provides social and legal solutions. Car owners attach symbolic value to their vehicles as objects of glory, power, convenience, and image. This is extended even further in criminality to include "machismo, strength, control, and attitude." The evidence presented shows that car thieves "display professional competence, skill, and pride through illegal and violent means." It is common practice for some men who are affected by romantic problems or insecurity issues to jump into their cars and act out their emotionality through risk-taking "bravado" in the form of vehicular-based violence.

The stories of violence committed with cars cover three "zones of relevance." The first is more distant in the sense that the automobile is used merely as convenient tool for getting to the scene of the crime. For instance, a drug dealer sells crack cocaine from his car. A robber gets to the victimized store by driving there. People use cars to get to overpasses, which become launching platforms for deadly projectiles that are either thrown or dropped onto other road users. About six per cent of all robberies in Canada occur in parking lots, which are also the source for half of all the cars that are stolen. The next relevant zone is the use of the vehicle to successfully complete a criminal act. For instance, a woman is sexually assaulted in a half-ton truck parked on the side of the road. Or, a road rager pursues another car, and shoots the driver. The closest zone of relevance that violence and vehicles have is the use of the car itself as the weapon of attack. For instance, police stop the driver of a suspected stolen vehicle, and the driver suddenly backs up, striking the officer who is approaching the stopped car.

The violent use of a vehicle also occurs in legal situations like the demolition derby. Rothe sees this practice as helping people take out their "automotive frustrations," yet he also worries that such derbies can "potentially increase aggressive driving in general." Even riskier are the "death-defying thrills" in motorcycle demolition derbies, where riders try to knock each other off their bikes–the winner being the last one standing. Illegal street racing in cities has become a "ubiquitous feature of our society" that causes hundreds of deaths each year. But it is likely to get much worse. One practice that is spreading is the "centipede," where young drivers form a convoy and play follow-the–leader, "darting in and around regular traffic at high speeds."

Rothe reviews statistics and research on the general connection between violence, alcohol, and illegal drugs. Half of all people accused of a crime in Canada have admitted to using alcohol or illegal drugs. Alcohol and crystal meth are two major factors that affect the increasing danger associated with the random violence to which motorists are exposed on city streets. Rothe is not trying to be alarmist, but wants to "help reveal our social context, which is replete with social problems that indirectly and directly affect our lives on the public roadway." While many people already experience this daily situation with concern and perhaps some anxiety, the specific details Rothe has collected in *Driven to Kill* can help lead to a general resolve to begin recovery procedures that counteract the deteriorating trend through adaptive social and educational practices.

In the final portion of the book, Rothe lays out his proposal for "social and psychological audits" to investigate the circumstances surrounding collisions and vehicle violence, and in particular, the "antecedent circumstances" that eventuate in the event. This kind of data gathering would involve personnel in investigation, criminology, justice, and traffic safety, and I might add, sociology and psychology. Rothe's proposal will require expanding the focus from the driver to "family, friends, colleagues, lovers, employers, and other individuals linked to potential aggressors." We learn from this book how it comes about that roadway violence is part of the regular pattern of actions that are practiced in a society. People are motivated to practice violence via many existing social psychological conditions that include image, power, control, gain, revenge, anger, and prejudice. By invoking the principle that "to be forewarned is to be forearmed," Rothe presents us with the vivid information about some of the frightening things that occur in the streets where we live, work, shop, drive, park, and recreate.

Leon James
Professor of Psychology
University of Hawaii
Co-author of *Road Rage and Aggressive Driving*
(Prometheus, 2000)

ACKNOWLEDGEMENTS

Acknowledgements are typically reserved for friends and colleagues who contributed to the success of a manuscript. This is not one of those acknowledgements. With the passing of my son to suicide, the days of my life have been a nightmare. Two very special women helped me out of the death-wish spiral. Linda, my new wife, whose deep love, patience, kindness, empathy, sympathy, and full understanding of my pain and anguish provided me the ongoing comfort that allowed me to be tearful. She helped me find the strength to complete this book. When my light was dimming, she caught the manuscript before it hit the flames. My sister, Bridgette, continually checked on me, shared her sadness and pain so freely, and supported me in ways that few ever would. She was a pillar of strength.

INTRODUCTION

L'enfer, c'est les autres.
Hell is other people.

— JEAN-PAUL SARTRE

Homicide, road rage, carjacking, drive-by shootings, smash and grabs, hit and runs, police chases, auto theft, auto break-ins: the list goes on. Thousands of North American drivers have become victims of such pernicious daily acts.

These are not the behaviours of just angry or impatient teens. Rather, they are easily the acts of mature men and women seeking revenge or enforcing their personal standards of roadway morality. They may be the acts of spurned lovers, sociopaths, or ideologues. Vehicular terror is ubiquitous.

In the past, most roadway violence was viewed as deliberate driving-related acts targeted at other roadway users (Drug and Crime Prevention Committee, 2005). However, this view overshadows such vehicle-based dangers as carjacking, armed robbery, physical assault against targeted victims, rape, premeditated gang shooting, or suicide (Law Reform Commission of Victoria, 1991).

It is time to give more than a cursory glance to our deeply troubled traffic system. The public must understand that significant traffic safety events have criminal intents: people use motor vehicles to create death, injury, social suffering, economic hardship, and emotional destruction. Vehicles that transport us safely to our destinations can also render widespread harm.

The descriptions in this book are not intended to be alarmist; rather, they serve as a reminder that we are all potential players in the drama of roadway violence, whether we are instigators, victims, or witnesses. Anyone can be a potential victim regardless of status or personal history. Everyone's destiny can be determined by other roadway users at any time of the day.

We benefit from the convenience of automobile travel, which may be why our abhorrence at vehicle-related mayhem quickly fades. Our initial shock at hearing of another vehicle-related crime becomes acceptance that auto-centred violence is a common subset of an increasingly violent society. It is not that we don't care. Rather, we don't understand the widespread impact. For example, few of us know or think about the fact that automobiles kill more people than do all weapons combined. In 2005, the homicide rate in the United States was 4.7 per 100 000 people (U.S. Department of Justice, 2006). In the same year, the motor vehicle accident death rate was 15.7 per 100 000 (Professional Research Consultants, 2005). The most dominant weapons are firearms. Yet, although we insist that firearms have strict controls placed on them, it would be diffi-cult to insist that motor vehicles require similar controls. If we raised the issue on a radio talk show, the airwaves would bounce with disbelief. Who would endorse, for example, the proposal that cars or half-ton trucks with more than 400 horsepower engines should be banned, or certain makes of cars should not be shown on television? How would the following suggestion resonate with television viewers: "If we don't get cars off the roads and keep them out of the hands of kids, we're going to have more bloodshed"?

Aggression is a cornerstone of violence and Darwinians remind us that hu-man beings require a level of aggression to survive. It is an essential part of being human. The intensity of aggression increases as we become more frus-trated or stressed, or as we become exposed to repeated intrusions into our lives. Furthermore, we live in a society of chaotic norms of conduct where previous vices like envy, gluttony, greed, lust, and wrath are now celebrated (Hankiss, 2006). We can now "kick ass," "show attitude," and "do our own thing" without normative censure.

When rage, retribution, or the urge to harm others enters a person's mind, a motor vehicle can be a convenient weapon-at-hand. The weapon can be directed outward to harm others or inward to harm oneself. Either way, the violence can easily be camouflaged as an accident, or it can be redefined as the result of an accident. By using vehicles for violent engagements, the perpetrators feel more secure about escaping detection and responsibility.

The problem of violence engendered by cars and trucks is serious, and should be acknowledged as such. This book recounts incidents of this violence in a di-rect manner. It seeks to answer questions such as the following:

» How does automobility generate violent intentions and actions?
» What does vehicle violence look like?
» Who are the victims and victimizers?
» How is vehicle-related violence produced, normalized, legitimized, supported, and dramatized?

Roadway violence is not an esoteric, melodramatic, or rare event. It is an escalating public problem. An interesting story was told to me at a conference. The story was about a social experiment that a professor performed with his undergraduate class. He asked students to respond to the following scenario:

» You're in a hurry to drive home, and you're tempted to take a shortcut across campus by driving around a barricade with a sign stating that the road is closed except to buses and emergency vehicles.
» Just as you start to drive around the barricade, an elderly stranger steps in front of your car.
» The stranger points to the barricade and tells you to back up.
» You ask him to move, but he won't get out of the way.
» What would you do to resolve the conflict with this pedestrian?

The majority of student responses were surprising. Rather than co-operation, they chose forms of violence as their first option. The most common response was that if they were the driver, they would not back off. The onus was on the pedestrian to move under the guise of threat. Common tactics of aggression were expressed and animated. Some students answered that they would tell the man to move or else they would hit him, inch their vehicle forward until he moves, or move him with their cars. Some students said they would yell obscenities, give the elderly stranger the finger, or otherwise show their displeasure before backing off. Rarely were students prepared to converse and co-operate with the pedestrian, asking him politely to stop blocking their way.

Such social experiments present us with more questions than answers. What should or can we do about people who confess they are prepared to assault others who obstruct their goals? Little can be achieved if we regard the problem as one of individual aggression. The bigger issue is to explore the extent to which violence in traffic has reached the silent majority—us.

How immediate and real is the situation? The Internet is full of sites detailing how to cut brake lines, engage in drive-by shootings, or purposefully run into a vehicle to make it look like an accident. As well, people have created many ways to use vehicles for violent intent. Children are drowned in sinking cars, pedestrians are run over, and robbery victims are locked in car trunks where they suffocate. Sometimes, vehicles are used to counter authority: they hit police officers or bomb government buildings. There are commercial ventures, such as organized car theft and the illegal transport of immigrant workers, who die of suffocation or hypothermia in trucks.

A FRAMEWORK FOR MAKING SENSE OF VEHICLE VIOLENCE

The phrase "vehicle violence" includes a wide array of intentional behaviours and social situations that result in death, physical and psychological harm, economic losses, and property damage. The violence varies in severity, frequency, immediacy, and the extent to which the vehicle serves as a primary or secondary platform for engaging in harmful activities. This variation presents a challenge in trying to develop a conceptual scaffold that is comprehensive.

Vehicle violence—sometimes called roadway violence—is usually conceptualized as a complex interplay of four major factors: the person, situation, vehicle, and culture. These factors interact when a driver confronts a "triggering" event (an event that causes or determinately influences a violent reaction).

Person-related factors include characteristics such as the perpetrator's personality, belief systems, age, gender, and transient states of being, such as stress and pressures at the time of an incident (Novaco et al., 1990; Novaco, 1991). It also includes individual attributes of impulsivity, mood, frustration, and propensity to take risks.

Situational factors include scenarios such as roadway congestion and traffic volume, work pressures and family strains—potential preconditions for anger and aggression.

Vehicular factors pertain to the different roles motor vehicles play in the commission or experience of violence. Cars are used as battering rams, shooting platforms, bomb sites, or accessories to crime. Their presence may convert a normal life situation into a crime scene, as in the case of robbery, assault, or theft.

Cultural factors signify generally accepted social rules of behaviour that prevail in a community. De facto issues in which norms, folkways, or mores influence our daily conduct are competition (e.g., survival of the fittest), profit (e.g., personal enterprise to succeed financially), sexual dominance (e.g., male's dominance over female), concept of justice (e.g., eye for an eye), revenge (e.g., get even). The extent to which we openly express anger and frustration, the right to arm oneself (in the United States), the right to self-defence, the right to defend personal property, and the right to spousal loyalty are a few social mores that, when threatened, can lead to violent response.

Most cultural norms are unremarked features of life. We know what we can and should do, but we don't need to think about why we do things. These norms serve as an unseen hand that guides us into action.

BASIC ASSUMPTIONS

A series of principles or working propositions were developed to serve as a worldview or horizon of meaning for vehicle violence.

- » People are inclined to view their motor vehicles as icons of modern times, instruments of glory, image, power, convenience, and fast transportation. They impute meaning to their cars and trucks on the basis of appearances, symbols, and messages, and the relationship among them.
- » Driver behaviour is influenced by media messages that introduce criminality as a preferred way of life—an urban, inner-city, romanticized notion of machismo, strength, control, and attitude.
- » The auto-centred transport system is seldom fundamentally challenged.
- » Traffic safety stakeholders have typically closed their minds to, or denied, the role played by industry in modelling distrust, dishonesty, self-interest, and criminality.
- » Males still dominate Western society, ruling "automobility."
- » Vehicle-related criminality often involves incumbent criminals who display professional competence, skill, and pride through illegal and violent means.
- » A type of bravado can characterize some emotions or feelings, especially in men who believe that personal problems such as a broken romance or loss of a job demand a dramatic release.
- » Human beings have control, authority, and primacy over the earth's dominion. As self-proclaimed stewards, they take what is good for humankind, regardless of the cost to nature.
- » People are not lone wolves. They are influenced and constrained by the groups to which they belong.
- » People have learned little from historical trends and even less from past illegal, immoral, or questionable actions such as state violence and terrorism. They live and believe in the present reality as it is constructed for them by influential spokespeople.
- » When something gets better, it often happens that something else has become worse.
- » People typically view vehicle violence as naturally occurring traffic safety accidents or normal events.
- » People are constantly negotiating their private self with their public self.

These principles guide the stories in this book. They provide an orientation by signifying relevant social patterns that help cultivate motor vehicle violence. They allow us to investigate changing traffic and/or social circumstances, and the differing social effects upon driver behaviour. They also give us a window through which we can better understand the pre-eminence of social psychological factors that play in the minds of perpetrators—their motivation, for example, to seek and perpetuate ideology, fulfill personal or corporate greed, become aggressive as a sign of self-image, or seek to become invincible.

ZONES OF RELEVANCE

When we speak of motor vehicles and violence, we distinguish violent enactments according to three zones (layers) of relevance: the mediate, intermediate, and immediate zones (Schutz, 1970). These zones reflect a kind of continuum, whereby each one represents a degree of closeness to the heart of a violent behaviour.

The first zone is referred to as "mediate." It includes perpetrators who use motor vehicles in a tangential way to produce violence. For example, a victim's car is stolen while she is asleep in her bed. She wakes up and confronts the thief, who then smashes her head with a tire iron. In another example, a drug dealer sells crack cocaine from his car, a criminal act. He gets out of his car and follows his customer to the coffee shop, where he knifes him for failure to pay cash. The car is merely a form of transportation and a place to operate a business venture, albeit an illegal one. In these situations, the vehicle provides a driver or passenger with access to violence. It plays only a mediate role. It serves as the prelude to violence, or an entry point for questionable behaviour that leads to further bad behaviour which escalates to physical violence.

In the "intermediate" zone, the vehicle plays a major role in the facilitation of violence but still falls short of being the blunt instrument. For example, a van is used to kidnap a corporate executive; a young woman is sexually assaulted in a half-ton truck parked on the side of a gravel road; a trucker is held up, robbed, and beaten by bandits; or a young gang member shoots a motorist from a moving sedan in front of a nightclub. In each case, the vehicle is vital in the launch of the intended violence, or it represents the platform from which violent outbursts are engaged.

The final zone encloses the violence and animates its pulse. We call it the "immediate" zone of relevance. The motor vehicle, akin to the smoking gun, is the instrument of terror. It is used to facilitate suicide, intentionally hit pedestrians, batter other cars, or become a mobile coffin in which kidnappers stuff victims in the trunk and kill them through neglect.

Although, at first blush, these three zones of relevance look like discrete entities, they are more integrated and fluid than they are distinct. They often interrelate, obscuring in practice what is unique about them. For example, a car is stolen. The victim loses her property but she is not physically harmed. However, the police spot the car driving down a city street and give chase. Officers stop the thieves and, while they are approaching the stolen car, the driver slams the car in reverse and strikes down one of the officers. Now the vehicle is directly involved in the violence. A stolen car becomes infused with a changed purpose and meaning. This example suggests a line of progression whereby each successive level of involvement towards the immediate violence subsumes its outer layer as the action becomes more aggressive (Rothe, 1979).

THE STORIES

To underline the social dimension of violence, this book acknowledges that violent incidents are experienced at the personal level. Incidents of vehicle violence siphon emotions, create worry and fear, deprive us of well-being, and create suffering and pain. The case studies throughout provide vivid images of victim and aggressor. They are summarized accounts of my previous research projects that have included data from court cases, medical examiner or coroner files, media stories, published and unpublished research reports that include anonymous interviews, and Internet articles. Please see the appendix of this book for more about how the research was compiled.

The lenses of this book are set on Canada and the United States, with a few selective excursions to elsewhere in the world. The goal is to portray events that are close to us, rather than loosely describe unfamiliar or even exotic events that give different meaning to vehicle-based violence.

To gather a comprehensive collection of all motor-vehicle violence would be a formidable task. Therefore, this book presents the tip of the iceberg. It is intended to create awareness and begin debate about traffic safety.

Finally, although this book started out as a scholarly work, it soon changed its orientation to reach a wider audience. The manuscript is grounded in scholarly analysis but can be read as a documentary, with occasional leaps into theoretical and philosophical debate.

SECTION I:
THE SOCIAL CONTEXT

The unexamined life is not worth living.

— SOCRATES

We are not isolated automatons living in a vacuum. We are located in a social context, within which we assign meanings to our activities and order to our priorities (Berger & Luckmann, 1967). We absorb normalized actions and thoughts offered by our elders, colleagues, friends, neighbours, lawmakers, business representatives, and politicians. We attend to shared rules and conventions assigned by the many institutions to give us some social and temporal certainty. Our social context not only embeds our actions, but it orients us towards appropriate and inappropriate behaviours.

Driving a vehicle involves complying with a number of social conventions. Many influences, however, contribute to the formation of a violent attitude and aggressive driver behaviour. These influences include institutions like the family (e.g., poor role modelling); education (e.g., student competition, bullying, co-operation); the media (e.g., violent movies, dramatization of the news); sports and recreation (e.g., demolition derbies, computer games); government policies (e.g., human rights, property ownership rights); and corporations (e.g., competition, executive greed, profit). Collectively, these and others form a social context with wide implications for our attitude and behaviour in general, and behaviour leading to vehicle violence in particular.

If different institutions in society consider risk taking as a positive characteristic and support it through word and deed, then it is likely that citizens may consider stretching social and legal norms as preferred ways of doing things. Furthermore, individuals are attentive to powerful symbols and metaphors expressed by institutions—such as "survival of the fittest," "the early bird gets the worm," "winner takes all," or "profit at all costs"—that represent ideological interests of corporatism, nationalism, competition, profit, ambition, power, and control.

This section explores the influence our social context has on behaviour, with an eye to understanding the grounding of vehicle violence in our social environment.

1
ROADS ET CETERA

THE DECEASED: Sandra West, a wealthy 37-year-old Beverly Hills socialite.

THE BEQUEST: Her estate worth about $3 million, most of which is left to her brother—provided he made sure she was buried "in my lace nightgown and my Ferrari, with the seat slanted comfortably."

WHAT HAPPENED: That's how she was buried, surrounding the Ferrari with concrete so no one would be tempted to dig it up and drive away.

— *The Best of Uncle John's Bathroom Reader*, 1995

First I crawled, then I walked, and then I rode a bike. Now I drive—travelling short and long distances. A few months ago, I bought a new Nissan Altima. All of my friends came to look it over, kick its tires, and congratulate me as if I had accomplished a great feat.

I am hooked on cars, taking life-threatening risks in order to save seconds on my way to the supermarket or to work. I drive four blocks to the gym, then circle the parking lot in search of the ideal spot that will save me ten steps. Now in the gym, I put on my workout clothes and head for the treadmill, where I spend thirty minutes walking at different speeds. Unfortunately, I am surrounded by others who have driven only to go jogging on an exercise machine. After a pleasant shower, I hop into my car and rush to my next destination.

At the heart of this daily routine is the symbolic meaning that motor vehicles have for North Americans, a value that has been ingrained in our minds through the media and consumer ideals. The motor vehicle is an icon of modern times, an instrument of glory, image, power, comfort, and immediate transportation. After years of living with our cars and trucks, we identify ourselves with vehicles on the basis of appearances, symbols, and messages of prestige. The pool of symbolic meanings has given rise to a car culture, which has become a pillar of our social context.

THE CAR CULTURE

Car culture results from our daily interactions with vehicles: our need and desire to own, show, and drive them, and the values we place on them. Cars are built and demolished. They are sold, leased, and stolen. They are given as gifts. They are raced. Insurance agents gamble on them. Lovers undress in them. Organizations magnify the importance of them. We talk to, plead with, threaten, and caress them. We give them male or female forms. "Today's troubadours no longer use mandolins but car horns," mocked the Russian composer Igor Stravinsky. "The way a man drives a car is the way he would like to be," joked Italian actress Anna Magnani.

The intense love affair between people and their cars is an outcome of corporate ideology expressed in marketing the motor vehicle as a symbol of convenience, excitement, glamour, self-esteem, personal identity, and expedient transportation. In the auto-promotion world, "Image is not everything. It is the only thing" (Moorhouse, 1983). We watch, listen, and buy into the message. We want the car not only for mobility but also for appearance and pleasure.

Keith Magee, the former general manager for Ford's Lincoln-Mercury division, noted that creating a positive image to the public "can add value beyond just what the individual product represents" (Serafin, 1995: 101). In a profit-driven car culture, auto manufacturers are "image shaping." The vehicle is often advertised as demonstrating affluence (luxury sedan), romance (limousine), family-based practicality (mini-van), sex (sports car), machismo (suv or half-ton pickup truck), or feminine-valued transportation (small, convenient, sporty Volkswagen Beetles) (Burns, 1999).

Cars are cool. Pop culture promotes the image of cars as an extension of cool people. Cars project both masculine and feminine imagery, carrying erotic appeal for both genders (Freund & Martin, 1993). Cool people execute cool physical acts, conversation, and symbolic showmanship with nonchalance and sophistication.

Different vehicles demand different driving styles. Young bloods roar their customized Hondas and Toyotas on city streets, strutting a cool reserved for "top guns." Urban cowboys broadcast their machismo by lane-hopping their oversized and overpowered half-ton trucks through traffic-congested city streets. Leather-clad bikers live their vision of devil-may-care freedom through their Harley-Davidson motorcycles. In each case, cool is based on what one person perceives another to think of him or her. It's cool to be different, live a high-risk lifestyle, pursue goals aggressively, and demonstrate symbolic violence.

Spin-doctors spend endless hours delving into people's cognitive processes so that advertisers can subliminally influence groups to behave certain ways (Lopiana-Misdom, 1997). Often the imagery created by advertisers subtly translates into threat, danger, and ferocity. Cool car names are an example. Jaguars, Cougars, Cobras, Lynxes, Broncos, Panthers, Firebirds, Vipers, and Thunderbirds symbolize powerful predators. Rapiers, Magnums, Lacers, Excaliburs, and Stealths represent weapons. Fuegos, Dusters, and Tornados refer to violent storms in the natural world (Marsh & Collett, 1986). MG Spitfires suggest World War II combat planes. Chrysler Intrepids reference fearless warriors. The mystique is extended into the world of motorcycles, with names like Triumph, Shadow, Virago, Screaming Eagle, Mean Streak, and Intruder. All of these vehicle names give the impression that by owning and driving one, we enter a metaphysical experience that makes us believe we can defeat the laws of physics and energy conservation (Hankiss, 2006).

In some cases, there is an association between the car maker and the desired characteristic of the car. For example, although there is a tendency for companies like Mercedes, BMW, Saab, Audi, and Lexus to emphasize the corporate name and not the model (e.g., Acura 3.5RL and 2.5TL), many of the names still evoke images of predation, weaponry, sleek aggression, and charisma. In fact, letters like EX, XT, SS, or LL placed behind a car maker's name generate a sense of vehicular performance and excitement. The metaphor can be further applied to auto design, where vehicle grills, headlights, and front-end architecture can create rush or repose. For example, the Dodge Durango, built by Chrysler, has a front end that looks like the face of a savage jungle feline. The vertical bars across the grill represent carnivorous teeth, while the vehicle's bulging fenders over the wheels give the appearance of clenched muscles in a vicious jaw. Meanwhile, the Mercedes sedan is designed to establish a more relaxing and distinguished feeling. Its features are symbolic of luxury, prestige, and aloofness.

ROADS AND HIGHWAYS

The lifeline of most Canadian and American communities is a grid of roadways. Roads dissect the landscape, and we use them as key indicators to develop a cognitive representation of geography. In an auto-saturated continent, drivers will always find enough streets to flex their muscles. As Jane Holz Kay discussed in her 1999 article, "The Overheated Car Culture," more than half of North American cities are asphalt roads and parking lots. They provide the infrastructure for increased use of the automobile, which seduces us to be increasingly reliant on the car and decreasingly on walking or biking.

Roads are considered part of the "commons," a resource for the individual and common good (Hardin, 1968). Unfortunately, heavy traffic congestion on many urban roadways during rush-hour traffic has limited people of their equal rights to reliable and timely transportation. Furthermore, some drivers' self-interest, narcissism, aggressive behaviour, and criminal intents have challenged our safe use of public roads, contributing to a tragedy of the roadway commons (Garrett, 1968). The roads are becoming increasingly high-risk to the point where the police can barely manage to keep them safe.

People seek and prize personal space, defined here as the region that surrounds a person, the area around our physical being that we consider to be our domain or territory. It is our comfort zone, an invisible boundary that, if crossed or violated, can produce or increase our tension levels significantly (Sommer, 1969). Personal space is culturally sensitive. According to Sommer, North Americans prefer more personal space than people in other parts of the world.

The personal space that we draw around ourselves is extended to the perimeter of our vehicle. For example, we may not like a person leaning on our new car when it is parked near a football field or in a parkade. Furthermore, when we drive, we assume that the roadway immediately in front of and behind us is ours, albeit for a brief moment. When we travel down the highway, we take ownership not only of the space within the vehicle, but also the psychological space in front of and behind it. We feel violated when other drivers infringe the zone by tailgating behind us or cutting too close in front of us. We have difficulty tolerating such manoeuvres, believing them to be belligerent or threatening. These actions can evoke our most primeval reactions (Marsh & Collett, 1986). We are quick to retaliate by disciplining the offensive driver (raising our middle digits, honking our horns, shouting obscenities), or by complaining bitterly to our passengers about the breach of our space. Our anger about tailgating may become so intense that we purposefully manoeuvre our vehicle to obstruct the other driver.

Modern North American roadways are designed primarily for motor vehicles and secondarily for pedestrians and bicycles. Large sums of money are spent each year to construct new roads and to resurface, restore, or rehabilitate old ones. Although the goal is to maintain roadways for efficient public transportation, some roadway designs offer situations that are ideal for constructing violent acts. For example, curvy mountain highways are ideal locations where drivers who want to take their own lives can do so by running off the road, smashing into the mountainside, or tumbling down a canyon. In some American cities, bandits can run up to cars stuck in traffic because of poor roadway design, smash the passenger windows, grab the purses, wallets, and laptops in the front seats, and flee on foot.

Cars on freeways can be moving targets for someone bent on criminal action. Millions of motorists travel at high speeds on four-, six-, or eight-lane freeways. A driver, passenger, or pedestrian can easily shoot at another's windows, or throw dangerous items at them (like rocks, hammers, or baseballs). The protagonist always has a good chance of escaping. In the autumn of 1996, gang members drove around California's freeways and threw hard projectiles, smashing more than 200 rear windows (Fotsch, 1999). This series of actions became part of a new pastime known as "moving vehicle vandalism."

OVERPASSES

Overpasses are convenient concrete roadway designs that are integral elements in urban and rural landscapes. They facilitate efficient and fast traffic, particularly at exit and entry points to freeways. Overpasses can also be pedestrian and bicycle bridges, most of which are not fenced. They can also be unprotected railway bridges.

Although transport planners and engineers develop overpasses for the convenience of drivers, the structures are routinely used for dangerous actions against innocent drivers. According to the U.S. National Highway Traffic Safety Administration (NHTSA, 2003), there are frequent reports of fatalities, major injuries, and property damage at overpasses. Projectiles vary from mannequins, bowling balls, tombstones, and kitchen appliances to cement blocks and boulders. The organization reported that in 2002, the United States had seventeen fatalities caused by thrown or dropped objects from overpasses. In Edmonton in 2006, a teenager dropped a basketball-sized boulder from an overpass on the Whitemud Freeway. The boulder smashed through the windshield of a school bus and killed its driver instantly. (CBC News, 2006).

PARKING

Vehicles must have space to rest when they are unoccupied, and so they are parked in lots, garages, and on streets. Most prominent are garages—commonly designed as featured parts of houses. Cities and other smaller urban areas are saturated with public and private spaces reserved for vehicles. Drivers use them for a minute, an hour, or a week for a set amount of money. As the number of vehicles on the road increases, so must resting stops. Parking lots and garages have become dominant features of urban landscapes, particularly in the business or downtown sectors of cities.

Unfortunately, parking lots and garages have become breeding grounds for criminal activity. Many lots are unattended, isolated, and poorly lit. Women in particular fear parking lots. Statistics Canada's Violence Against Women Survey was completed in 1993 with 12 300 women who were 18 years of age and older. The survey asked respondents to rate how worried they would feel if alone at night in four situations: a) walking in their neighbourhood at night, b) taking public transport, c) using a parking garage, and d) being home. Of those who reported using public transport, 3 out of 4 stated they were somewhat or very worried using this service after dark when alone. Approximately 4 out of 5 women who used cars stated that they were very or somewhat worried when entering parking lots at night (Scott, 2003).

Women have good reason to be scared. About 6% of all robberies in Canada occur in parking lots (Statistics Canada, 2005) and about 50% of vehicles stolen are removed from parking lots. A review of Juristat's Canadian Crime Statistics (2003) tells us that the location of criminal violence against persons includes the category of "parking lots." Whereas the majority of violations in 2002 occurred in private residence, 3.6% of all homicides, 4.1% of all assaults, and 5.7% of all robberies happened in parking lots (Juristat, 2003).

Drivers and passengers are easy targets for assailants or thieves. Eiseland (1990) detailed how a young nurse fell prey to a murderer in an unattended four-storey parking garage located in a "low crime" area of Sioux Falls, South Dakota. The predator was hiding in the shadows of the dimly lit parking structure. After carefully observing his prey's movements, he attacked. He beat the nurse, forced her into his car, and drove out of the garage undetected. He later raped and murdered her (Eiseland, 1990).

The attack was severe, but not unusual. Parking lot assaults occur frequently and they have an international scope. The Liability Consultants in Massachusetts analyzed 1000 premise liability lawsuits between the years 1992 and 2001. They found that almost one-third of all cases reviewed comprised murder, rape, robbery, or assault that occurred in a parking lot or parking garage. Verhoek-Oftedahl and Silverman (2002) reviewed research on family violence. They reported that of the rape and sexual assaults recorded in four national American surveys, consisting of 78 000 female respondents, 3.5% of the stranger-stranger and 2.5% of the non-stranger type of assaults happened in parking lots or garages. (Incidents were classified as "strangers" if the victim identified the offender as a stranger, did not see or recognize the offender, or knew the offender only by sight.)

Parking lots vary greatly in shape, size, and use. They may be giant high-rises, subterranean multi-level structures, or flat lots at small retail centres. But one thing overrides all structures: potential safety. Three factors determine parking lot safety: the design of the parking lot, crime history, and location (McGoey, 2002). The crime rate of a parking lot can be affected positively or negatively by its design. For example, large high-rise or subterranean structures can have poor visibility because of walls, pillars, and elevation changes. Large, flat parking lots attached to regional malls can offer car thieves or assailants ideal opportunities to watch for security measures and plan escape routes. The time of day, amount of traffic, and the use of parking lots make a difference to the relative safety of each particular lot. As the evening's darkness creeps in, some parking lots become blacked-out entities with no available witnesses to observe what goes on (McGoey, 2002). Employees working late are vulnerable to attack as they approach their vehicles.

Parking lots outside of nightclubs or bars have different problems from those adjacent to a day-use professional office building. Nightclub and bar parking lots typically have a history of crime, especially if they are located in low socio-economic parts of the city where there is a high crime rate and where there is poor lighting for drivers and passengers to see potential threats at night. Parking lot lighting plays a central role in safety and security for the people who come in and out of bars when it is dark.

Predators like to hang out in parking lots to find potential victims. To camouflage their intent, they pretend to talk on nearby telephones, walk nonchalantly near parked cars, or sit in their car and spy on others, sometimes behind the façade of a newspaper. The aggressors like to get close to their intended victims before they strike. Shoppers often walk to and from their vehicles lost in their own thoughts, unaware of what is going on around them. They fumble for their keys in their pockets or purses as they try to hold on to their purchases. They turn their backs and attention completely away from individuals nearby to load their shopping bags into the car, and settle their children inside the vehicle (McGoey, 2002). Would-be assailants take note and act.

Although drivers need to be cautious in parking lots, the responsibility for a lot's safety is incumbent on businesses that own or lease them. A federal judge in Texas fined Wal-Mart $18 million because it gave incomplete and false evidence in a lawsuit involving an abduction from a Wal-Mart parking lot. The abduction had resulted in rape. The judge found that Wal-Mart had falsely stated that it had never conducted a study of crime prevention in its parking lots, did not disclose the identity of the vice-president involved in the study, did not disclose articles he wrote about the study, and did not disclose previous lawsuits against the retailer about sexual assault in its parking lots (Norman, 2004).

From a design perspective, new parking lots are more likely to incorporate Crime Prevention through Environmental Design (CPTED) principles, such as proper lighting, visible pay phones, open areas for escape, with markings that are easily seen by people experiencing emergencies. Roaming cameras are more commonly used with increased surveillance staffing. Still, there are many smaller parking lots whose owners do not subscribe to these principles or cannot afford to implement them.

Parking lots are also sites of increasing stress. Our nerves get frayed when we return to our parked vehicle and find a dent in it because another driver settled into a parking space beside us and recklessly opened the door. Our frustration and anger has little opportunity for constructive release other than transforming into disdain for other drivers. Whereas most drivers do a slow burn and get over it later, some drivers bang the doors of the other vehicle or bump into it as they leave the lot—a symbolic form of competition.

But who can blame the careless door openers? Parking spaces in many shopping malls are eight feet wide. Place three luxury-sized cars or half-ton trucks side by side and door-opening space becomes a fraction of what is needed. Planners, squeezing that one last space into a parkade, often leave patrons with navigation problems and dented doors.

RACETRACKS

With the motor vehicle's iconic value to our lives, it is consistent that we celebrate motor vehicle rituals. Arguably, motor sports are top spectator sports in the United States and Canada. NASCAR racing is presently rated as the most watched sports event in the United States. Formula 1 races are legendary, a celebration of technology, speed, skill, and drama. Road rally racing, another popular competition, involves skilled drivers and navigators driving highly modified production cars, challenging time, weather, and roadways. Stock car competition, a variant of touring races, involves modified stock cars racing around an oval. In drag racing, the drivers pit their highly developed speed machines against the clock, completing a 400-metre, straight strip of road in the shortest time possible. Other forms of racing are karting, off-road racing, sports car racing (LeMans Endurance Series), truck racing, and various forms of motorcycle racing. People pay large sums of money to sit in the stands and cheer high-risk performance.

Spectators can be injured when parts fly off stock cars. A car can hit racing officials and pit crew members are always in danger of getting run over. Drag races are probably the worst. Cars that use altered or rocket fuels are at serious risk. Engines can explode, and when parachutes fail to open, extremely serious crashes occur. Mark Hamrick (2004), quoting from findings published in the Associated Press, reported that twenty people involved in drag racing died in 2003, and there have been 318 drag car racing deaths since 1990.

One of the most controversial, yet prevalent, cultural celebrations is the demolition derby. In our car culture we not only prize and adore the vehicle, but we brutalize it to celebrate it. Participants purchase and build cars to destroy them intentionally. The last car still moving wins.

We may argue convincingly that drivers use demolition derbies as physical outlets, a kind of running of the bulls that would make Hemingway squirm. Eight to twelve specially prepared cars are sealed into a gravel bull pen, measuring around 50 by 100 feet, where they pummel each other until only one—the winner—is left running. Demolition derbies are more than mere sport for the audience. They help take out a person's automotive frustrations in a (relatively) safe, controlled forum. Nevertheless, they can potentially increase aggressive driving in general. Albert Bandura (1973) asserted that a culture can produce highly aggressive people by valuing aggressive accomplishments, furnishing successful models, and ensuring that aggressive actions secure rewarding effects.

While in a conventional auto race, the winner is the car that finishes first, in a demolition derby, the winner is the car that finishes. Period! A demolition derby connoisseur named Conniff (1999) suggested that to appreciate a demolition derby, you don't have to understand racing: "You don't have to understand anything." It is an "unspeakable charm of destruction. Drivers put their brains in boxes and go hell bent to destroy and win."

Some risk takers have developed this search for destruction and death-defying thrills to unusual lengths in motorcycle demolition derbies. Riders try their hardest to knock each other off the bikes. The last biker still riding is crowned the winner and takes home the trophy or prize money. Helmets are required, but hurting one another is not only allowed, it is promoted.

The demolition fad has spread to the use of school buses, where participants drive the buses into a blocked off arena, listen to a countdown, and once the green light is given, back into each other at high speed in order to disable each other. The last bus running is the winner. Because school buses have an extended rear overhang, they sometimes crush the back ends until the buses are shortened up to the rear wheel wells. This adds to the excitement and brings a roar from the audience. According to a popular bus demolition website, "Kids love this sport because they love to see the buses they hate get destroyed" (Members Tripod, undated).

Organized motor sports reflect the norms and pulse of a society. Sport psychologist Lynn Jamieson (2002) suggested that we have a society where people are increasingly infatuated with violence, whereby violence is one of the leading causes of death for people aged fifteen to forty-four worldwide. A person's sensation of violence and aggression is easily transferred to professional sporting events like motor sports—especially demolition derbies, where spectators imagine themselves to be potential combatants. Spectators feed off the savage actions of sporting figures, venting their frustration and diverting their attention from their own problems, potentially blurring the line between racing violence and everyday life. A large part of the social context reflects the need to satisfy increasingly aggressive individuals by creating such violence-based opportunities.

STREET RACING IN CITIES

City streets are usually considered to be transportation routes lined by commercial outlets, service centres, residences, and other buildings. But in many

North American cities, such as Vancouver or San Diego, the streets are not the commons for all to use for transportation. They are racetracks. Supercharged, rebuilt engines are transplanted into sleek, customized cars that launch down city streets in a hiss of nitrous oxide and high-octane fury. Street racing is an illegal and highly dangerous event. Young people put their lives on the line for financial rewards, glory, and self-respect.

Street racing has become a ubiquitous feature of our society where the competitive impulse is characterized by customized, high-speed cars on public roadways, as represented in the movie *The Fast and the Furious*. The National Hot Rod Association (2003) quoted the NHTSA's finding that in 2001, illegal street racing in the United States produced 135 fatal crashes, an increase of 72 from the year before. San Diego, often referred to as the capital of street racing, reported that 16 deaths and 31 injuries were directly related to illegal street racing (NHRA, 2003). The following case from British Columbia in 2006 demonstrates the spontaneous nature of a street race that led to the death of an innocent bystander. Names and other identifiable information have been changed to preserve anonymity.

Sandy, who had prior convictions for breaking and entering and a poor driving record, drove a yellow BMW. At 2:30 one morning in Vancouver, he was returning home from an evening of playing computer games when a white Mitsubishi Gallant came up behind him, repeatedly flashed its lights, and then passed him. Sandy sped up so that he could catch up to the Gallant. A street race ensued. A customized Toyota Matrix joined the BMW and Gallant in their race.

As the three cars roared towards an intersection, Sandy's BMW was in third position, travelling between 180 to 200 kilometres per hour. He was weaving in and out of traffic to help him advance his position relative to the Gallant and Matrix. No one slowed down. Mr. Leery, a retired local citizen, had just disembarked from a southbound bus and was walking at the crosswalk. He had crossed at least four traffic lanes when he was struck down by the BMW. According to Sandy, the collision occurred in the curb lane, while his competitors were in the other two northbound lanes.

It is a wonder that the two lead vehicles just missed the pedestrian, who was more than halfway across the street when the racers suddenly appeared to his right. Mr. Leery dashed toward the east side of the road when Sandy struck him. It is likely that Sandy and the pedestrian did not see each other until the last moment because the other two racers blocked their views. Mr. Leery died on the spot.

The judge who heard the case told the court that the accused knowingly and willfully risked his life and the lives of others. As a consequence, he killed someone. The judge stated that society is determined to isolate and punish those associated with such behaviour. He sentenced Sandy to four years in prison for causing the death of Mr. Leery by criminal negligence. He further sentenced the young man to six months' imprisonment concurrent for hit and run. Sandy was prohibited from driving anywhere in Canada for ten years and from possessing firearms, ammunition, or explosives for ten years. Finally, Sandy was ordered to provide a body sample for DNA analysis.

In another case in Toronto in 2006, two eighteen-year-olds were racing in a posh Toronto neighbourhood. One of the racers hit a taxicab, killing the driver immediately. A copy of a popular video game simulating car races was found in one of the cars (CBC News, 2006, January 28).

In the United States, according to figures from the NHTSA, street racing caused 125 deaths in 2004 (Valiquet, 2006). In Canada, data are difficult to obtain about street racing because neither the Canadian federal government nor the insurance industry tracks related casualties. One unofficial report, based on media tracking, indicates that at least fifty people in Canada die each year because of street racing (Neil, 1999). Because street racing is unofficial racing where the course is improvised and timekeepers, spectators, and racers appear through an informal underground network, official statistics are difficult to find (Peak & Glensor, 2004).

Street racers also participate in side attractions. One event is the "centipede," where young people form a convoy of vehicles and play follow-the-leader, darting in and around regular traffic at high speeds, or they engage in 360-degree burnouts at intersections. Most noticeable is the arrival of a novel, yet high-risk, version of street racing called "drifting," where the operator drives sideways down a road at high speed. Rather than straighten out the swerving car, the driver over-counters so that his car goes into another drift and swerves the other way. The ideal setting for the sport is a mountain road where there are numerous sharp "S" turns strung together. To prepare for the mountain challenges, young men and women in their early twenties practise in parking lots. Toyota Corollas are popular drifting cars.

Drifting circuits are gaining popularity as adjunct motor events that are warm-ups to major car races like the Grand Prix. Travelling at increasingly high velocity from 20 to 120 kilometres per hour, the driver tries to lose traction by popping the clutch or pulling the side or hand brake (Morton, 2006). He begins to swerve and move into a full drift, with the vehicle pointing in one direction while the driver's head points in the other.

The growing interest in drifting is idealized in the movie Fast and Furious 3: Tokyo Drift, a favourite with teens and young adults. Although drifting is always dangerous, drifters deny the sport's high risk by saying they are not about to "injure the car on the wall."

IN SUMMARY

We can speak of roads, parking lots, overpasses, and racetracks as vital features for sustaining and promoting our reliance on motor vehicles and, at the same time, for contributing to violence. The spatio-temporal arrangements that give vehicles an elitist standing are part of a social context that supports and sustains an ideology of automobility (Freund & Martin, 1993).

DOMINATING
SOCIAL ISSUES

An artist must know how to
convince others of the truth of his lies.

— PABLO PICASSO

It is folk wisdom that is commonly shared in bars, living rooms, and on street corners anywhere in North America. We appear to live in an increasingly violent society. Criminologists and public health professionals agree that there is more violence in our homes, workplaces, public institutions, schools, healthcare facilities, and streets. The violence ranges from people with disturbed mental states who lash out in a fit of rage, to those who engage in planned acts calculated to gain advantage.

Statistics prove the point. The United States Preliminary Semiannual Uniform Crime Report, publicized by the U.S. Department of Justice (2006), has synthesized violent crime data into a table that shows percentage increases in crime between the years 2002 and 2006. American law enforcement agencies have noted sharp increases in violent crime (3.7%), murder (1.4%), robbery (9.7%), aggravated assault (1.2%), and arson (6.8%). In Canada, the adult violent crime rate, as calculated per 100 000 people, has decreased by 1.7% during the same four years (Statistics Canada, 2006). Still, 2006 provided 605 homicides, of which the killers most likely responsible were males aged 18 to 24 years, followed by males aged 30 to 39 (Statistics Canada, 2006). Furthermore, more than 84 000 young people aged 12 to 17 were charged with criminal offences in 2003.

Unfortunately, these numbers show merely the tip of the iceberg because statistics are collected only after the police become involved. The statistics do not accurately portray such incidents as sexual or physical assault because victims may not report their cases due to fear of reprisal by the attacker, suspicion by the police and courts, shame of being a victim, personal inconvenience, or the belief that nothing will come of the report. An earlier estimate by the U.S. Department of Justice, Office of Juvenile Justice and Delinquency Prevention (1999) stated that only 28% of violent crimes against juveniles become known to the police. This figure is substantially higher than the one for unreported adult victims. It is a reality shared by Canada.

Many claims about growing violence in society are related to imagery and text reported in the media such as the Internet and television. Websites present a continuous serving of gruesome footage of beheadings, torture, animal mutilation, sexual assault, and other sadistic acts. The spate of media-related research, however, still pertains to public television. For example, one prominent body of research literature demonstrated that watching television in the twenty-first century contributed to an increase in people's aggressive behaviour. Programming and information presented on television influenced people to place greater value on using aggression and violence to solve personal problems and conflicts (Huston et al., 1992). Furthermore, it increased people's desensitization of the seriousness of violence and instilled a greater tolerance of it. On the other end of the spectrum, some literature suggested that viewing excess violence on television produces a "mean-world syndrome," where viewers overestimate their risk of becoming a victim (Gerbner, 1994).

A third body of research literature proclaimed that blaming the media is too simplistic. Karen Sternheimer, a sociologist at the University of Southern California and researcher at the Center for Media Literacy, represented this perspective when she wrote to the American Sociological Association. She proposed that, contrary to the U.S. surgeon general's claim that the media causes violence, "If we want to understand why young people become homicidal, we need to look beyond the games they play." Placing the blame on the media exonerates the environment that a child lives in which might be nurturing the violence: poverty, instability, family violence, unemployment, and mental illness (Sternheimer, 2007). She criticized the surgeon general's cause and effect theory as being too simplistic because it did not include context and meaning. Sternheimer rationalized that society is saturated with social toxins like increased social stress, marital breakup, competition for survival, unemployment, and drug and alcohol abuse, which influence people's attitudes and behaviour towards each other. Violence or violent thoughts materialize, in part, because of such antecedent factors.

SOCIAL STRESS

Some call it "emotional stress," others refer to it as "dealing with daily pressures," and others suggest it is physical or emotional demands that people generally can't handle. Social psychologists call it "social stress": people's reaction to difficult situations in which social demands are placed on them that exceed their adaptive capacity to deal with them.

For example, research has shown that hostile behaviour during marital conflict seriously damages coping skills and mental health (Kiecolt-Glaser et al., 2003). It is no surprise, therefore, that divorce is a dominant stressor (Amato, 2000). In the United States in 2003, there were 3.8 divorces for every 1000 citizens (National Center for Health Statistics, 2004). In Canada, the divorce rate has been fairly stable over the last ten years: 2.31 per 1000 inhabitants (Statistics Canada, 2003c). The impetus for Canada's divorce rates was the implementation of the "no fault divorce" act and the reduced minimum separation time for spouses from three years to one year.

Divorce usually brings with it emotional turmoil, sadness, depression, and/or forms of aggression. As a culture, we have tried to minimize the devastation of divorce by providing support systems for divorcees and children. We take solace in the view that divorced partners go on to find happiness with a new mate. However, it is not that simple. The National Institute for Health Care Research (1998) suggests that a significant number of divorcees and their children experience emotional problems throughout their lives, showing up in increased emotional trauma, physical risk, and destructive behaviours.

When husbands and wives divorce, they split the family, severely altering the relationships children have with their father and mother. As a result, children can lose their sense of family, security, and attachment. They fear abandonment and experience first-hand the hostility between parents. They may be frightened and confused by the threat to their security, becoming vulnerable to physical and mental illness (American Academy of Child and Adolescent Psychiatry, 2004). Furthermore, children may hold anger within themselves, become more accident-prone, or become increasingly aggressive—all factors for engendering personal harm. Especially in their teenage years, children of divorced parents may become more resentful and angry, and may become involved in high-risk and violent behaviours (DeBord, 2004).

Divorce is not the only culprit. Social stress is also caused by such factors as unemployment, financial insecurity, bureaucracies, death, health problems, and increase in responsibility. As well, Chicago sociologists suggest that cities are inherently stressful because the high density of settlement causes anxiety and tension, creating conflict within and between individuals (Berger & Berger, 1975).

Social stress is often displayed as fear, anxiety, anger, and aggression among children (Lam, 1999) and adults (Carrère, et al., 2005). It can be readily apparent in traffic. For example, Selzer and associates (1968) reported in their hallmark study on anger and driving that a motorist's inability to deal effectively with anger can seriously degrade driving performance. People increased their risk of road rage or aggressive driving after they had recent experiences that left them uncertain and anxious, that were considered to be beyond control, or that were judged to be threatening. After statistically analyzing fatal collisions, the researchers reported that 20% involved drivers who had been in aggressive altercations within a six-hour period before their deaths. In Australia, the Victorian Community Council Against Violence (1999) concluded that social stress, caused by increased economic/workplace and social uncertainty, contributes to a greater probability of drivers becoming involved in aggressive and high-risk driving behaviours. Health professionals generally attribute part of the increase in driving "pugnacity" to social factors such as swelling congestion, urbanization, dual-income families, workplace downsizing that increases crowding, family discord, job dissatisfaction, and physical illness (James & Nahl, 2002).

Addictions researchers agree that many people turn to alcohol to help them cope with social stress (Cappell & Greeley, 1987; Krause, 1991). Stressful life events are correlated with alcohol dependence, which eventually results in health problems (Johnson & Pandina, 1993; Welte & Mirand, 1995). One of those problems is aggression and the propensity to become violent with a vehicle.

ALCOHOL

A common scene in North America is a young bartender working the lounge bar late Friday afternoon. It's the busiest day of the week, a perfect time to earn big tips. Office workers in the surrounding buildings look forward to Happy Hour so they can release the stress of a highly patterned workday. Some are aching from family troubles or financial problems; others hate their work or their colleagues, or they can't handle the responsibilities assigned to them. All are looking to have a few drinks to dull their worries temporarily.

This scenario is not unique. Alcohol is consumed to reduce stress and anxiety—to feel good. When problems erupt into our patterned lives, some of us increase our alcohol consumption to the point of alcohol abuse, which increases the potential for violence. We drink to feel stronger and in control when parts of our lives are out of control. Research in the United States shows that men drink primarily to deal with the stresses of life, escape problems, boost self-confidence, and feel more empowered. Research has further established that people for whom limited personal power is a concern continue to consume more liquor, triggering violent reactions in pressured situations (Parker & Rebhun, 1995).

Studies have also shown that injury and death due to intentional trauma are among the most important consequences of alcohol misuse (Gruenewald et al., 2002; McLeod et al., 2003). In the United States, the NHTSA announced that in

2005, 16 885 people died in alcohol-related motor vehicle crashes, representing 39% of all traffic-related deaths (NHTSA, 2006). The Canadian figure is slightly lower at 36%. Robert Mann (2004) took it one step further. He reported an overlap between road rage and alcohol abuse that results in low self-control, with frequent rule-breaking behaviour and general disregard for legal sanctions.

In 2005, the U.S. Department of Justice, Bureau of Justice Statistics found that about 30% of violent crimes involved an offender who had been drinking alcohol. About 66% of the victims who suffered violence by an intimate (a current or former spouse, boyfriend, or girlfriend) reported that alcohol was a factor. Among spousal victims, 3 out of 4 incidents involved an offender who had been drinking. By contrast, an estimated 31% of stranger victimizations were perceived to be alcohol-related (U.S. Department of Justice, 2006).

It is a truism that inebriated people are less likely to have control over their actions than those who are sober. For example, a husband is drunk and talks with his wife about their worsening financial situation. Conversation leads to quarrelling, which may lead to confrontation. The episode can easily end in violence, an escalation that is more likely to happen when alcohol is involved (Begona et al., 2000).

The prevalence of alcohol abuse in the family is a significant social problem. The U.S. Department of Health and Human Services (undated) quoted an American Journal of Public Health study from 2000 that found approximately one in four children aged 0–17 were exposed at some time before age 18 to familial alcoholism, alcohol abuse, or both. The American Academy of Child and Adolescent Psychiatry (1999) stated that a child living with alcoholic parents is more susceptible to self-injury, violence, and injury to others than children who grow up in more stable home environments.

Despite the intimate connection between alcohol and violence, we attend to a social standard that proclaims drinking alcohol is a "time out" from rules of normal social behaviour. "I was drunk at the time" is often used as an excuse for avoiding personal or legal responsibility (Shepherd, 1994). This excuse, however, is seldom accepted in court.

Whatever the cause for consuming alcohol may be, a factor that increases its use, and thereby increases the chance of violence, is access to alcohol. Government policies such as deregulation of liquor sales in some communities may be a contributing factor to people taking less social responsibility for their behaviour, as demonstrated in cases of fetal alcohol syndrome, obnoxious public and private behaviour, impaired driving, and a range of social and emotional trauma. The trend appears to be for more sales, more drinks, and more risky behaviour. For example, in Calgary, the number of liquor stores has increased more than tenfold from 23 in 1995 to almost 300 in 2003. Many are in close proximity of each other. Alberta has had the highest per adult alcohol consumption rate among the Canadian provinces, between 8.5 and 8.7 litres of alcohol per adult for fiscal years 1997–98 to 2001–02 (Flanagan, 2003).

This kind of proliferation of private liquor stores changes the character of a community. Police reports in Calgary document a rise in impaired driving charges and family violence cases in areas of the city with the highest density of liquor stores (BC Government Employees' Union, 2003). The finding is consistent with peer-reviewed research by Rossow (2002) and Ramstedt (2002) that demonstrated greater volume of alcohol consumption is related to higher levels of mortality for violent deaths and suicides. The findings are consistent with a position paper published by the Centre for Addiction and Mental Health (2004), which stated that one of the mandates of alcohol monopolies—to control drinking-related harm—has eroded. Meanwhile, alcohol marketing and promotion agendas have gained ground.

Robert Nash Parker (Parker & Rebhun, 1995) wrote an interesting book about the relationship between homicide and alcohol outlet density. After he acknowledged the causes of inner-city violence, such as poverty, ethnicity, and family structure, Parker established that high liquor-outlet density is a major factor for high levels of violence in the areas in which the outlets are located. His twenty-year study of 256 American cities demonstrated that the country's increase in outlet density from 1960 to 1980 played a significant role in the skyrocketing violence during those years.

After the Cohen research team (2003) completed a thorough review of alcohol research literature, they concluded that "wetter" neighbourhoods have higher levels of alcohol consumption, traffic crashes, and violence. Su (2002) presented more local research on the relationship between liquor licence density and domestic violence in Baltimore, Maryland, by analyzing domestic violence and liquor licence data gathered from the Baltimore country police department and the Baltimore Liquor Board. He concluded that every unit increase in liquor licence density is associated with a 9% increase in domestic violence density. Gruenewald et al. (2002) concentrated entirely on bars located in communities. The study concluded that the density of bars is strongly associated with greater rates of assault on streets, in the home, and in motor vehicles.

Violence and alcohol consumption can happen in one of two ways. Violence may be the unintended outcome; for example, a drunk gets into a fight about car keys. Or it can be deliberate, where alcohol is consumed to create or facilitate violence. For example, the majority of people who attempt suicide consume alcohol beforehand, and some men will swig a number of drinks before they initiate fights with other bar patrons.

There is also a measurable relationship between drug abuse and violent crime. Both are part of a lifestyle that involves antisocial and deviant behaviour (Parker & Auerhahn, 1998). Rather than one causing the other, it is more appropriate to say that drugs and violence exacerbate each other. Some users become violent under the influence of drugs. Others engage in violence in order to obtain money for drugs. Drug dealers become violent to avoid police arrest, to compete with other pushers for a piece of the drug market, or to respond to a business deal where someone was cheated. P.J. Goldstein (1985) outlined the following aggressive patterns of interaction within the drug distribution and use system:

» disputes over territory between rival drug dealers
» assaults and homicides committed within dealing hierarchies as a means of enforcing normative codes
» robberies of drug dealers and usually violent retaliation by the dealer or his/her bosses
» elimination of informers
» punishment for selling adulterated or phony drugs
» punishment for failing to pay one's debts
» disputes over drugs or drug paraphernalia
» robbery violence related to the social ecology of local policing

A Canadian study of drug dealers on probation illustrated the extent to which their illegal behaviour is lubricated by violence: over half the drug dealers (56%) admitted they had used violence some time in their illicit activities (Casavant & Collin, 2001).

Although drug-related violence is common in American and Canadian cities, it is more likely to be featured in the media when territorial battles erupt between competing criminal organizations or gangs that are involved in drug smuggling (Criminal Intelligence Service Canada, 1999). The available data show that in Canada, between 1994 and 1998, there were 103 homicides, 124 murder attempts, 9 missing persons, 84 bombings, and 130 incidents of arson related to drug dealing and processing.

A crucial element of the association between drugs and violence is the chemical impact illicit drugs have on human behaviour. Some drugs are known to increase aggression, while others have a calming effect. For example, users who ingest large doses of amphetamines, cocaine, LSD, or PCP may experience violent outbursts (Rothe, 1994). Of special importance is PCP, whose chemical name is phencyclidine and is colloquially referred to as "angel dust," because it is second only to alcohol as the drug most often associated with violence (Boyd, 1991). It is well known for inducing violent behaviours and physical reactions such as seizures, coma, and death. It stimulates the nervous system, simultaneously acting like a hallucinogen, stimulant, depressant, and anaesthetic.

Methamphetamine, commonly referred to as "crystal meth," has spread quickly into mainstream society. It was once the drug of choice for bikers and truckers, especially for the latter when they wanted to stay awake on long journeys. It has now become popular with people from all walks of life. It affects the central nervous system and gives users a temporary high, which can manifest as unpredictable violent behaviour. The drug can lead to hallucinations, paranoia, and aggressive psychotic behaviour. Wild rages and mood swings are common, a state of mind that is particularly dangerous when or if the user operates a motor vehicle.

Some users of crystal meth experience the state of "tweaking": the crash at the end of the high that is accompanied by feelings of sadness and emptiness. During this time, they can pose a serious danger to others, who are perceived to be a threat to the tweaker. It can produce unpredictable, violent behaviour whereby the user confronts and assaults those whom he believes may threaten him. In the case of driving, those threatening a tweaker may be other motorists, casual pedestrians, or friends and family members in the vehicle.

Although there are no statistics to help define the nature or extent of the problem, the dangers posed by crystal meth users are evident in motor vehicles. The following case illustrates a real-life incident. Names and other identifiable information have been changed to preserve anonymity.

Jerry had been erratically driving a one-ton rental vehicle at speeds exceeding eighty kilometres per hour in a fifty zone, when he sideswiped the passenger side of a car that he passed at high speed. Instead of stopping, Jerry stepped on the gas pedal and made a run for it, heading west. He didn't get far. Heavy traffic congestion blocked his escape.

Jerry stomped on the accelerator and drove between two lanes of eastbound traffic, striking seven parked vehicles. Fortunately, there were no injuries. Although Jerry's truck had its front wheel sheared off, he refused to slow down. He tried to control the truck on three wheels at high speed but lost control. The truck went off the opposite side of the road and smashed against a light pole.

Onlookers surrounded Jerry while he considered escaping on foot. He spat on the paramedics that arrived. He was angry but not badly hurt. His stunt caused more than $80 000 in damage and scared the daylights out of the other drivers.

When Jerry presented his story to the judge, he talked about being high on methamphetamines at the time of the violent event. He had started a crystal meth binge the day before the wild ride, and he was high when the police caught him. He did not know the details of the incident; his mind was blank.

Jerry had been taking crystal meth for about two years before the orgy of destruction. On a previous occasion, he had been arrested for domestic assault and uttering threats while he was high. Jerry was always angry, experiencing aggressive urges. In court, he confessed to being an addict.

Jerry pleaded guilty to charges of attempted theft, mischief causing damage under $5000, physical assault, dangerous driving, and one count of hit and run after an accident. He was originally charged with fourteen offences under the Criminal Code.

The judge concluded that the crystal meth had undoubtedly aggravated the driving offences. He ordered Jerry to serve twenty-two months in prison with a twenty-five-month probation period. Jerry was considered likely to reoffend because of his addiction to crystal meth.

Jerry's court case illustrates the direct relationship between the use of crystal meth, property damage, and violent vehicular crime. Users may experience severe, terrifying thoughts and feelings—fear of losing control, fear of insanity and death, suspicion of everyone, anxiety and despair—while using the drug. They can feel several different emotions at once or swing rapidly from one emotion to another. The drug can produce delusions and visual hallucinations. Paranoia often sets in, where users believe that other people want to harm them. Hallucinations or delusions can result in violence, homicide, suicide, or self-mutilations (National Institute on Drug Abuse, 2005). When users are behind the wheel, incidents such as reckless or suicidal driving can follow.

Statistics Canada published a 1998 survey entitled *Homicide in Canada* in which the head researcher, Orest Fedorowycz, concluded that approximately 50% of accused persons had used alcohol or illegal drugs before committing their crimes. In 1999 another Canadian research team (Brochu et al., 1999) distributed questionnaires to all new prisoners who were incarcerated in federal penitentiaries. The answers showed that slightly more than half (50.6%) of the inmates had used drugs and/or alcohol on the day they committed the offence for which they were incarcerated. Among this group, approximately 16% had used illegal drugs only, and 13% had ingested a combination of drugs.

In Canada and the United States, some people use illegal psychoactive (mood-altering) drugs like cocaine and cannabis for recreation and ceremony. They produce euphoria, influence mood, change activity levels, reduce tension and anxiety, decrease fatigue and boredom, improve social interactions, temporarily escape reality, and heighten the body's senses. The majority of common citizens, however, ingest legal psychoactive drugs like caffeine, nicotine, prescription drugs (sleeping pills, pain killers, and general anesthetics), and over-the-counter medications like cough syrup and pain relievers every day. For many people, consuming these drugs has become routine. But, like cocaine, an overdose of sleeping pills or over-the-counter medications may cause an individual to become irritated and agressive while driving an automobile.

SOCIAL COMPETITION

Chicago sociologists Parks and Burgess (1925) theorized that social life consists of competition, which breaks down the structure of our communities and leads to social disorganization. Increased competition among individuals is considered to be an ideal basis for developing our society's leaders in government, education, and industry.

Competition is now a fact of everyday life in North America. We compete for our necessities: food, clothing, shelter. We also compete for wealth, power, luxuries, and social standing. Our educational system is based on competition, one student against another for the highest marks. Our federal, provincial, and local governments are themselves built on competitions called "elections" where candidates win or lose. Furthermore, people from different backgrounds compete against one another to gain favour with the government and to lobby their needs. As consumers we are always looking for the best deals—quality products at the lowest possible price. Our society is consumerist and profit-driven. It highlights self-interest, illustrated by the statement, "If I don't get all I want now, someone else will, which means there will be less for me." This self-interest can spur people to take additional risks at work, at home, or on city streets.

Self-interest in traffic stems from the assumption that people are the centre of their own worlds, seeking what they believe is in their best interest and avoiding that which is not in their interest. The search for personal best interest beyond all other goals leads us into competitive situations with others who also seek what is best for them. Nowhere is this more evident than on our public roadways. For instance, conflict theory suggests a struggle between different road users exists in traffic, whereby users compete for space and time to reach their destinations or achieve their transport goals. Each driver strives for a piece of roadway, for which other roadway users also aim, whether they are pedestrians, cyclists, truckers, motorcyclists, or general motorists. From a competitive point of view, we lay claim to the immediate area before our car, a space to which others are not welcomed. Witness the excess passing that occurs on extended roadways where trucks, buses, and slow-moving vehicles are usually passed so that drivers can gain clear views of the road, release themselves from confined driving, and provide themselves opportunities to drive fast and unobstructed.

It is the job of traffic planners and highway engineers to develop systems that limit competition and induce consensus. Unfortunately, such systems mostly assign priority to the automobile: they design lanes, roadways, and intersections for convenience of the driver. By formalizing the priority of the car, planners have tried to reduce the competition between pedestrians, cyclists, and motor vehicles (Surface Transportation Policy Project, 2003). Still, a competition remains. Pedestrians try to beat cars as they scurry across the street and cyclists seek room on busy roadways. Drivers jump red lights or screech off the mark when a signal light turns green to gain advantage. Unfortunately, that advantage is often little more than a gained car length at the next traffic light. A hollow victory!

UNEMPLOYMENT AND POVERTY

Our lives revolve around our capacity to buy. Economics is the locomotive that allows us to live the way we do. It is no surprise that economic inequalities, such as low-earning capacity and unemployment contribute to property and violent crimes (Hagan & Peterson, 1995). The discrepancy in opportunities for differing socio-economic groups within society is a key factor in criminal behaviour, and is manifested in such motor vehicle-related crimes as auto theft and vandalism.

Widespread and chronic unemployment within a community fosters a social context that could be described as a "culture of unemployment," where people routinely experience low self-esteem and motivation, have normalized poverty as status quo, and where unemployment is inherited by the next generation. Research has shown that people living in poverty are more likely to be victims of or witnesses to intentional violence (Cohen et al., 2003).

Poverty may be described as erosion of hope and opportunity. The poor are disempowered from making important social and economic decisions that affect their lives. Individuals are marginalized. By being consistently denied privilege and power, they can easily internalize their disempowerment into an "I am less worthy" attitude. This mindset can lead to a search for escape through drugs and alcohol, which may contribute to violent acts.

Economic deprivation reaches straight into the cities, which have excessive concentrations of people living in assisted housing in segregated poor communities. As cities increasingly become privatized, investment-oriented, consumer entities, the underemployed and unemployed poor become relegated to geographical zones, with the spillover effect of losing social services and or having reduced physical services, such as roadway maintenance and street lighting. The potential for delinquency, crime, and gang violence increases in these neighbourhoods, and, as we note later in this book, the presence of street gangs increases the possibility of drive-by shootings.

Furthermore, the poor are less likely to be able to afford safety products such as bicycle helmets, or to properly maintain their vehicles. Children from impoverished families are more likely to play on public roadways and come into harm's way than children with greater economic resources. National Safe Kids in the United States and Safe Kids Canada report that low-income children are twice as likely to die as pedestrians in motor vehicle collisions, four times more likely to drown, and five times more likely to die in fires than children from households that are not low-income (National Safe Kids, 2004: 2).

Poverty has generational consequences as crime is perpetuated over time. For example, children who grow up in impoverished neighbourhoods have an increased probability of committing property crimes and engaging in violent acts (McCord et al., 2001). The opportunities for car crime, such as auto theft, drive-by shooting, and carjacking, are accentuated (Nettler, 1989).

IN SUMMARY

When we transpose social problems onto the roadway, we become more aware that when we are in our automobiles, there is a reasonable chance of meeting a road user who has abused drugs or alcohol, is desperate, or whose behaviour is unconventional and risky. The intention of this statement is not to be alarmist but rather to help reveal our social context, which is replete with social problems that indirectly and directly affect our lives on the public roadway.

SYMBOLS AND MESSAGES

Bad faith consists in pretending to ourselves and
others that things could not be otherwise—that
we are bound to our way of life, and that we could
not escape it even if we wanted to.

— MARY WARNOCK,
The Philosophy of Sartre, p. 53

Many of us remember with smiles on our faces how Bugs Bunny asked his foe, "What's up, Doc?" We laughed when Wile E. Coyote tried to catch the Roadrunner through deadly technological innovations. Yosemite Sam tried to blow up Bugs Bunny; Pepé Le Pew sexually harassed a female cat for romance. Trains, trucks, and cars ran over Elmer Fudd while he tried to shoot Bugs Bunny or Daffy Duck. Sylvester the Cat fell off high buildings or was electrocuted while trying to catch Tweety Bird.

These cartoons signify competition, conflict, violence, and aggression wrapped within humour. Bugs Bunny, a cunning, outspoken rabbit, was not belligerent, but a mischievous respondent who used his wits to outmanoeuvre opponents intent on violence. Yet one of Bugs's catchphrases was, "Of course, you know this means war." Notably, much of the violence included vehicle chases and vehicles purposely running over the characters.

Bugs Bunny is part of American pop culture. His image is iconic, symbolizing that hate, revenge, and envy are cultural realities that can be overcome by creative tricks. Opponents are seeking violence, death, and destruction—but they lose. Violence is normalized and laughed at via television. The cartoons were first aired in the 1950s and they are still being shown today. Many of those still watching are adults.

It is often said that North America is a media-mad society. We place an overwhelming trust in media and rely on it for everything from information and entertainment to interaction for romance and friendship. Any description of vehicle-induced violence must include the media's influence on the glamouriza- tion of symbols, images, and textual messages that contributes to that violence as an everyday phenomenon. Violence always attracts attention, creates intense reaction, and mobilizes the presses.

THE MEDIA CULTURE

Images are manufactured and managed to influence impressions. Signs and symbols are manipulated to give an impression of "what is, and what should be." In the corporate and political worlds, especially, "Image is everything." Car makers spend millions of dollars to convey favourable images to consumers, investors, and their own employees through specialized use of words and vi- suals (Serafin, 1995). Silver convertible coupes force city dwellers to turn their heads and gasp enviously. SUVs can climb mountains. Sports cars are faster than fighter planes. Because we are easily seduced by such images, automak- ers search the globe for spin-doctors to create corporate and product identities through metaphors, names, slogans, symbols, repackaged ideals, automobile de- signs, and the promise of a better and brighter motorized future (Burns, 1999).

Images are constructed to guide people in making sense of the world in pre- defined ways. Hence, people use media-generated images to construct mean- ing about political, social, legal and economic issues (Burns, 1999). Media offer people explicit or subliminal frames to solve problems or take future action, as demonstrated in a commercial about a Pontiac sub-compact car that suggested a driver being chased by the police is a game of wits that the car wins.

Recently the American Medical Association's chair of the Board of Trustees discussed how television constitutes the backdrop to a child's life. He quoted a Kaiser Family Foundation study in which researchers Rideout, Vandewater, and Wartella (2003) concluded that children over eight years old watch nearly twenty hours of television each week. Children develop brand identification at a very young age. Young children were able to recall the advertising slogans for certain breweries like Budweiser. Through their exposure to beer commercials, the children had internalized that drinking beer is acceptable practice. Media strategies used were symbolization, normalization, glamorization, glorifica- tion, recognition, and sublimation. Similar tactics are used in the auto industry. Automakers and affiliated industries are leaders in image-making, whether that be nationalism (Americans drive a certain kind of vehicle to baseball or basketball games), sportsmanship (SUV drivers help stranded skiers up a snow- packed mountain), elegance (couples drive a slick black sedan to a college gradu- ation ceremony), adventure (half-ton trucks sit precariously on mountain ledges for extreme sight seeing), blue-collar reliance (construction workers use tough four-wheel trucks to pull huge trailers), femininity (young, beautiful women wrap themselves around cars on the beach), freedom (semi-trailer trucks roar on a lonely desert road at dusk), and family stability (mini-vans are filled with children and parents laughing and playing).

Seductive media slogans, such as "Live heavenly and raise hell," "Just do it," or "Get it while you can," also may produce images of sensation seeking, exploitation, and risk taking. They can serve as moral imperatives. In January 2008, Ford Canada pulled their advertisement from a Winnipeg newspaper because, in hindsight, they recognized the power of symbols. The ad read, "Drive it like you stole it," followed by "Built for Life in Manitoba" (*CBC News*, 2008). Still, symbols of sexuality, power, aggression, triumph, speed, revenge, war, and explosion appear in all kinds of advertising, news stories, television shows, and movies. Such symbols have now become mainstay features on many websites and in video and computer games.

Typically, media portrays two forms of extreme violence: assault on innocent citizens by thugs roaming the streets; and organized violence where calculating professionals or victimizers pursue their quarry, who are socially but not personally known to the criminal. For example, movies portray a member of an organized crime syndicate pointing a gun at the head of a disarmed rival gang member and telling him, "Don't take this personal. It is only business."

But FBI and RCMP statistics show that in past homicides, three out of four victims knew their assailants (Catalano, 2003). Domestic or family violence topped the list of murder cases, usually carried out by men against women and/or children, caused by suspected or real spousal disloyalty, arguments over finances, male dominance over women, or family break-ups (Catalano, 2003). Yet, in polls held across North America, citizens are more likely to fear being killed or raped at the hands of a complete stranger. It is an undue fear of victimization dependent on media images of frightening events that is independent of crime rates. They remind people that danger can strike at any time or location, and that life is tenuous and precious (Warr, 2000).

Media expert Mark Fishman (1978) noted that competition for audience share in a hot adversarial media climate encourages media sources to be the first to "get the story," even if it is based on distorted or incomplete understanding of the facts. This situation has evolved into a basic truism as witnessed by the constant battle for viewer ratings between Fox TV and CNN (Rutenberg, 2002). The one-upmanship has been further magnified with the introduction of quick and sensational news items reported in blogs and citizen journalism on the Internet. As well, television now offers around-the-clock cable news. Once an event such as murder-suicide by car has been identified and reported, other related stories on, for example, traffic mortality or vehicular violence, have a greater chance of being covered. The aggregate of these stories can lead to an epidemic of media coverage (Hartman & Golub, 1999). Who was the victim? Was there political intrigue? Was the act shameful? Was it sex-related? Could it happen again elsewhere? Road rage is a case in point here: more than half the driving population in the United States, and close to that in Canada, believes they can become victims of road rage (James & Nahl, 2000). Their fear of victimization is fuelled both by the ongoing media stories that highlight sensational stories of extreme road rage violence and the high number of road rage events that have been documented recently in the research. The statistics are reported in dramatic ways that suggest anyone can be a serious victim at any time.

To begin to understand why the media has an impact, we must first recognize the explanatory power of the "theory of suggestion," otherwise referred to as the "imitation effect." Some people are so seduced by bouts of violence that they experiment, plan, undertake, mimic, or try to execute an act better than the original perpetrator did. Imitators are drawn to an original act featured in the media because of its uniqueness, the excitement of evil, the anticipated notoriety, the competitive potential to do better than the original actor, or to fulfill a hidden desire to do what someone has previously done. Ray Surette (1994), a prominent criminologist who has done extensive research on copycat crimes, contended that copycat crime is a persistent social phenomenon. However, the specific relationship between media coverage and the occurrence of copycat crime is still largely unknown, and specific factors in a social context influencing copycat crimes have not been identified.

Surette (1994) argued that copycat crimes readily fall within one of two North American groups that reveal themselves in the world of driving. On the one hand, "mode" copiers intend to commit a crime already and become informed of a successful method from the media. For example, a potential car thief learns how to break into and hot wire a car after watching a television police drama. On the other hand, "group" copiers imitate acts in groups. For example, a group of teens swarm an old man in the street because, earlier in the same week, other attackers had been granted probation rather than prison (Surette, 1994). Serious roadway violence that demonstrates copycat scenarios includes drive-by shootings, car bombings, and mechanical tampering of brakes to create a serious crash.

A significant area of imitation is vehicular suicide. Studies have shown that single car crash suicide attempts increase after the media has reported traffic suicides. Research in the 1970s demonstrated the existence of "cluster suicides" in which the local television reporting of teen suicides caused copycat suicides of impressionable youth. Potentially suicidal teenagers say to themselves, "I'll show everyone who has been mean to me," or "I know how to get my picture on TV" (Gould et al., 2003).

Bollen and Phillips (1981) were interested in the relationship between published stories of suicides and suicide attempt rates. They concluded that when a newspaper publicized an article on suicide, which was sometimes disguised as motor vehicle fatalities, there was a 31% increase in California motor vehicle suicides on the third day after the story was publicized. The study was replicated in Detroit. The increase in that city ranged from 35% to 40%.

The cause of crime is seldom uni-dimensional. However, different forms of media, with their power to reach mass and selected audiences, provide an ongoing barrage of symbols that have an impact on people's thoughts, feelings, and actions (Nettler, 1989). Media can stimulate benign sentiment and noble deeds as well as malign emotion and wicked acts.

MOVIES

In our culture, vehicular violence is replayed many times in the movies. Indeed, to look at the annals of movie history is to become familiar with the onslaught of vehicular violence on ordinary and extraordinary people. A car was rigged to transport moonshine in *Thunder Road*, to become a killing machine in James Bond movies, and a suicide vehicle in *Thelma and Louise*. In Steven Spielberg's early thriller, *Duel*, an anonymous, faceless trucker plays a deadly game of cat and mouse with a salesman (Dennis Weaver). The large eighteen-wheeler takes on the persona of a stalking machine seeking to kill a salesman driving a family sedan. In *Bullitt*, Steve McQueen is involved in a car chase that many critics consider to be one of the quintessential portrayals of speed, high risk, and excitement. *Smokey and the Bandit* is about a car chase between the police and a bandit (Burt Reynolds), taking us on a wild ride across the United States. *Christine* is about a dorky high-school student who enters into a dysfunctional relationship with his homicidal car. In 2005, the old television series *The Dukes of Hazzard* was given new life as a movie. Once again, Bo and Luke Duke use their souped-up 1969 Dodge Challenger to taunt the police into wild car chases with no legal or moral consequences.

More recently, the fad has moved towards street-racing movies. *The Fast and the Furious* (followed up by *The Fast and the Furious 2: Tokyo Drift*) details an inside look at the world of street racing. It has many wild car chases on city streets and the action is intense and illegal. Power, adrenaline, and victory are imprinted on the viewer's mind. In David Cronenberg's fetishist movie, *Crash*, traffic-crash death and carnage are portrayed as a sexual turn-on, and its on-the-edge eroticism mingles with the glory of the automobile.

Discussions about violent movies invariably turn to copycat behaviour. A Toronto police officer was of the opinion that *The Fast and the Furious* might have inspired a high-speed crash that left two dead and sent five young people to hospital (*National Post*, 2001). Vancouver police said that they were bracing for an upsurge in street racing after the release of the same movie. In Ottawa, a twenty-one-year-old man died after imitating a scene from the movie *The Program* in which young men proved their bravery and team spirit by lying in the middle of a busy highway (*New York Times*, 1993). After similar deaths in the United States, Touchstone Pictures cut the highway scene from the film. Many more stories have been reported in the newspapers about movie-related imitation crimes.

There seems to be an endless variety of movies that provide the audience with a populist framework for which risk taking and thrill seeking is cool, worthwhile, and advantageous. A number of movies glorify criminality through sensational stunt driving that, if imitated by ordinary drivers, would make a mockery of traffic laws. Some young people try copycatting high-risk driving. They admire the actors' clothes, physical appearances, accents, use of slang, sleek vehicles, and attitude towards taking risks and extreme actions. They desire to be like them (Woodrick, 1977).

VIDEO GAMES

We hijack a high-powered car, race it to a busy intersection, jump out, and start shooting everyone in sight. The police and rescue workers arrive on the scene. We blow them away with automatic weapons. We jump back into the car and head towards the mall, killing even more people. Carnage is everywhere. A disaster? No, this is a video game called *Grand Theft Auto: Vice City*. Parents hate it; retailers love it; teens play it. Video games have entered the mainstream media.

Programmers design these games, played extensively by teens, to glamourize aggressive and morbid elements such as torture, death, and maiming. They normalize extreme violence and the challenging of authority. According to psychologist Albert Bandura (1986), video games promote aggressive tendencies, leading to aggressive behaviour. His General Aggression Model (GAM) became the framework later used by researchers such as Anderson and Bushman (2002) to hypothesize that violent video games influence behaviour by promoting aggressive attitudes and desensitizing players to aggression.

A counter-claim to the General Aggression Model is the Catharsis Theory (Bushman and Huesmann, 2000) which states that playing aggressive video games has a relaxing effect on players because it channels latent aggression and tension, much like watching violent football or rugby games. The effect is positive. Aggression is dissipated through participation in the games. Participants and members of the audience can let off steam in a safe environment. Their aggressive urges and impulses can be purged by playing violent video games.

Although the Catharsis Theory offers an interesting point of view, it has been severely contested in the media literature, especially with the incredible growth of violent and graphic computer games.

MSNBC quoted sales figures produced by NPD *Funworld*, a trade publication that tracks video game sales and development sales. Video game software and hardware topped $12.5 billion in 2006, a 6% increase from 2004. Games rated "mature" because of violent content are the fastest growing segment of the game market, accounting for more than 13% of sales, compared to 6% in 2001. The market leader in 2002 was the mature-rated video *Grand Theft Auto 3* which sold more than five million copies (NPD *Funworld*, 2003). After having been betrayed by a girl during a bank robbery, the player is in a getaway car and intent on revenge. Mafia bosses need a favour, crooked cops need help, and street gangs want the player dead. So the participant is assigned missions to rob, steal, injure, and kill. There are more than 100 characters, and over 50 vehicles ranging from sports cars to ice cream trucks and boats to buses. Players have at their disposal a huge array of weapons to fight full-blown gang wars or undertake drive-by shootings. Is there an unintended message in the game? For many the answer is "yes." It implies that crime can be profitable. It assumes that violence in society is not only acceptable, but it is preferred. The motor vehicle is designed to be a dominant weapon.

Carmageddon 2, considered by video game officiados as "eye candy" to the gaming audience, like its predecessor, is all about racing and carnage. It is programmed for players to wreck cars, maim, and kill. Players earn points by driving over victims and animals. Bonus points are awarded for style. Within the same genre of games is *Midnight Club: Street Racing*, where players make their way up the ranks of outlaw racing clubs. Performance-enhanced cars are driven on busy city streets until a member of the illusive Midnight Club challenges one of these drivers to race. And so it begins! Players roar around city streets at breakneck speeds with little concern for property or life.

Violent video games present a dark mood of excitement. The visuals are movie-like superb representations of the real world. Cars blow up and crash. Players shoot, punch, kill, injure, and crunch without suffering or feeling pain. They die and gracefully depart; there are no funerals, bankruptcies, bereavements, or legal, moral, social, or cultural repercussions. The desensitization is similar to the training methods used in the military to motivate soldiers to shoot and kill the enemy without conscience or remorse. The games are examples of classical operant conditioning and role modelling. Young people learn to associate violence with pleasure, strategy, enjoyment, cunning, cynicism, competition, reward, excitement, and preferred lifestyle. A fear is that as young people become adults, they may interpret life events as a video game where violence is normal and acceptable.

POPULAR LITERATURE

Glossy magazines are filled with dramatic, far-out, practical, sexual, economical, and reverent images of motor vehicles. With photographs that tempt the eye, magazines penetrate the reader's consciousness, suggesting that everyone can realize their dreams or reinvent their lives by driving a featured vehicle. Readers can customize their cars so they look like Toronto dudes, Arizona desert bandits, Wall Street executives, Arkansas good old boys, or Alberta para militarists. Glossy magazines provide unlimited expectations, many of which cross the line of immorality and illegality. For example, Bonnie and Clyde, two of the most notorious American gangsters, have their get-away car iconized through endless magazine stories.

Today's magazines are specifically marketed to special interests, such as vintage and classic cars, street racing, lifestyle, youth, vehicle maintenance, sex and vehicles, violence and automobiles, militia action and vehicles, and so on. A glossy picture-saturated magazine named *DUB* has become a major player in the urban car scene, featuring outrageous customized cars of rappers and professional athletes with a suggestion of male assertion and sexy women.

NEWS STORIES

Many of us begin the day by flipping through the newspaper or clicking through an online news site while we sip our coffee and prepare to enter the outside world. We glance at the headlines and skim articles about earthquakes, political scandals, and traffic crashes. Our appetite for catastrophe is quickly satisfied. Yet, although we search for the dramatic, we expect news reporting to be truthful and objective.

The news is a social construct, manufactured from life events for public consumption. News writers employ a variety of techniques that help sensationalize events because that is what sells newspapers or gets ratings. Headlines are linguistic devices to attract the attention of the reader. Schudson (1995), a media analyst, suggested that newspapers are usually more than mere transmitters and receivers. They set the tenor of the story or they add something to every story they report. They are producers and interpreters (Frascara, 2004).

When newspapers, television, radio, or websites report news to the public, they confer legitimacy to stories. People read or listen to them and believe them, unaware that news writers amplify a certain perspective of events that often carry moralistic and ideological overtones.

"There is no terror in the bang, only in the anticipation of it," said the ultimate master of terror, Alfred Hitchcock (Glassner, 2000). Some news writers embrace this truism. Through the use of foreshadowing anecdotes, reporters can place an incident into the domain of imminent doom. In that domain, demented drivers, rather than poor public policies, inadequate policing, or inferior roadway infrastructure, occupy centre stage in the coverage of severe motor vehicle crashes. Stories about road rage seldom address government planning policies that allow for greater traffic volume than the roadway design allows, speed limits that are out of tune with traffic flow, and obstructions that restrict driver movement—situations that routinely cause drivers to lose their patience. Gunplay and drive-by shootings are reported as criminal acts of revenge rather than the unforeseen consequences of problematic government policies.

Do news stories contribute to greater violence? Reporters interpret events according to their beliefs and their editors' ideologies. Presenting such interpretation as fact may have measurable consequences. News stories that include inordinate portrayal of violence may also lead to copycat crimes, commonly referred to as the "hypodermic model" of crime.

A significant part of daily newspapers are the letters to the editor. They are a basic form of advocacy serving to demonstrate community sentiment on controversial issues. A wide range of opinions and concerns, agreements, or disagreements is served to the reader. For example, a popular issue is cyclists. Some letters have expressed violent thoughts, as is illustrated in this opinion printed in the Editorial Page of the *Edmonton Sun*: "We have these bozos who think it's a good idea to ride their bikes on icy roads...People should get tax credits for mowing these idiots down" (*Edmonton Sun*, Sunday Comment, 2007).

TALK-BACK RADIO

A popular forum of current affairs interaction in cities is the talk-radio show, many of which take on ideological overtones. Broadcasters sometimes use this radio format to feature dominant scandals, government policies, or social problems.

In a more controversial form of talk radio, shock jocks make contentious remarks to arouse listeners and increase ratings. They fuel controversy by challenging human rights policies and behaviours. For example, they may offer strong sentiments against the rights of bicyclists, pedestrians, or motorcyclists, which may incite listeners to act violently against one of these groups. Clear Channel Communications operates radio stations in San Jose, Cleveland, Houston, and Raleigh. In 2003, their morning talk-show hosts joked about vigilante action against cyclists. They urged listeners to call in to share stories about harassing cyclists. The hosts offered suggestions on how to run cyclists off the road, and they proposed that listeners pelt them with empty pop bottles. According to the shock jocks, bicyclists had no right to be on the road (*Raleigh News & Observer*, 2003). Some listeners agreed with the radio personalities. One listener phoned to tell of a man in her neighbourhood who shot pellets at bicyclists when they rode by his house, attempting to hit their tires and force them to crash.

Cycle lobbyists wrote protest letters to Clear Channel Communications as well as the Federal Communications Commission, state and local prosecutors, and the radio station's sponsors. On November 3, 2003, a member of the cycling community wrote to the radio station: "You need to do a major healing with the cycling community. As President of Southeastern Communications I have instructed my people to avoid your products, and protest your stations and concert venues until restitution has been made."

On November 5, the vice-president of marketing and communications at Clear Channel Communications responded that he was taking the matter seriously and regretted the incident. He stated that Clear Channel Radio does not condone the advocacy of violence and that the radio hosts had been suspended or terminated. He invited the cycling community to partner with the radio network to promote cycling safety. To show good faith, Clear Channel radio stations donated $10 000 for the promotion of safe cycling routes in Cleveland. The cycling community was satisfied with Clear Channel's response.

Although this illustration was an extreme event, many more radio episodes are on the air where shock jocks criticize the right of bicyclists to be on the road in inclement weather, pedestrians who hold up traffic because they wish to cross the street, or motorcyclists riding side by side, using their legitimate portion of a lane on a four-lane highway.

RAP MUSIC

Music has always been a medium with a message. It has always been sensitive to social issues like alienation, loneliness, poverty, revenge, conflict, and violence. Social commentary found in folk music, the blues, and pop music has segued to hip hop, ghetto, and rap music. The latter goes hand in glove with violence. Of particular importance is a form of rap called gangsta rap, popular in North America's urban centres. Death Row Records, a recording label, brought gangsta rap from the streets of Los Angeles into record stores across North America. The company's symbol is a hooded figure strapped into an electric chair.

Gangsta rap songs are marketed for their violence. The lyrics introduce rage behind the wheel, conflict with the police, bombings, and drive-by shootings followed by tire-squealing escapes. They detail an animated inner-city life comprising drugs, alcohol, rape, killing, and hot cars.

Cars play a major role in the songs. They are "pimped" for illegal street racing, outrunning the police, drive-by shootings, and carjackings. They are a symbol of aggression and violent response to the streets; they exemplify power to hurt.

Some condemn gangsta rap as promoting violence and romanticizing outlaws (Best & Kellner, 1999). Others think of it as just another form of expression, a depiction of the inner-city citizen's struggle to survive in harsh social environments. Regardless, the portrayal of a violent lifestyle that includes cars has become a major music art form.

INTERNET SITES

The Internet is contributing a new dimension to the issue of media violence. Anyone online can download violent music lyrics (including gangsta rap lyrics removed from retail versions of songs). With the click of a mouse, they can also access violent images, video clips, and games.

The Internet is replete with websites that offer graphic scenes and text on murder, gore, racism, wife and child beatings, violent pornography (including child images), mutilations, bomb making, gun play and vehicle tampering (e.g., brake lines cut), and intentional high-speed car crashes. They show horrifying executions, murders, suicides, and genocides in wincing detail. The sites tend to illicit support for or participation in violent behaviours.

IN SUMMARY

The media is a highly visible and influential part of society that must be kept at the forefront of any analysis of violence. It has the power to lead people to aggressive behaviour, or to minimize the repercussions of violence in commercials, movies, television shows, websites, or video games. More importantly, media contributes to normalization of violence in our communities. Media violence is embedded in our social context, a kind of "psychic air" that we breathe (Cantor, 2002).

CORPORATE INTERESTS

Behind every great fortune there is a crime.

— HONORÉ DE BALZAC

The downtown core of many cities is saturated with skyscrapers, monuments for corporations and other businesses. Corporations are part of a complex network of social institutions that either constrain or liberalize our behaviour. When we look closer, we find that corporations can be intrusive giants that help shape our cultures, values, and lives. In their common attempt to increase profits, reduce competition, and gain control of markets, large corporations have become interlocked with government branches, political parties, and trade associations (Mills, 1951). They have become a centrepiece in our social fabric.

Ideally, the relationship between corporations and the community should be a social contract for the benefit of citizens. That relationship, however, has given way to greed and profiteering (Moir, 2001; Key & Popkin, 1998). A spate of highly publicized scandals within corporate giants like Enron and WorldCom has produced a public perception of moral weakness in the corporate world. Public confidence in corporations has steadily eroded, and cynicism has set in.

The social contract is a moral platform that was originally designed by Jean-Jacques Rousseau in 1762 to establish a basis for how we can live together without succumbing to the coercion of others. Through the social contract, free and equal persons come together and agree to create themselves anew as a single body, directed to the good of all considered together. Today, that contract has become unremittingly shaky. Corporations focus on serving their shareholders, whose profit motives often reach beyond community standards of safety, morality, legality, and other social concerns. Their considerable attention to research, development, and marketing strategies may lead to greater sales and higher dividends for shareholders, but can contribute to unsafe, impractical, and low-quality products.

An example of the conflict between the interests of public safety and profit is the production of pocket motorcycles: two-foot-long miniature machines that are replicates of Kawasaki or Harley-Davidson motorcycles. They have the capability of reaching speeds up of fifty kilometres per hour. They do not meet motorcycle safety standards, are poorly built, and are low to the ground, meaning that other motorists can't see them. These are high-risk, dangerous machines with gyro wheels that are too small for an average-sized rider to handle on trails or in fields. They operate best on hard street surfaces, where most provincial and state jurisdictions do not allow them to be driven legally. Hence, many pocket bike enthusiasts drive them illegally on public roads or sidewalks. Furthermore, riders generally do not wear protective equipment (Canada Safety Council, 2004). What responsibility do corporations have for building and selling pocket motorcycles knowing that they will likely be used in an unsafe and illegal manner?

Questionable commercial practices cover the transportation gambit. There is ample evidence that the Canadian Competition Board, various attorney general offices in the United States, and the American Congress have periodically investigated allegations of attempted price fixing in the gasoline industry. A class action suit is before the Chicago courts that accuses Exxon Mobil, Marathon Oil, Citgo Petroleum, and American affiliates of Royal Dutch Shell and BP of intentionally limiting available gasoline supply, driving up prices, and hiking profits (*Bloomberg News*, 2007). The petroleum producers, however, have not been charged. Similar concerns have been raised with the car insurance industry. Provincial governments such as Alberta and Nova Scotia have publicly reprimanded auto insurance companies for charging excessively high premiums. Three previous provincial governments of British Columbia, Saskatchewan, and Manitoba established Crown corporations to reduce high premiums and to increase the low level of crash support that drivers received with private insurers.

The circle widens. Transportation-related industries, such as automakers and dealers, the trucking industry, and tire manufacturers, have a questionable history of white-collar crime, defined by the American FBI as illegal acts of deception, concealment, or violation of trust (U.S. Department of Justice, 1989).

Legal charges against automakers have included fraud, racketeering, dishonesty, slave labour, political cronyism, industrial espionage, restriction of access to information, unsafe work conditions, unsafe products, willful breaking of maintenance contracts, non-adherence to warranty promises, and conspiracy to monopolize the market. Such charges serve as a backdrop for individual citizen attitude, decision making, and behaviour. Social learning theory, as proposed by Albert Bandura (1986), states that people's behaviours and thoughts result from observing role models like family members, friends, work colleagues, mass media, public figures, and corporate leaders. People identify with corporate leaders. Chief executive officers and senior administrators are public figures who have influence on what people define as desired goals and how they can achieve them. They are part of the social psyche that surrounds citizens when they cheat on their taxes, speed in traffic, steal from the workplace, abuse those who are less fortunate, accept bribes, or seek power at the expense of others.

AUTOMAKERS AND WHITE-COLLAR CRIME

It is called white-collar crime: corporations engaging in illegal activities in the course of doing their business dealings (Sutherland, 1949). Repeated involvement of deviant business actions represents a "criminogenic" (crime-causing) corporate culture that demonstrates a kind of ethical numbness or insensitivity to people. It becomes intrusive into the social fabric of society and gains importance as role modelling for individual behaviour (Hills, 1987).

Although criminologists and members of the FBI Financial Crimes Division estimate that the total cost of white-collar crime is about $300 billion a year— that is, more than eighty times the total amount stolen in all thefts and robberies in the United States—corporate involvement in white-collar crime has not received its just amount of public attention (Reinmer, 1998; Evans & Lundman, 1987; Lichter & Rothman, 1994). It does not typically resonate with conventional crime imagery held by most Canadians and Americans. There is a public perception that the "real" criminals in the United States and Canada are young, low-income males, while the corporate criminals are more likely to be older, affluent, white males (Reinmer, 1998; Katz, 1995). People are more likely to consider corporate criminals as professionals who, despite their indiscretions, are still engaged and doing a good job. Furthermore, corporate crime is not as horrifying as street crimes like carjacking, breaking and entering, murder, or robbery. As Gerber and Fritsch (1993) pointed out, mugging vulnerable groups like senior citizens is visible, but anti-trust violations by large corporations are usually hidden and not recognized as problematic. Although the media has more recently pushed for stories on prominent figureheads involved in white-collar crime as part of a trend in "Schadenfreude" (delight in a person of stature's misfortune), white-collar crime remains underreported. White-collar crime is often difficult to detect or prove, and reporting it may arise in lawsuits. As well, large media outlets may be owned by international corporations and have, therefore, a pro-business orientation.

There are profound and dangerous examples of white-collar legal accusations that directly relate to violence and the auto industry. The Ford Pinto, a compact car sold in the early 1970s, was rushed onto the market to compete with the Volkswagen Beetle. Three young women driving a 1973 Ford Pinto were involved in a rear-end crash when the automobile burst into flames. The Ford Motor Company was charged with reckless homicide (Strobel, 1980). The state alleged that the corporate managers were aware that the car's gas tank could easily rupture in a rear-end collision, spew gas, and engulf passengers and drivers in fire. Critics argued that the vehicle's lack of a true rear bumper, as well as any reinforcing structure between the rear panel and the tank, meant that in certain collisions, the tank would be thrust forward into the differential, which had a number of protruding bolts that could puncture the tank. It made the car a potential death trap.

Ford had originally planned to include an inexpensive rubber bladder inside the gas tank that would have prevented most of the car's explosive crashes. But company accountants thought that the costs of the bladder could raise the price of the vehicle enough to lose customers. Another solution was considered to be simpler and cheaper. A piece of plastic for about $11 per car would solve the problem. Again, the decision was made not to include the product. The president of Ford and his executives did their own number crunching, comparing the cost of installing the plastic to each vehicle with the estimated cost of settlement payments for future crash and burn victims. The bottom line was that the cost of changes to the vehicles was more than the potential cost of liability for projected crashes and mortality. The following economic cost-benefit ratio was located in the Ford files:

Benefits
Savings: 180 burn deaths, 180 serious burn injuries, 2100 burned vehicles
Unit Cost: $200 000 per death, $67 000 per injury, $700 per vehicle
Total Benefit: 180 x ($200 000) + 180 x ($67 000) + 2100 x ($700) = $49.5 million

Costs
Sales: 11 million cars, 1.5 million light trucks
Unit Cost: $11 per car, $11 per truck
Total Cost: 11 000 000 x ($11) + 1 500 000 x ($11) = $137.5 million
(Strobel, 1980)

It appears that Ford executives decided it was cheaper to pay liability claims for people who burnt to death than to introduce preventative measures for new vehicles. Their decision led to the fiery deaths of several hundred drivers and passengers, and to the physical disfigurement of many more (Henslin, 1994).

A lengthy court case followed. The automaker was accused of recklessly designing, manufacturing, and marketing the Pinto's unsafe fuel tank system. In the end, the Ford Motor Company was acquitted. Ford's lawyers sidestepped the charge by resting the defence entirely on the legal entity of an American corporation. According to company lawyers, Ford as a corporation could not be guilty of a criminal offence. There was no identifiable specific wrongdoer or single agent who intended to commit an illegal act. No one was responsible—not senior management, not shareholders, not the corporation, not the president. The plaintiff's argument was that the corporation was to be presumed innocent until proven guilty, and guilt requires the establishment of a guilty mind. This argument suggested that corporations could not be held criminally responsible because they did not act; they did not have a mind capable of guilt (Glasbeek, 1989). As a result, the American legal system helped immunize corporations like Ford from criminal prosecutions and increased the incentive for corporate wrongdoing if the reward was substantial enough (Glasbeek, 2003; Russell & Weissman, 2003).

This case is a high-profile example of a corporation breaking the social contract. A large automaker overlooked human rights and human obligations entrusted to a rational and decent society. After the lawsuit, however, Ford finally did modify the Pinto fuel tanks in the 1971 to 1976 models.

While the Ford company fiasco was still fresh in consumers' minds, General Motors (GM) offered a vehicle that also had the possibility of exploding. Each year the *Corporate Rap Sheet*, a consumer vigilante newsletter, features the ten most irresponsible American corporations that have been charged with some "form of plunder, criminal negligence, environmental destruction, or betrayal." The sixth corporation listed for 1992 was GM because of the following accusations made by the Center for Auto Safety:

» GM manufactured and marketed pickup trucks with hazardous gas tanks that led to over 300 deaths—a death rate ten times higher than that of the Ford Pinto.
» GM covered up the problem and decided not to install safety liners, which would have reduced crash fires in the vehicles.
» The defect stems from GM's decision to install side-mounted fuel tanks outside of the frame rails on all "C" and "K" style pickup trucks manufactured between 1972 and 1987. The design exposes the tanks to direct hits and resulting ruptures in side collisions.
» Other manufacturers placed their pickup truck fuel tanks inside protective frame rail structures during the same model years.

(Mokhiber et al., 1992)

Similar events happened again in 1994 when the company was listed as the fourth worst corporation because, critics claimed, without a recall and repairs, the gas tanks of the company's trucks were susceptible to explosion when broadsided in a collision (Mokhiber, 1994). The company has also been accused of being involved in such questionable acts as interference with collective bargaining practices through espionage and labour spies; switching engine and other automobile parts to and from models of varying prices; attempting to influence government regulators by presenting misleading data; criminally conspiring to eliminate electric transportation and monopolize the sale of buses; ignoring safety-related problems associated with several of its vehicles (for example, the Corvair and CK model pickup trucks); cutting costs by replacing standard parts with less expensive inferior substitutes; refusing to repair vehicle parts even after they were responsible for a disproportionate number of crashes; refusing to replace unsafe and defective parts; covering up mechanical problems and withholding important information; polluting the environment; and unnecessarily using animals in lab tests (Burns, 1999).

Perhaps the most questionable moral accusation made against General Motors occurred in 1999 when the *Corporate Rap Sheet* again featured the automaker as the fourth worst corporation in the United States (Mokhiber, 1998). General Motors was accused of having been "an integral part of the Nazi war efforts" (Dobbs, 1998). According to the researcher, during the last quarter of 1939, GM converted its 432-acre Opel complex in Rüsselsheim to war-plane production. From 1939 to 1945, the GM Rüsselsheim facility built 50% of all the propulsion systems produced for Germany's Luftwaffe. Bradford Snell reported that the Nazi armaments chief, Albert Speer, spoke of how Hitler "would never have considered invading Poland" without synthetic fuel technology provided by General Motors (Dobbs, 1998: A11). The Ford Motor Company is also implicated. The famous "Blitztruck" used in the Poland attack was manufactured by German Ford. To show his gratitude, Hitler decorated executives of Ford and General Motors with the highest medal bestowed on a foreigner, the Grand Cross of the German Eagle. These automakers have declined all requests for access to their wartime archives.

On a similar note, a BBC news reporter claimed that between 1941 and 1945, the giant German automaker, Volkswagen, employed about 7000 slave labourers to make mines, V-1 missiles, and anti-tank rocket launchers for the German Nazis. The labourers were badly mistreated, and many died in appalling conditions in hidden military complexes. As a compromise, the German car maker agreed to participate in the 1999 Holocaust compensation fund, which made limited retroactive payments to former slave labourers such as those used by Volkswagen (BBC News, 1999).

In 1996 the Ford Motor Company was hit with class action lawsuits that aimed to reverse the company's refusal to replace faulty ignition switches and their refusal to advise their customers that the problem may cause fires (Dever, 1996). Kenneth Moll, the attorney who initiated the Ford class action suit, suggested that the goals of the action were to ensure a fully inclusive and fully reimbursable recall of all automobiles that were equipped with distributor-mounted TFI modules and compensate all persons who suffered economic damages as the result of vehicles equipped with those modules (NBC 5 News, 1996).

In 1999, Ford offered each family of the workers killed and injured in a boiler explosion $1 million along with additional benefits to supposedly refrain from talking publicly about the incident. There had been a massive boiler explosion at its Rouge complex power plant in Dearborn, Michigan, on February 1. The offer came while evidence was mounting on the unsafe working conditions at the seventy-eight-year-old facility. According to a socialist newsletter, legal analysts and occupational health safety experts judged the money as a bribe to prevent victims from speaking out about the plant's violations of safety standards (White, 1999).

Another corporate problem appeared when USA Today reported that Ford had asked the U.S. Supreme Court to hear its appeal of $290 million in punitive damages, which had been awarded by a California jury. The jury had ruled that Ford's personnel knew the roof of its Bronco SUV could not properly withstand a rollover. The case arose from a 1993 crash in which three people were killed. Ford had claimed that the Bronco's roof met federal regulations and engineering standards (Kiley, 2003). The case proved to be a milestone where the courts awarded punitive instead of compensatory damages, meaning that the Ford corporation was judged to be engaged in "willful" wrongdoing. The California high court denied Ford's request to review the punitive damages award (Accident Reconstruction Network, undated; Romo v. Ford, 2003). In fact, the Court of Appeal offered the following profound treatise that is relevant not only to the Ford Bronco case but also to the Ford Pinto case.

It would be unacceptable public policy to establish a system in which it is less expensive for a defendant's malicious conduct to kill rather than injure a victim. Thus, the state has an extremely strong interest in being able to impose sufficiently high punitive damages in malicious-conduct wrongful death actions to deter a "cheaper to kill them" mind set. The proportionality inquiry must focus, in any event, on the relationship of punitive damages to the harm of the deceased. (White, 2005: 105)

In short, corporations must desist from accounting principles that provide a positive cost benefit for killing an innocent customer. According to White (2005), the court referred to Ford's conduct as a malicious conduct to kill.

Across the Pacific, we find the case of Japanese automaker Mitsubishi Motors. From 1993 to 2004, the automaker engaged in systematic cover-ups of auto defects that nearly bankrupted the company. For four years the company maintained that the reason the wheels were falling off its heavy trucks while moving was poor maintenance. It was, in fact, a mechanical defect. The automaker kept silent about its knowledge that its trucks had problems with fractured clutch housings that could result in transmission parts falling off (Schuman, 2004). The flaws contributed to seventy-three collisions and two fatalities. One woman was killed when a wheel flew off a truck and hit her.

In June 2004, Mitsubishi Motors recalled 155 000 cars in Japan to repair twenty-six mechanical defects that it had failed to report since 1993 (Schuman, 2004). Shortly after, the Japanese police arrested the president of the corporation on charges of criminal negligence.

Court challenges against automakers, and automaker aggressive stances in favour of profit, seem to continue. For example, the *Detroit News* reported in April 2004 that, according to federal statistics, an estimated 7000 people are killed or seriously injured each year when the roofs of their vehicles collapse. The newspaper discovered that in 1971, Ford and General Motors led an industry-wide effort to persuade federal officials to adopt a minimum standard for roof strength after their vehicle fleets failed the government's first proposed test. According to documents presented at a court case in Florida in 2005, the Ford Explorer's roof was made weaker after two redesigns in the 1990s, even though engineers had recommended strengthening the roof. In 1995, the Ford Explorer had a roof strength-to-weight ratio of 1.72. In 1999, the number had fallen to 1.56, barely over the federal minimum of 1.5. Internal Ford e-mails unsealed at the trial revealed the concern company engineers had with the slim margin of safety. The company has since had four court verdicts against it contesting the design of the Explorer roof, the most recent of which was in Florida where a jury, on March 18, 2005, ruled the Explorer's roof was defective and ordered the company to pay $10.2 million for economic damages, pain, and suffering (Crashworthiness, 2005).

Other major automakers could also be involved, suggesting that the wrongdoings of automakers are more than occasional events. They have become part of our social context. Such business behaviour is at best morally questionable and at worst reprehensible.

CAR DEALERS

Deceit and immoral conduct do not stop at the gates of the automakers. They appear at the premises of some auto dealerships, whose unscrupulous dealers have been charged with turning back odometers, salvaging titles, repairing flood-damaged vehicles without properly advising customers, and cloning vehicle identification numbers (VINs). The latter act begins with a criminal obtaining an identification number from a local vehicle. He then steals a vehicle that resembles the description of the vehicle whose identification number he noted, and brands the stolen vehicle with the same number. The vehicle is then sold or dealt through dealerships, or via "curbsiders" through newspaper classified ads or Internet auto sites, sometimes to the full knowledge of the dealers.

More questionable acts happen when vehicles that were involved in serious crashes and were declared total write-offs in Canada are repaired and then shipped to the United States for sale, to the full knowledge of some dealers (Mello, 2002). Similar treatment may be given to vehicles that received serious flood damage.

The most blatant of these crimes is odometer fraud, which Herzog (2005) estimated involves more than 89 000 vehicles per year that reach the Canadian marketplace. It costs consumers nearly $4 million. The following is an example of such an experience.

Healey, a fifty-four-year-old forklift operator, worked at a local brewery. He went shopping for a mini-van at a long-established GM dealer in Newmarket, Ontario. He spotted a white 1998 Chevy Venture LS whose odometer registered only 34 214 kilometres. The dealer informed him that the mini-van was a lease-return vehicle that had just arrived on the lot.

The van's exterior paint and body were in good condition, and it was loaded with options. He took the vehicle for a test drive and was pleased with the results. The van's registration papers and safety inspection certificate appeared to be in order. Healey was satisfied that he was receiving value for his money, so he handed the salesman a cheque for $21 625.

Shortly after Healey drove the mini-van home, signs of trouble appeared: odd start-up sounds and leaking fluids on the driveway: conditions not becoming a vehicle that had been driven for only 34 000 kilometres. Becoming suspicious, Healey pulled out a platinum spark plug and noted that it was completely burnt out. Healey purchased Ontario's Used Vehicle Information Package (UVIP) to establish the van's history. The papers indicated his van had several previous owners, none of whom were private individuals.

The man decided to contact the van's original owner, an Ontario fleet leasing firm. He learned that the leasing company sold the vehicle with an odometer reading of 153 138 kilometres—that is, 120 000 kilometres more than were registered on the vehicle sitting on the sales lot.

Armed with the evidence, Healey returned to the car dealership to confront the salesman. As soon as he began to lay out the information, the dealer agreed to give Healey a full refund, no questions asked. Janeshewski (2004), the journalist who covered the story, suggested that such a response is not entirely unexpected. When dealers are confronted with hard evidence, they usually negotiate a financial settlement with the customer to avoid negative publicity and potential civil or criminal proceedings.

The example is not unique or isolated. Odometer tampering is common fraud. In 2002, Morgan completed a study for the NHTSA. He summarized that the United States has about 452 000 cases of odometer fraud per year. There is a 3.5% chance that a vehicle had its odometer rolled back at any point during the first eleven years of its life. The difference between the inflated price that consumers actually paid for rolled-back vehicles and the price they would have been willing to pay if they had known the true mileage averages $2336 per case of odometer fraud. The final tally amounts to $106 million per year (Morgan, 2002). Odometer rollback is most common on newer vehicles that have acquired significant use over a short period of time through lease and rental agreement, or through heavy company or business travel (Herzog, 2005).

Canada is implicated in many of the American odometer rollbacks. A significant number of Canadian registered vehicles have their odometers rolled back before they are sold in the United States for large profits. It is part of the grey zone in the used auto trade between Canada and the United States (Mello, 2002). Although profits were significant because of the favourable monetary exchange rate between the two countries (Geranios, 2002), they have since been reduced because of the dollar parity between Canada and the United States.

Computer technology has made it easier to reverse odometer readings, making it even more commonplace. Websites cater to enthusiasts. Anyone can log on and read blogs by an array of people who spend their time rolling back odometers on resale vehicles. Some websites advertise kits that instruct Internet users on how to become successful rollback artists (Herzog, 2005).

Janeshewski (2004), working on a media story about odometer rollback scams, interviewed personnel from General Motors to gain a corporate point of view. A spokesperson for the car manufacturer confirmed that the company's computers were capable of catching odometer tampering. However, according to the director of public relations for GM Canada, there is no legal obligation for General Motors to notify the authorities that odometer tampering had occurred (Janeshewski, 2004).

According to Consumer Affairs (2003), a report distributed by Public Citizen, a consumer advocacy organization founded by Ralph Nader, consumers are routinely fleeced of hundreds and sometimes thousands of dollars apiece by fraudulent auto sales representatives. The allegations are supported by documents obtained by auto sales industry whistleblower Duane Overholt, who worked in Florida auto sales for twenty years. The consumer group outlined cheating strategies such as boosting the manufacturer's suggested retail price with extras (some of which already come with the vehicle); running credit reports on potential buyers without their permission; using add-on worksheets to get customers to pay more than the price they had just agreed upon; demanding customers to sign blank bank forms that the dealer fills in later; and adding products to the sales contract after the customer leaves. Public Citizen recommended that state and local law enforcement authorities enforce consumer protection laws and that state and federal lawmakers mandate that financial and dealership documents be contained in a single file available to the consumer on request (Consumer Affairs, 2003).

TIRE MAKERS

The influence of corporations on the health and welfare of roadway users extends into the tire manufacturing industry. Although tires are an essential part of a vehicle, drivers typically take them for granted. We attend to them only when they go flat or blow out—or when news about defects are made public.

In August 2002, Bridgestone/Firestone recalled seventeen million tires shortly after a class action suit by Florida motorists on behalf of those injured and killed while driving on tires branded as the Firestone radial ATX, radial ATX II, and the Wilderness AT brands (Barancik, 2000). Bruce Kaster, the attorney representing the claimants, told the press that Bridgestone/Firestone had known for decades that under extreme conditions their steel-belted radial tires were prone to breaking apart, which could kill drivers and passengers. He revealed that company engineers had long known about the problem and that they could solve it at a cost of about $1 per tire (Barancik, 2000).

Similar to the Ford Pinto case described earlier, the newly minted company Bridgestone/Firestone did not make the changes because it likely wanted to maintain its margin of profit. Consequently, at least 271 people were reported killed and hundreds more injured in collisions that involved Firestone ATX tires. The company finally yielded to pressure and recalled its tires at the cost of $1 billion (Gouras, 2004).

Four retired Firestone employees came forward and talked about the company's emphasis on "quantity over quality." In sworn depositions against the tire maker, the retirees questioned the company's quality control, claiming that the manufacturer used outdated rubber for its new tires. They furthermore claimed that company management demanded that employees work twelve-hour shifts, which led to fatigue and contributed to poor workmanship (Kelly, 2000). Reporters were told that employees spent only ten to twenty seconds inspecting each tire. Tires sometimes moved so quickly through the production line that they slipped through the quality control station. There was insufficient time for workers to inspect them properly. One employee claimed that factory workers were involved in the unsafe practice of lancing tires to fix blisters and using old rubber for manufacturing new tires (Kelly, 2000). Finally, workers claimed that the steel-belt cords were exposed to humidity, which permits condensation to form, causing corrosion. Another worker signed an affidavit claiming that workers, who were paid on a piecework salary program, protested—to no avail—that quality was being sacrificed for quantity (Voehl, 2000).

After the U.S. Court of Appeals for the Sixth Circuit heard the case, it ruled that the accusations had enough substance for a lawsuit (Kelly, 2000). It was around this time that another case yielded a verdict of guilty against Bridgestone for having produced faulty tires. The court decided that the company's tires caused or contributed to crashes on Ford Explorers, creating an orgy of blame. Ford Motors blamed Bridgestone for manufacturing unsafe tires, while the tire manufacturer blamed Ford for improper inflation instructions. Furthermore, the tire company held Ford Explorer drivers responsible for underinflating their tires. As if that were not enough, a Riverside, California judge agreed to consider a plaintiff's bid to pursue a national class action lawsuit claiming defects in Firestone Steeltex tires while Bridgestone was being charged.

The accusation gained momentum when New Hampshire's Attorney General Philip McLaughlin joined fifty-two other jurisdictions and filed lawsuits against Bridgestone/Firestone. He demanded a $51.5 million nationwide settlement from the company for its allegedly selling defective tires and for misrepresenting its tire replacement process by promoting another allegedly defective tire. Bridgestone/Firestone denied wrongdoing under the settlement terms (New Hampshire Department of Justice, 2001, November 8). The case is still before the courts.

To regenerate public confidence, the attorney general demanded the following permanent injunction provisions:

» Bridgestone/Firestone shall not misrepresent the characteristics, manufacture or appropriate uses of a tire.
» The company must be able to substantiate with competent and reliable scientific evidence any specific claims of tire safety, performance or durability.
» The company may not make misrepresentations during a recall or customer satisfaction program.
» The company shall not provide or facilitate inconsistent information to consumers about tire pressure.
» The company must not make misrepresentations in or retroactively change any guarantee or warranty.
» The company shall not misrepresent that they have given an expert all requested information.

- » The company shall not misrepresent the expected life or wear pattern of a tire tread.
- » The company must handle consumer complaints in a truthful, ethical and timely manner.

(New Hampshire Department of Justice, 2001, November 8)

Typical of white-collar crime, the tire manufacturer put the desire for profit ahead of people's safety. Botched tires were sold to the public. The issue is best expressed by the investigative journalist F. Voehl (2002) when he summarized his research:

In my opinion, which I know will be controversial, the case placed dollars over the value of human lives, and those making that decision are as guilty of those deaths as any of those charged and convicted in international incidents/crimes we have seen over the years, whenever economic gain was achieved at the expense of the death of innocent people. Indeed, I believe that the incident involves intrinsically non-integrious, criminal behavior on the part of those holding organizational decision authority.

INSURANCE COMPANIES

Insurance companies play a vital role in the pulse of daily traffic. Motor vehicle insurance is usually an unremarked feature of driving. The fundamentals are easy. The state decrees that drivers must have insurance. Most times we do not need it, but we can't drive legally without it. Insurance companies charge vehicle owners premiums and, in the event of crashes, they pay out claims. Hiding within this transaction is the potential for secrecy and fraud, in which the insurance companies may be victims or instigators.

As victims of fraud, auto insurers pass on its cost to policyholders and the general public, who pick up the tab through higher insurance rates. The Insurance Research Council (IRC) in the United States estimated that insurance fraud added between $4.3 and $5.8 billion to auto injury settlements in 2005. These figures represented between 11% and 15% of all money paid for private passenger auto injury insurance claims that year. The IRC reported that fraud (the misrepresentation of key facts of a claim) and fraud build-up (a claim in which the injury is exaggerated and/or the injury is excessive) existed in about one in ten paid bodily injury liability (BI) claims, and one in twenty paid personal injury protection (PIP) claims. Insurance fraud is estimated to cost Americans about $80 billion each year, or $950 per family, according to Charles Folti, Attorney General of Louisiana (2004). Parallel numbers are difficult to find in Canada because the insurance industry, although alleging that fraud increases premiums, has not openly revealed the financial impact of fraud to their policyholders (Saksida, 2006).

Insurance fraud usually constitutes a well-thought-out plan that involves conspirators, often friends, colleagues, or professionals like medical doctors or insurance adjusters. One example is commonly referred to as "paper only collision," in which lawyers, doctors, and insurance agents conspire to process fake paper claims made by drivers. The fraud may also involve members from the auto repair and salvage industries who falsely document services on collisions that exist only on paper. To minimize their risk of being exposed, the conspirators try to keep claims below $10 000, an informal benchmark insurance companies use to decide whether they should send investigators for further examination.

Closely related to paper-only collision is the hit-and-run claim where a perpetrator with a witness reports a fictitious hit and run to the insurance company. Again, the amount of money claimed is important to the success of the fraud. If the amount of the claim is moderate or low, the insurance company may decide that the claim is not worth further investigation.

More sophisticated teamwork is required for scams known in the insurance business as the "swoop and squat" and "sideswipe." Both imply a form of roadway violence without the consequence of mortality. The "swoop and squat" involves two vehicles working as a team to set up a crash. One vehicle pulls in front of an innocent driver and the other alongside, blocking in the victim. The lead car stops short, causing the victim to rear-end it. The partner serves as an official witness. To embellish the claim, the fraud artists may engage their own medical doctors or chiropractors to diagnose whiplash.

The fraud commonly referred to as the "sideswipe" usually occurs at an intersection that has two left-turn lanes. The perpetrator crosses the centre line, intentionally sideswipes the victim's car, and then alleges that the victim caused the collision by entering the lane.

Another fraudulent manoeuvre is the "t-bone." The instigator waits at an intersection until no witnesses are present, and then intentionally rams into a car as it passes. When the police arrive, bogus witnesses are planted to tell the investigating police officers that the victim ran a stop sign or red light, resulting in a collision. A similar ploy is used in the "hand-wave." In heavy traffic, the instigator waves his hand to offer an unsuspecting driver the right of way. As the victim begins to merge, the fraud artist quickly speeds up and purposefully hits the vehicle. When the police arrive, the perpetrator denies ever giving up the right of way.

A scam that occurs within body shops involves air bags. Employees remove deployed air bags from vehicles and fill the cavity with garbage materials like old rags, beer, and pop cans. Management then falsely bills the driver's auto policy for a new air bag. This scam puts drivers' lives at risk as they unknowingly drive their cars without air bags.

A review of news stories produces an armful of cases on auto insurance fraud. The following is an example:

> TORONTO (CP)—The cyclist thought he had his insurance-claim tracks covered: he had his girlfriend run him over with her car, and then stuck a toothpick up his nose to aggravate his bleeding.
>
> The ingenious bike-rider copped $22,000 in compensation.
>
> But the scam—among the Insurance Bureau of Canada's top 10 frauds of 2003—backfired.
>
> The cyclist was later taken to court when insurance investigators discovered the man had his girlfriend deliberately run into him, and then stuck a toothpick up his nose to get blood—and the insurance money—flowing. (Habib, Canadian Press, 2003, December 17)

A news story in the *Los Angeles Times* spoke of a mass arrest of eighty-six people charged with "bilking insurance companies out of more than $500,000 in one of the largest auto insurance fraud cases ever filed in Los Angeles County" (*Los Angeles News*, 2007, January 5). Employees from twelve law offices referred crash victims to chiropractors who, in conjunction with the law offices, worked out a strategy to overcharge insurance companies. More than 100 people were indicted for participating in the scheme, including 13 office administrators, 2 attorneys, and 87 insurance claimants.

Insurance companies are victims of fraud, yet they can also be the initiators of questionable legal tactics against drivers. For example, some insurers ask claimants to release information that impinges on their right to privacy, and without telling claimants that the information can be used against them. Insurance companies often fail to advise claimants that the insurers are in an adversarial relationship to claimants.

Moreover, insurance company adjusters are in an ideal position to misrepresent the information they give to unsuspecting claimants. For example, adjusters may direct claimants to have their vehicles repaired at a particular body shop, from which the insurer may be receiving discounts for recommended business. The body shop's loyalty is to the insurance company and not to the claimant because, ultimately, the insurance company pays the repair bills.

A non-profit group called Fight Bad Faith Insurance Companies (FBIC) maintains a website about questionable insurance practices. This lobby group asserts that insurance companies commonly deny legitimate claims and breach contracts. The following statement is from FBIC's website:

According to an enormous number of knowledgeable bad faith insurance experts and plaintiff attorneys in the field and voluminous amounts of statistical and other consumer information available, FBIC estimates that there are many times more breach of contract and bad faith insurance practices and denials of claims perpetrated by bad faith insurers against policyholders and claimants than there are fraudulent claims made by consumers against insurance companies...exceedingly upwards of 100 times more. (FBIC, 2005)

The FBIC sponsors an ongoing survey designed to establish the level of service covered by different insurance companies. The three best and worst are then publicized on the website. They describe the extent to which the insurers breach contracts with their policyholders.

Jordan Stanzler (2003) quoted the chair of the Dow Corning Corporation as saying, "It has become standard operating procedure for some insurance companies to procrastinate and dispute rather than honor policies with companies that become embroiled in litigation." Stanzler asks his readers to reflect on the honesty and trustworthiness of their insurer, and the expectations they have of that insurer in the event of an accident.

TRUCKING COMPANIES

Freight companies are in business to haul maximum loads in minimum time. But to do so, North American carriers are mandated to abide by a series of policies, legalities, licenses, certificates, permits, and other official documents that allow them to move goods across state, provincial, and country borders. They need to find the competitive edge within this jungle of official demands and expectations.

To succeed in the highly competitive enterprise of transportation, drivers and/or freight executives may cut corners to reduce trip time, save storage costs, decrease operating expenses, or increase the size of loads. The police routinely charge truckers for improper load securement, operating oversized or overweight loads (especially dump trucks), exceeding their legal hours of driving, operating unsafe equipment, cheating on logbook entries, engaging in improper placarding, and a host of other illegal acts, most of which occur due to the pressure shippers, dispatchers, and often managers impose on truckers (Rothe, 1990).

Whether the truck is independently owned or is part of a corporate fleet, violations are not uncommon. They are an inconvenience, scoffed at by some truckers as just another "cost of doing business." When the police focus on the driver and the machine, however, they are missing the role played by dispatchers and shippers who may be pressuring, manipulating, or threatening the trucker to breach certain laws for the sake of profit and efficiency. Although dispatchers and shippers are accountable for their influence on trucker's driving behaviours, they are seldom assigned legal responsibility for what happens next.

In a noteworthy case in New Jersey, an enforcement officer caught a trucker hauling an oversized load with a weight exceeding that of his permit (*Times News*, undated). Furthermore, the driver neither properly secured the load, nor correctly displayed an oversized load sign on the rear of his rig. As a result, the officer confiscated the truck at the side of the road. We know that the trucker broke a series of laws, but do we know what could have happened if the trucker had refused to "bend" the law for his employer? Truckers can lose their jobs, be officially sanctioned for unsatisfactory behaviour, be forced to haul unprofitable loads, be ordered to operate sub-par equipment, be expected to wait longer periods of time for their next hauls, or experience longer wait-over periods in distant places before new loads are assigned to them (Rothe, 1990). Independent-thinking truckers could easily lose the confidence of the corporate dispatch office or the freight company management.

Unsecured loads are a constant worry. Nails, bricks, cement bags, wire, pipes, building materials, equipment parts, and logs can easily fall off and create carnage on the road. A short news item in the newsletter *Health and Safety Alert* (2005) illustrates the seriousness of breaching the load securement laws: "On 22 January 2003 three children were killed in a motor vehicle accident when the vehicle they were travelling in ran over steel plates which had earlier fallen from a pallet on a road train." Peter Kissinger, president of the American Automobile Association Foundation for Traffic Safety, told the media that new research found that vehicle parts, cargo, or other material that has fallen or that was thrown from vehicles onto the roadway is estimated to cause over 25 000 crashes per year in North America, resulting in approximately eighty to ninety fatalities per year (AAA Media Release, 2008, January 4).

SPEED ENFORCEMENT COMPANIES

Some people have called photo speed enforcement both a cash grab and a tool to regulate and reduce speeding on public roads. A computerized radar gun, usually located within specifically designed vehicles or mounted on power poles, tracks speeding vehicles, then snaps a picture. A computer records the licence plate number from the photo, then a ticket is mailed to the registered owner of the vehicle. The operation is run by trained personnel.

Affiliated Computer Services (ACS) is a Dallas-based company that offers mobile or fixed photo radar technologies to reduce speeding. Its website makes the following claim:

The Photo Radar System combines image capturing with advanced radar technology to yield photographic evidence of vehicles exceeding the speed limit. Photo Radar allows communities to consistently enforce speed limits. Moreover, Photo Radar enhances traffic safety by eliminating potentially dangerous police pursuits.

ACS contracts out their technical, logistical, and financial resources to police services across North America. The Canadian Department of Justice, however, has formally charged ACS with bribing public officials over a six-year period between January 1, 1998, and June 24, 2004. Two Edmonton police officers were charged with breach of trust and accepting secret commissions following an investigation by the RCMP. The photo-radar company was also charged with offering secret commissions (Russel, 2007). Both officers were cleared of all charges in November 2007.

The accusation that ACS has continued to offer gifts to the police department in Edmonton, in direct violation of ethics rules that are standard throughout Canada, was thrown out by a judge because of "legal confusion" (630 CHED, 2007). Still, the Edmonton Police Commission has recommended that the municipal government control the photo radar program. A consulting firm found that the city could do the job for $2.6 million—about $600 000 less than the cost of paying a private contractor like ACS (Beazley, 2007).

In April 2006, the *Winnipeg Free Press* asked for the memos, reports, and e-mails surrounding the process used to select ACS to be the city's photo enforcement vendor. A city auditor's report released in March raised a number of issues, including how the city lost millions in expected profit and questions about the technology's effectiveness in reducing crashes. Unlike Edmonton, Winnipeg city council has not initiated formal investigation of the company.

IN SUMMARY

The intentional violence perpetrated on our roads is enveloped in a general trend of corruption and deceit, whereby transportation-related commercial interests may undermine the interests and health of individual consumers. We should be aware of the behind-the-scenes meaning of corporate activity: the breach of rules for corporate gain, the use of deceit or misinformation for cover-up, and the subtle consent to engage in aggressive or immoral behaviour for corporate well being.

The issue is a paradox. Corporations that are entrusted to provide us with safe and efficient transportation sources and services may be producing products, processes, and policies that harm us. They may breach the social contract between people and corporate demands, placing in doubt our trust and good-will towards them.

Edwin Sutherland (1949), the most distinguished criminologist ever to study white-collar crime, proclaimed that our decision to follow or breach a law is guided by observing others (such as corporate executives). Although corporate actions do not causally determine an individual's behaviour, they serve as a range of possibilities from which we all may draw.

STATE-SPONSORED VIOLENCE

How soon we forget history...Government is not reason.
Government is not eloquence. It is force. And, like fire, it is a
dangerous servant and a fearful master.

— GEORGE WASHINGTON

Although the military is periphery to this book, brief mention of it graphically illustrates how motor vehicles can be used to provoke and sometimes curb violence.

Our political leaders represent our governments. They are arguably the pillar of our social context, the centre from which orderliness, fiduciary responsibility, fairness, security, and trust radiate. Three points on a triangle constitute a government: power, authority, and legitimacy. Power is the central focus for this chapter. It is hereby defined in this context as the probability that a government will be able to carry out its will, even against resistance, regardless of the means by which such resistance is overcome (Weber, 1947). The government may even threaten recalcitrant citizens with disagreeable consequences, which may be the legitimate use of physical force.

Governments have control of the armed forces and police enforcement. They can exercise their power by threatening violence externally on other nations, or internally on their own citizens. They can create conflict or clashes with those opposed to the government. The violent exercise of power can become a habituated act whereby the government thinks that violence is the essence of the state or a principle of everyday governing. In the seventeenth century, Thomas Hobbes (1999) wrote that the state has the authority to use force for establishing and maintaining an orderly society. Consistent with Hobbes's principles, throughout the ages political leaders have justified their actions according to the argument that the state has the right to arm and use violence to maintain law and order (Shearing & Ericson, 1991).

The behaviours and attitudes of earlier leaders help form our social context; our forefathers have left a legacy that often guides state rulers today (Schutz, 1970). They have established avenues of authoritarian rule that echo in some modern leaders' minds. One of those historical venues is the use of motor vehicles for state-supported aggression and genocide.

The state's authority to use violence as a display of power is facilitated by access to specifically designed motor vehicles, such as machine gun-mounted jeeps, artillery pulling trucks, and rapid deployment vans. There is an obvious interplay among government leaders, the availability of armed personnel, and access to strategic means such as vehicles designed for conflict.

STATE GENOCIDE

Discussion about state-sponsored violence invariably leads to inquiries on genocide. The 1948 United Nations Convention on the Prevention and Punishment of the Crime of Genocide defined genocide in Article II as:

> Any of the following acts committed with intent to destroy, in whole or in part, a national, ethnical, racial or religious group, as such: killing members of the group; causing serious bodily or mental harm to members of the group; deliberately inflicting on the group conditions of life calculated to bring about its physical destruction in whole or in part; imposing measures intended to prevent births within the group; forcibly transferring children of the group to another group.

Irving Horowitz (1982), the eminent scholar on state violence, proposed that genocide is a structural and systematic destruction of innocent people by a state bureaucratic apparatus. It usually entails mass crimes against humanity. Death is at the hands of the state.

For most of the twentieth century, specially armed motor vehicles constituted an important asset for governments bent on genocide. They contributed to the ultimate dehumanization of people by treating death as a unit of production. The Nazi regime systematically annihilated millions of Jews, Gypsies, mentally and physically disabled citizens, and other minorities. Historical documents tell that gas chambers were major instruments of death. However, there was also the systematic use of vehicles referred to as "gas vans," or "Sonderwagen." These vehicles were specifically engineered to channel carbon monoxide, generated by the trucks' engines, into sealed chambers. This method was initially used as part of the "euthanasia" program, in which the Nazis killed physically and mentally handicapped Germans. Later, the gas vans were used to kill Soviet prisoners in the Sachsenhausen concentration camp and the Chelmno extermination camp. Conservative estimates suggest that gas vans were used in the murder of approximately 700,000 people throughout Nazi-dominated Europe.

The idea of the gas van originated with SS-Brigadeführer Artur Nebe, commander of a special unit called the Einsatzgruppe B, which operated in territories close to the central European front. The Einsatzgruppe B had carried out large-scale shootings of Jews, communists, and other so-called "asocial elements" in Belorussia. Nebe, a former leader of the Reich's Criminal Police Department (Kripo), was instrumental in the deployment of the euthanasia program and killing by gas (Arad, 1987).

Government officials supplied the gas vans to the special unit stationed at the Chelmno death camp in November 1941. The killing in Chelmno began on December 8, 1941. By the middle of 1942, about thirty gas vans had been produced by a private manufacturer (Nationalsozialistische Massentotungen, undated). They were used throughout Europe and Russia. Erich Gnewuch, a former Nazi soldier, testified about the use of gas vans in occupied Russia from 1942 to 1943:

> On orders from my department, I too drove a gas-van from Berlin to Minsk. These vans had been constructed with a lockable cargo compartment, like a moving van.... I was detailed with the gas-van to about twelve convoys of arriving Jews. It was in 1942. There were about a thousand Jews in each convoy. With each arrival I made five or six trips with my van. Some of the Jews were shot. I myself never shot a single Jew; I only gassed them. (Kogon et al., 1993: 57)

To highlight how the Nazis disassociated themselves from humanity and considered the use of gas vans to be nothing more than a business transaction, Kogon, Langbein, and Ruecker (1993) published the following correspondence between a senior SS officer and Dr. Becker, a junior officer, regarding the construction and implementation of gas vans:

> The special vans manufactured by us are at this time in operation pursuant to the order of the Chief of the Security Police and the SD. There are more vans under construction, whose delivery is however dependent upon the appropriate shipping orders being issued by the General Plenipotentiary for Vehicles [GEK]. At what point in time the GEK will confirm the state of preparedness is not known...

Since I assume that the Mauthausen concentration camp cannot wait indefinitely for the delivery, I request that you use steel bottles with carbon monoxide or respectively other remedies to get things started. (Kogon et al., 1993: 58)

More recently, state genocide operations in Yugoslavia, Albania, Zimbabwe, and Sudan among other countries were activated with the deployment of armies who used vehicle-based weapons to fulfill their goals. Machine guns were mounted on the backs of trucks, or on smaller vehicles like jeeps, to shoot indiscriminately at suspicious opponents or so-called "enemies of the state."

CROWD MANAGEMENT AND CONTROL

Of concern to states today is crowd management and crowd control. "Crowd management" involves techniques used to manage lawful public assemblies before, during, and after the event. The purpose is to maintain the lawful status of the public assembly. Crowd management can be accomplished in part through coordination with event planners and group leaders, permit monitoring, and by critiquing past events.

"Crowd control" involves techniques used to address unlawful public assemblies, including a display of formidable numbers of police officers, crowd containment and dispersal tactics, and arrest procedures. Crowd control can be either lethal or non-lethal. In many Western countries, crowd control is non-lethal, with authorities using equipment that exerts minimum force. The main instrument is a vehicle-mounted water cannon, the most modern version of which can add dye and tear gas to the water.

Most countries have strict restrictions on the use of crowd-control equipment that is used for defensive purposes. Motor vehicles are favourite instruments. They provide protection, mobility, and shock effect. Vehicles can also be outfitted with searchlights, close circuit television, water cannon, public address, and psychological warfare systems. The United States has developed an advanced crowd-control vehicle called Sheriff, which is a Humvee with a mounted millimetre-wave electromagnetic energy system to be used for controlling urban areas (World Tribune, 2005). It is a new "non-lethal" weapon that uses a directed energy beam to inflict a painful but brief burning sensation.

In some countries, security forces favour taking an offensive stance in crowd control. Again, motor vehicles are ideal instruments. They can be driven directly into crowds to induce panic and force rioters to scatter, allowing dismounted personnel to arrest small groups of rioters. Certain repressive regimes, such as Burma, are less scrupulous in adopting strategies that punish or terrorize the local population. Their vehicles of choice are jeeps with weapons like 7.62 millimetre machine guns, which are lethal weapons intended to create casualties. Lasers, which damage eyes, are also used on top of Land Rover jeeps to cause blindness.

IN SUMMARY

Regardless of ideology or form of government, nearly every country has a military or national police force that possesses special vehicles to control civilians when necessary. They are visible elements of a military or police force designed to protect a belief system and way of life, or to defend a cadre of leaders who want to maintain political power and authority.

VIOLENCE AGAINST NATURE

Until he extends the circle of compassion to all
living things, man will not himself find peace.

— ALBERT SCHWEITZER

While human beings are part of the natural world, we work unceasingly to stand apart from our natural environment, developing new technologies to master it according to our needs and wants. Plants and animals have become "our" natural resources, to be "harvested" at our whim. We have developed a relationship to nature that can be described by metaphors such as "conquest," "assault," "dominion," or "control," each of which denotes violence and reflects an ideology of nature's subjugation at the hands of human beings. This is no better exemplified than by people needlessly killing and torturing wild animals.

For some people, hunting animals is a vexed activity. For others, the distinctive outcomes of hunting are the insurance of a good balance of healthy wildlife, a vibrant rural economy, a food source, and a cornerstone of cultural identity. This second group believes their behaviour to be culturally legitimate and socially approved, sanctioned by earlier generations (Keller, 1996). Underlying these rationalizations are the assumptions that hunters respect natural and societal laws, the essence and dignity of the animal, and the finality of the kill. These assumptions can be questioned. There has long been a crisis of hunt saboteurs who shoot defenceless animals at the side of roads, from within, on top of, or aside of a truck, sports utility, or all-terrain vehicle, often using spotlights to blind and confuse the animals. They use motor vehicles to compound an animal's vulnerability, reduce its chance of escape, and to increase the hunter's odds of successful kills. Hence, the argument that hunters replicate the natural selection of animals is spurious and indefensible.

Modern technology has given hunters the power to control the odds of a successful kill. One of the technological innovations used to support hunting is a modified motor vehicle. Many websites advertise the "perfect vehicle" for a hunt. As one hunting enthusiast described on his web page, a hunting truck should be a mid-size, crew cab, 4x4, short-bed pickup with a cab-height canopy. The truck should provide comfortable seating for four adults, be durable and practical. Four-wheel drive is a must. Although ethically debatable, hunting with specialized vehicles is an acceptable part of North American life. It forms part of our social context. It is common for friends to encourage hunters with supportive comments like "Happy four-wheelin,' and good hunting!" and "How many did you bag?"

WILDLIFE POACHING

Poaching is the illegal hunting, killing, or capturing of animals. Poachers devastate nature by breaking laws that are designed to ensure proper wildlife management and species survival. They kill animals without a licence or permit, use prohibited weapons or technology, shoot animals outside of the designated time of day or year, and kill animals of a prohibited sex or life stage. They kill wildlife for their meat, skins, internal organs, and external extremities, and for sport.

Poaching is typically a crime of secrecy and stealth, whose full damage is largely unknown. In North America, much of the illegal hunting or trapping on land includes killing bear, elk, moose, lynx, and deer. Much of this poaching occurs with the support of motor vehicles.

Finding statistics on poaching is nearly impossible. However, a report by Alberta Rural Crime Watch highlighted the number of occurrences of poaching investigated through its Report a Poacher program. The report stated that, in 2000, there were 2529 illegal wildlife hunting activities and 73 illegal fur trapping activities. In 2001, those numbers changed to 2667 illegal wildlife hunting activities and 63 illegal fur trapping activities (Alberta Rural Crime Watch, 2002). The statistics are based on tips that law enforcement officers received from concerned citizens. Although the numbers have limited or no power of generalization, they do point out that poaching is a large problem in Alberta, and perhaps in the rest of North America.

Poaching depends on motor vehicles to gain access to the animals' wilderness habitats and to transport carcasses or animal parts from the kill sites. Opportunistic motorists also shoot deer and elk from the roadside. Both kinds of poachers are likely to shoot from off the backs of moving or stationary pickup trucks.

Because of their design and utility, certain pickup trucks and ATVs (all-terrain vehicles) are natural tools in the poachers' tool kits. In Canada and the United

States, however, it is illegal to hunt from motor vehicles. It is illegal to use motor vehicles to search for, locate, "push bush," or flush out game under any circumstances. Motor vehicles cannot be used off established roads and trails in state wildlife management areas, U.S. Forest Service National Grasslands, Bureau of Land Management lands, federal waterfowl production areas, federal refuges, state school lands, and any areas where motor-driven vehicles are restricted. Motor vehicles are allowed only for transporting hunters, supplies, or equipment to or from hunting destinations. In most, but not all, areas, vehicles may be used to retrieve a big game kill like deer, elk, or moose by the most direct route. Still, the carcasses of poached animals are routinely transported in car trunks, in hidden boxes, or stacked under leaves and plastic garbage bags in the back of pickup trucks.

To help reduce poaching, some provincial and state governments in Canada and the United States have regulated the use of motor vehicles for hunting. For example, the state of North Dakota and the province of Quebec have explicitly forbidden the use of motor vehicles to pursue game. Few other states or provinces have been as forthcoming.

How extensive is the practice of shooting animals from vehicles? The question is nearly impossible to answer directly. There are, however, selected media stories that clearly illustrate animals having been wantonly shot from vehicles. Poachers On-line documented a case in which two juvenile boys from Campbell County, Wyoming were fined over $1000 and given 45 days in jail, 6 months probation, and the revocation of hunting privileges for six years. The two young men were convicted of killing a big game animal by shooting from a vehicle.

One of the most effective measures used to stop poaching is the implementation of Poaching Hotlines, where citizens are urged to call if they suspect poaching happening somewhere in the United States. A successful ending to a serious poaching incident happened in Gillette, Wyoming. An anonymous caller to the Poaching Hotline left a message about several deer, including a mule buck and antelope, having been shot and left to rot in February 2005. Two game wardens investigated the area and found two doe antelope and a doe deer carcass. After further investigation, the game wardens arrested two male hunters and a 17-year-old juvenile for killing the animals from their vehicles while driving on county roads. Their weapons were .243, .223 and .22 calibre and 7.62-millimetre rifles. One of the wardens said the following:

> We aren't sure how many animals were actually killed because they were shooting into herds as they saw them. Unfortunately, this type of activity happens more often than we'd like to think. This time, things worked out because someone came forward and provided critical information that was needed to begin an investigation. Without the

help of this informant, these poachers probably may not have been caught. (Poachers On-line, undated)

A common outcome of hunting from vehicles is that the animal's head is sliced off for a trophy and the carcass is left to rot in the wild.

In a Louisiana experiment, game wardens placed a deer decoy near the side of a road at different times of the day and for different time spans. Officers monitored the number of motorists who stopped and shot the decoy. Different time segments produced similar findings: drivers shot the decoy from moving and stopped vehicles. All actions were illegal. In the first day, the authorities issued twenty-four citations to ten people for hunting from a road, hunting from a moving vehicle, and hunting deer during illegal hours. On another day, seven hunters shot at the decoy. Again, citations were handed out for hunting from a road and for hunting from a moving vehicle. This trend continued for at least another month until the decoy was taken down (Outdoor Central News Network, 2003). The experiment illustrates the extent to which illegal shooting from vehicles happens on a regular basis. If left unchecked, it would undoubtedly increase significantly.

Shooting moose from vehicles became an outrage in Cape Breton, Nova Scotia. In 2005, Aboriginal people in the area were becoming upset about moose being shot from the backs of trucks. In a story reported by Wes Stewart (2005), truckloads of hunters patrolled the highland area and shot moose from vehicles at night. Night-vision goggles were used to track the prey. Tony Nette, manager of wildlife resources with the Department of Natural Resources that year, told the local newspaper that abuse of moose hunting was a big problem carried out by a few Aboriginal and a lot more non-Aboriginal hunters. He said, "Hunters are up there riding ATVs, rifles slung over their shoulders, or hunting from the back of a pickup...there are an awful lot of unethical practices going on." (Stewart, 2005: A1)

On an equally sad and dramatic note is the issue of shooting grizzly bears from vehicles. One of the last remaining areas where grizzly bears still roam free is near Jasper National Park, around the forests and clearings of Hinton, Alberta. A biologist has verified that twenty-six grizzlies were shot and killed in the area during a four-year period ending in 2001. It is believed that many deaths go undetected. By using the 50/50 formula, whereby for every dead bear found there is another undiscovered, the biologist suggested that the actual death rate for grizzlies in the area for a four-year period is about fifty. The numbers are serious because there are less than a thousand grizzlies in Alberta (McDiarmid, 2002).

The main cause of the wanton destruction is the increased use of motor vehicles in the area. Because of logging, gas and other natural resource exploration and development, and agriculture, more roads have been graded in the Rocky Mountain area. These roads offer increasing access into bear habitat. Poachers use the roads to seek out elk, sheep, or grizzly bears in formerly remote and pristine natural areas. Such was the fate of Mary, a beloved local grizzly living near the town of Hinton, who was found dead near a gravel road. The biologist suggested that the bear was shot from the road, or the poacher drove into the ditch and killed the bear within metres of the road (McDiarmid, 2002). The poachers' accomplice was the vehicle—and the many roads that provided access to the bear.

Poaching activities can be further refined to night hunting, where motor vehicles are equipped with powerful spotlights to find animals at night. Blinded and confused, animals stagger in front of vehicles, becoming easy targets. Hunters easily shoot them for recreation, fast meat, or trophies.

The use of off-road vehicles for hunting has increased over the years. There is less need for hunters to "walk and stalk," which is part of the traditional "fair chase" of elk, moose, or deer through rugged countryside. A pro-ATV newsletter suggested the following:

> Over the past couple of decades, ATVs have embedded themselves deep into the hunting culture. They've become such an important tool that many hunters now wonder how they ever got along without them. However, the use of ATVs by hunters has also sparked controversy, and it usually is the result of some riders not following common-sense courtesy rules or fair-chase procedures. (*Dirt Wheels Magazine*, 2004: 1)

The following is a description from one of many case studies. Names and locations have been altered for anonymity.

> An undercover officer met Belinda and Dale in the local bar. After getting to know the two, the officer was invited to go hunting with the couple on the following Sunday. He subsequently joined them on a total of 48 hunting trips. The undercover work led to the couple being charged with 61 counts of poaching-related offences.
>
> On the first trip, the officer drove his regular pickup truck with Dale in the passenger seat and Belinda sitting in the middle.
>
> Once the team arrived north west of the Edson area they travelled between the forest reserves. As they entered the area, Belinda told the two men to get their rifles out. She got out her 270 rifle and left the Lee Enfield 303 behind the seat. Although the truck was moving, the rifle was fully loaded, sitting in the front seat on the passenger side. The muzzle end was down towards the floorboards of the truck.

Belinda suddenly jolted the undercover officer to stop because she had spotted some deer down the hill. Dale told Belinda that the deer were about 400 yards away and that he was not willing to pack the dead animal that far. But Belinda was curious to see if she could kill an animal from this distance. She sat in the truck (with the door shut), aimed at the deer from the window, and pulled the trigger. But the gun did not go off. So she used the bolt action, loaded another shell into the rifle and fired. At first Belinda thought she missed. After leaving the scene, Belinda told the two men that she thought that one of the deer did flinch. Maybe she had hit it, but she didn't feel like checking.

The trio went on another hunting trip the following week. This time they packed a bag with a spotlight, a rope, knives, and firearms. A fourth person asked to come along for the hunt. The four hunters continued going west on a main road that had turned from pavement to gravel, when Dale suddenly told the driver to stop. He had seen a moose to the left of the truck.

Belinda and Dale got out and stood beside the left quarter panel on the backside of the truck. Belinda raised her rifle and shot freehand. Two shots were fired. Dale also fired off two shots from the side of the truck. The moose dropped on Belinda's shot. Both went to the moose with knives to "finish it off."

In September of the same year, the trio was driving through a wildlife sanctuary when they spotted a couple of wolves crossing the road in front of them. As they drove through the sanctuary, Belinda said she should have shot the wolves, skinned them, and sold the hides. A short while later the group stopped the truck, and Belinda got the firearms out. It was still dark. Belinda took out a spotlight to improve her vision so early in the morning. She told the two men that if they saw a deer or moose she would give the driver the spotlight to hold on the animal while she pulled the trigger.

Later in September, the three took with them a spotlight to help search for animals. While on a straight stretch of oiled road, the trio came upon three whitetail deer, which the undercover officer judged to be mule deer. Belinda jumped out of the truck and rested her rifle between the cab and the open door. The bullet tore through the rib cage of the first deer, the mother, then broke the backbone of one of her fawns. Belinda hit the doe and fawn with one shot. Both animals dropped. Belinda wanted to go after the third deer because she didn't think it would stay alive over the long winter, but it ran off.

After the carcasses were thrown onto the back of the truck, the trio set out to shoot moose. Just southeast the driver noted three moose in different locations. Belinda went after the first one. She missed. She came back to the truck. The trio drove a little ways, and she shot at a second moose. Then a third one. She went in looking for them, but she missed. The trio left the area at noon, stopping at a campground to string up the two deer in a tree, and to skin and gut them.

On the way back to the city, the three discussed what to do with the deer. Neither Belinda nor Dale wanted them. So they decided to transport them to Calgary where a friend would buy them for $125.00. The deer were piled into Belinda's mini-van, with the doe lying underneath the fawn. (They transferred the carcasses to the mini-van because the back of the truck was full of blood and guts.) The exchange ended with each member of the trio receiving only $30.00 cash.

More events like this happened. About forty-eight of them! Belinda was found guilty of 22 of the 61 counts, and Dale 13 of 61 counts.

Experts say that poachers are arming themselves with increasingly sophisticated equipment, weapons, ATVs and SUVs, and high-technology items such as global positioning systems and night vision equipment. It gives poachers better odds of escaping capture (Colorado Division of Wildlife, 2003), while increasingly threatening wildlife.

ROAD KILL

Each year thousands, if not millions, of animals are killed on public roadways. Deer, skunks, porcupines, squirrels, groundhogs, birds, mice, and rabbits are dominant species that die under the wheels of the automobile. The problem is becoming more serious as the number of vehicles on the road increases. For example, collisions involving wildlife and domestic animals in Alberta have nearly doubled from 5997 cases in 1991 to 11 412 in 2001. Similar statistics are evident in other Canadian provinces (Canada Safety Council, 2004).

The Highway Safety Information System (HSIS) in the United States studied animal crashes. The report drew the following conclusions:

» Animal crashes, both in terms of total numbers and as a percentage of all reported crashes, have steadily increased.
» Animal crashes tend to occur more frequently in rural areas.
» November has substantially more animal crashes than any other month.
» Animal crashes occur more frequently at night.
» In terms of time of day, the greatest number of animal crashes occur in the early morning hours (between 4 to 6 a.m.) and the evening hours (between 6 and 11 p.m.).

» Using a "sliding scale" approach, animal crash clusters (0.5-km-long sections with an average of more than one reported animal crash per year) were identified in each of the States.

(HSIS, 1995)

The American Insurance Institute for Highway Safety analyzed federal crash reports and concluded that during 1998 and 2002, there were 201 fatal crashes that involved animals, an increase of 27% from the previous four years (IIHS, 2005). Some studies have shown that while drivers avoid some animals, they actually aim for others. A snake was laid out in the road and observed by a class of sociology students. It appeared that drivers aimed for the rubber snake. One driver slowed down, drove over it, then reversed and drove over it again. An oncoming truck driver steered his vehicle to the wrong side of the road to hit the snake. It appears that, for some drivers, certain animals are fair game.

IN SUMMARY

Motor vehicles play a significant role in the domination of human beings over animals. They can be designed, equipped, marketed, and used for hunting purposes or for the purpose of exploiting nature. Hunting and poaching with the use of motor vehicles is a calculated practice that reflects on our values. Moreover, some people contend that violence against animals is a potential forerunner for social antagonism, violence among individuals, or a gateway crime for future violent crimes (Leiss, 1972).

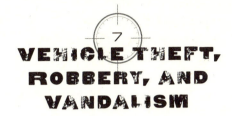

VEHICLE THEFT, ROBBERY, AND VANDALISM

The world is round. Only one third of its people are asleep
at any one time. The other two thirds are awake and
causing mischief somewhere.

— DEAN RUSK, U.S. SECRETARY OF STATE

Everyone seems to have an opinion about car theft. Some think it is merely joyriding, a non-violent crime, a societal nuisance. Thousands of thefts happen every year with few receiving special attention. Yet car theft is a serious crime that does impact the victims' lives.

The simplest definition of auto theft is someone takes a motor vehicle from someone else and deprives that person of ownership. At best, it is a thief jimmying the lock while the owner is shopping or sleeping. At worst, it is a criminal threatening or imposing physical violence on an owner before forcefully taking the vehicle. Once stolen, the vehicle may be used for immediate transportation, joyriding, dealing drugs, robbing convenience stores or other businesses, or threatening to harm and kill people.

Despite booming Canadian and American economies of the late 1990s and subsequent years, the gap between the rich and poor continues to grow (Gray, 1998). Liberal criminologists propose that poverty or the lack of personal resources is a leading contributor to theft and robbery. Some "have-nots" may become desperate and steal from the "haves" because they do not have or perceive to have legitimate opportunities to benefit from the economic dream. They steal as situations present themselves: for example, when a car with keys in the ignition sits in front of a convenience store. Others engage in car theft as a planned activity, a pre-defined strategy that includes vehicle location, theft engagement, and subsequent resale.

Another theory of crime especially relevant to vehicle theft is the bio-psychological theory, which states that people, when given a choice, will choose a course of action that provides them with more benefits than drawbacks (Wilson & Hermstein, 1985). The potential benefits are material gains (e.g., the stolen vehicle), emotional benefit (e.g., stealing a car for thrill rides), approval of one's peers (e.g., friends approve of stealing as an activity), and the ability to satisfy an individual's sense of justice (e.g., stealing as revenge).

Regardless of the theory to make sense of car theft, there is still the stark reality that stealing motor vehicles is a normative feature of our times. The Insurance Information Institute (2005) reported that motor vehicle theft in the United States happens at a rate of a vehicle stolen every twenty-five seconds. In Canada, one in ten households reported that they were victims of motor vehicle theft (Nathans Centre for the Study of Organized Crime, 2003). The odds of a motor vehicle being stolen in the United States are about 1 in 190. In Canada, it is about 5 per 1000 people or 6.5 thefts per 1000 insured vehicles (Statistics Canada, 2006; Insurance Bureau of Canada, 2006). Furthermore, 2 out of 100 registered motor vehicles were robbed of automotive parts, or personal property was stolen from them. A consistent pattern in the data is that Canadians are twice as likely as Americans to have a pickup truck, mini-van, or suv stolen, but less likely to have a car stolen (Statistics Canada, 2001). If auto theft were a legitimate business, it would be ranked fiftieth among the Fortune 500 companies. According to the FBI, motor vehicle theft is an estimated $7.5 billion business in the United States that continues to grow as the demand for stolen vehicles grows in countries throughout the world (U.S. Department of Justice, 2005).

Motor vehicle theft has become a part of our social context. We objectively acknowledge that it happens, then curse when it happens to family and friends, only to shrug it off later as just another everyday crime that gets limited attention from police. Most of us habitually lock the car doors to help prevent theft. By doing so we reduce the likelihood of a domino effect whereby a stolen vehicle can be used in the commission of a subsequent crime, or the likelihood of a police chase at high speed that results in death or injury to the criminals or innocent bystanders.

THE SIGNIFICANCE OF AUTO THEFT AS A CRIME

As cars replaced horses, horse thieves upgraded their skills and began to steal automobiles. Not a day goes by without instances of motor vehicles being stolen from shopping malls, curbsides, residential driveways, parking lots, and garages.

The FBI distributes a Uniform Crime Report that illustrates the occurrences of certain crimes. McGoey (2000b) established from those reports that nearly 1.4 million vehicles are stolen annually in the United States. The crime is most dominant in the urban regions where large metropolitan areas of the United States sport an annual vehicle theft rate of 1223 per 100 000 people. Small cities with less than 10 000 inhabitants reported a car theft rate of 247 per 100 000 people, and rural counties had a rate of only 126 per capita (McGoey, 2000b).

As high population density, urbanism, and megalopolises become more prominent, so does the motor vehicle theft rate. The presence of so many vehicles and the large number of streets presents a problem for the police to identify stolen vehicles visually when there are thousands of similar-looking vehicles in traffic every day. Sometimes, aggressive police officers do recover stolen vehicles when they stop drivers for traffic infractions, such as speeding or running red lights (McGoey, 2000a).

The Insurance Bureau of Canada noted that auto theft costs Canada close to $1 billion a year, considering insurance, police, health care and judiciary costs. Insurance companies paid $600 million annually with an additional $250 million paid for police, health care, judiciary costs, and correctional services in 1997 (Standard & Poor's, 2000). The Insurance Crime Prevention Bureau reported that auto theft rates in Canada translate to more than $43 per premium annually (Insurance Bureau of Canada, 2004). They are most problematic in Alberta, Quebec, and British Columbia, which have some of the highest per capita theft rates in North America. About 25% of stolen vehicles in Canada are never recovered.

In their study to identify the relationship between auto theft and mortality, the National Committee to Reduce Auto Theft (2002) indicated that there is no comprehensive reporting system that captures and links incidents involving stolen vehicles and related injuries and deaths in Canada. However, the authors of the study reviewed newspaper articles published between 1999 and 2001 and established that, for those years, eighty-one persons were killed as a direct result of auto theft, and another 127 suffered injuries. The analysts further estimated that young people account for more than 40% of those charged with motor vehicle theft, resulting in 20 road fatalities per year in Canada. Overall, vehicle theft produced an average of 27 fatalities and 117 injuries per year in Canada between 1999 and 2001, without any indications that these numbers are likely to decline in the future (Parks, 2002).

Motor vehicle theft transcends boundaries between neighbourhood, province, and country. Before an owner realizes that the car is missing, well-organized gangs can steal a Mercedes in Canada, ship it to France, and have it driven unimpeded to the Russian border at Kaliningrad (Kupchinsky, 2003). Another car theft pipeline is located in western Canada where vehicles are stolen in

Calgary, transferred to the United States, and shipped to international markets in the Middle East or Central and South America.

PROFESSIONAL CAR THIEVES

For some thieves, stealing vehicles is an occupation practised with pride, skill, and technique. Professional car thieves are masters of technology, quick assessors of motor vehicle quality and worth, business contractors, and, if need be, professional stunt drivers. Car theft is a career for them. A common belief among car thieves is that they are no different from businesses that sell bad or unnecessary merchandise to naïve customers or auto mechanics who perform unnecessary repairs (Henslin, 1996). Like other businesses, car thieves can operate independently or as team members. They steal and sell as single operators or they fulfill contracts for organized crime or crime co-operatives.

The auto theft professionals are skillful, strategically opportunistic, brazen, organized, networked, and financially aggressive. This was well illustrated in the following description of car thieves in White Plains, New York:

> They stripped cars in the garage while the owners were asleep inside
> the house. Other times they used computer equipment described as
> "steal kits"—disconnecting a car's computer system and connecting
> their own to bypass alarms and start the car. The thieves could switch
> a car's computer system in six or seven minutes. (Liebson, 2003, June 5)

When the police cracked this case the professional gang had stolen approximately $1 million worth of vehicles during a three-month period. Ironically, authorities caught the thieves by stealing one of the thieves' cars. They fitted it with a tracking system, then followed the thieves as they stole cars from driveways and garages.

In 2006, thieves used laptop computers to steal soccer star David Beckham's BMW. The high-tech criminals used a laptop and transmitter to open the locks and start the ignition of Beckham's armour-plated BMW X5. Six months later, a second BMW X5 was stolen from Beckham using the same technology (Holl, 2006).

Vehicle theft, although typically involving individuals acting alone, is often part of a larger enterprise that includes a team of thieves, computer technicians, vehicle repair shops, and salespersons. It gives the appearance of a criminal corporate venue. The professional auto thief, much like a salesperson, has a business plan designed to fulfill market needs. Michael Miller (1987), an expert on motor vehicle crime, argued that organized crime rings select vehicle models for theft from a shopping list of highly profitable vehicles that customers want. Specific cars are targeted, boosted, and quickly driven to a central location, from which they are then shipped to international markets. The scope of sales is large. For example, in Canada alone, 170 000 vehicles were stolen in 2006, of which 20 000 stolen vehicles were exported (Insurance Canada, 2006).

Stolen cars are also marketed locally. Curbsiders advertise them in newspaper want ads as used vehicles for sale. There are always enough unsuspecting customers to make the scam profitable. As with international sales, the type of vehicle stolen may be determined by the characteristics of the local market and facilitated by individuals who know the system (Field et al., 1991).

The following is a description of an inside job. Names, dates, type of vehicle, location, and other identifiable information have been altered for anonymity.

Awari, a forty-five-year-old Canadian citizen, emigrated from Lebanon to start a new life in Canada in the early 1960s. He lived in Prince George, British Columbia, and worked at K & L Auto Sales. He had no criminal record prior to being indicted with two counts of being in possession of two different motor vehicles, knowing that they were stolen. The first count related to a 1996 Toyota Celica and the second count, three years later, featured a 1998 Audi.

The Toyota Celica belonged to Isobel, who reported it stolen from a Vancouver car dealership, where her son had left it for repairs. Her son had placed the keys in the dealership's drop box. When Isobel phoned the dealership the next morning to inquire about the car she learned that it had been stolen.

The car was eventually found parked near Awari's West Vancouver residence. Awari had used it as his personal vehicle for several months. After the vehicle was recovered, the police checked its Vehicle Identification Number near the windshield. The number on the plate was different from the vehicle number found on other parts of the car. The new number on the Toyota came from K & L Auto Sales, a company that rebuilds and repairs motor vehicles and engines, often from salvage vehicles obtained from the provincial Crown insurance company.

Awari had worked for K & L for six years as a body man and mechanic. When asked by the courts about the false identification number on the Toyota, he had no satisfactory exculpatory explanation. He pleaded guilty.

Awari was sentenced to four months imprisonment, to be served in the community, and probation for an additional twelve months.

SITUATIONAL AUTO THEFT

Auto theft can be a means for people to get their hands on quick cash. It provides an income for those who don't have access to work opportunities or who are unwilling to work in traditional employment. Furthermore, some young people hoist cars to experience the thrill of the theft and the joyride that follows. Unfortunately, the term "joyriding" minimizes the seriousness of the offence and the potential loss of life or injury that can result from it. There's nothing joyful about a twelve-year-old losing control of two tonnes of steel through a crowd of innocent people.

Canadian crime statistics for 2001, which are still quoted today, provide a breakdown of youth and auto theft (Juristats cited in Legal Notices, 2003). Forty-two percent of those charged with motor vehicle theft were aged twelve to seventeen, compared with 20% for other Criminal Code offences. More precisely, as the Solicitor General of Canada concluded in 2003, the average age of a young car thief is sixteen (Public Safety Canada, 2003). Similarly, in the United States, an estimated 175 400 car thieves were arrested in 1996. Of those arrested, 42% were eighteen years old or younger and their primary purpose was joyriding (McGoey, 2001).

An extraordinary outgrowth of joyriding is the use of cars as "driverless missiles." Joyriders steal a car and rig it to continue running after the driver has jumped out. They jam the accelerator pedal and send the empty vehicle flying down back lanes and highways, across lakes and ditches, smashing through fences, garages, utility poles, and buildings (Canadian Press, in Cormier, 2004). Driverless missiles are not just silly freshman pranks. They carry heavy financial burdens on victims of the car theft, and they have the potential to injure, as in a case in Winnipeg, when a sedan crashed through the wall of an apartment building and landed on a bed. Fortunately, the tenant was not home at the time (Canadian Press, 2005).

The impact of auto theft on the individual victim is grief and pain. The following example describes the psychological impact on a mother when her vehicle was stolen. Her story was given at an interview held in 2006. Names and other identifiable information have been altered for anonymity.

Lorna had just turned fifty, slowly regrouping from a difficult divorce. She had three children, two teenaged sons and a daughter.

One evening, Lorna drove to the city library to return books she had on loan. She stopped her black 1997 Dodge Caravan mini-van in the No Parking zone directly in front of the library's front door and left it running. Her purse was flopped on the passenger seat, partially open.

Lorna scooped up the books she wanted to return and went in the front doors of the library, heading toward the book return slot beside the front desk. A young man was walking out as she entered. Lorna dropped off the books and returned outside.

Just as she left the library, she spotted her van reversing out of the No Parking zone. She ran up to the back window and pounded on it, yelling for help. But the van roared off. Lorna ran into the library to ask the clerk to dial 9-1-1.

A police car appeared in minutes. After talking to the officers, Lorna called her daughter to pick her up.

Lorna thought about the many things that needed to be done. She had to call the credit card companies and cancel her credit cards. She had to call her insurance company, and her driver's licence and other laminated documents had to be reported stolen.

In the hours after the theft, Lorna became a nervous wreck. She rehashed the story to her children several times, and spent the night tossing and turning, crying silently, trying to control her fears. The thief had her insurance and registration documents, which provided him with her address. And he had her house keys—a potential invitation to come to her home.

The police called early the next morning. They had spotted her van in the suburbs, being driven recklessly on icy streets. Because of the weather and road conditions, the police couldn't give immediate chase. They thought the van was packed with electronic wares that were stolen from a recent break-in at a home-entertainment store.

Lorna became anxious that her vehicle of six years would become a police target and be involved in a chase ending in a smash-up. Then, she received a call from the RCMP saying the van was spotted in a nearby town, again being driven erratically, and again the police were unable to stop it. A house break-in was reported in the town, and the van was reported to be near the scene of the crime.

At 3:45 the next morning, a city patrol car noted a grey mini-van speeding down the street. An officer took up pursuit while his partner checked the licence plates on the computer. The van had been stolen and the driver was a suspect for local breaking and entering. There was fresh snow on the city's roadways, making driving slick, but there was not much traffic. The police car gave chase. The driver of the van, a nineteen-year-old man, sped up, but lost control and smashed into the front end of another oncoming police car. The van careened off and struck a tree. The thief suffered a broken arm and broken ribs from the side impact, and his passengers had cuts and bruises. The van was a write-off.

Although the incident had a violent ending, Lorna was relieved when she heard the outcome. She no longer had to fear for her family's safety. In her mind, however, her mini-van had transformed into an object of dread. She did not want to see it ever again.

Lorna's story illustrates that vehicle theft involves more than just the loss of a vehicle. The harm resulting from a car theft transcends inconvenience or financial loss. The victim feels vulnerable and suffers on different levels. This story also exemplifies the fact that car thieves are 200 times more likely to have a serious crash with a vehicle than its owner ever will (*Overdrive*, 2001). Stolen vehicles are moving targets for high-speed police chases that often result in violent endings.

STEALING VEHICLE PARTS

Vehicles that are expensive because of their form and image are often stolen to be stripped down for their parts, and are subsequently sold on the black market, Internet auctions, or in other marketing operations.

Recycled or used car parts are desired items. Illicit workshops or "chop shops" strip stolen vehicles of parts that are quickly sold to both aware and unaware customers. Auto insurers claim that a $20 000 stolen vehicle can be stripped and sold into $30 000 worth of parts inventory to unscrupulous scrap and auto-body shops (McGoey, 2000b). Truckers can order a second-hand transmission or clutch assembly at half the price of a new one. For years, truckers needed only to call ahead for a transaction at an agreed-upon location (Rothe, 1990).

As part of the economy, recycled vehicle parts can experience market fluctuations. As more gadgets and mechanical innovations are introduced into new motor vehicles, the value of the vehicle increases on the black market. For example, recent years have seen a significant rise in the theft of air bags, which are costly to produce and relatively easy to steal. The U.S. National Insurance Crime Bureau (2003) confirmed that more than 75 000 air bags are dismembered from their cars every year, costing insurers and vehicle owners more than $50 million per year. While new air bags bought from car dealers cost about $1000 each, stolen ones bought on the black market range from $20 to $200 each. Unbeknownst to the vehicle owner, a $20 air bag is installed, but the owner pays $2000 for what he thinks is a new air bag (State Farm Insurance, undated; *CBC News*, 2007). Criminal elements pocket the difference between the cost of new parts and those stolen (Gregoire, 2001). Unfortunately, precise figures are not available in Canada because no one seems to be tracking specific numbers (Harvey, 2005).

Damaged air bags that are replaced by used ones create a significant safety problem. In 2000, a fifty-three-year-old Vancouver woman was killed after the air bag in her car didn't deploy. There are no guarantees of safety when body shops install stolen or malfunctioning air bags in vehicles.

Dealing in stolen air bags has become more lucrative than the historical favourite of slicing stereo systems out of car dashboards. Air bags are easy to dismantle, they have no serial number, and are hard to trace. Furthermore, those who steal air bags are highly trained professionals, who have specific tools for the job. A thirty-five-year-old victim of an air bag theft described the professionalism of the theft as follows:

> Thieves left no debris and no other damage. It was done with the precision of a cardiologist, I can tell you. It was nice and clean, almost like honor among thieves. I'm surprised they didn't wash it. (Gregoire, 2001: 1)

The stolen parts market operates like any other business in a free enterprise system, according to the law of supply and demand. The rule of thumb is that vehicles which are the most likely targets for theft of parts are also top selling models. The demand for recycled parts for such vehicles increases with their popularity. Xenon headlights have become popular with thieves, as have global positioning systems (Insurance Information Institute, 2005).

New hot cars mean new hot equipment. Few items are hotter than Momo wheel packages. Parts dealers charge customers upwards of $8000 for a set. The same set can be bought for $3000 on the black market. Although there are huge savings, the real attraction of stolen Momos is their perceived coolness among young people.

Momo wheel packages are not the only hot ticket item. In California, thieves pick on Honda Civics and Acura Integras to poach sleek body types and engine parts for use in the growing street-racing subculture. Ironically, the GPS security systems, such as LoJack or OnStar, designed to stop car theft, are stolen by thieves and sold on the streets to customers who want to protect themselves from car theft.

The media plays a significant role in marketing trendy car features. It glamourizes car parts like "spoilers" on television or movie screens, creating a "demand and supply" though the black market. The highlighting of specific vehicle accessories in music videos, ads, movies, and computer games contributes to an underground marketplace for drivers who want to become like the people portrayed in the media. Wheel covers, headlights, mirrors, air intakes, sound systems, bumpers, and grills are coveted items. The Escalade is the vehicle of choice for the rap-music videos, and the Momo package rules for young entrepreneurs.

The contemporary cult of vehicle break-ins includes the theft of valued possessions, such as CD players. Although these are relatively low-cost items in the crime severity scale, their theft often transforms the car. To get at these personal pieces, thieves break windows, slash convertible roofs, or mutilate car doors, often creating monetary damage in the range of $300 to $3000. One prevalent practice is the "smash and grab." Thieves locate a target vehicle, smash its window, and scoop items sitting on the seat or on the floor. They escape on foot and are seldom caught. The following Crime Stoppers warning in Regina, Saskatchewan describes the impact of smash and grab thieves:

> Over the course of Monday December 25th and Tuesday December 26th, the Regina Police Service received numerous reports of vehicle damage. Almost all of the reported incidents involved the windows of vehicles being damaged or destroyed, and articles being stolen from inside. The 12 reported incidents occurred mostly in northwest Regina, however, there had been similar incidents reported in the south end of the city a few days prior. (Regina Police Service, Crime Stoppers, 2007, March 9)

Thieves constantly scan for easy targets like tourists who drive rental vehicles in recreation areas. Travellers are likely to carry more money and valuables than local residents. Because tourists are easily lulled by the seeming serenity of local sights, they often fail to take simple theft precautions such as rolling up windows, stowing away valuables in the trunk, parking in brightly lit areas of the city, or locking their cars (Wakefield, 1998). There is plenty of opportunity for motivated thieves to either steal the car and dismantle it for parts, or grab purses and cameras left lying on the back seat.

Auto theft has become a form of pop crime that can be easily learned through the Internet, where there is quality and quantity of information for would-be auto thieves. Tools like the "Slim Jim," a lock pick instrument, were recently marketed for easy forced entry. Automakers countered the use of the tool by either placing covers over the locking mechanism or by moving the door-lock mechanisms to a place in the door where it is difficult to get at with a Slim Jim. In response, the American Locksmith Service introduced a new and improved Slim Jim, priced at $6, which is thirty inches long and three-quarters of an inch wide. It is capable of slipping through the new car lock cover inside the car.

Thieves who want to upgrade can use a door-opening kit that includes six carbon lockout tools for about $30. Some thieves shop at certain supply stores who still sell "tryout keys" for most cars, for the nominal cost of about $20 per set. Other gadgets designed for easy vehicle entry are lock aid guns, thermal lances, needle-picking vibrators, and cobra picks. Despite these easily accessible tools for illegal vehicle entry, Statistics Canada reported that the most common technique for gaining criminal access to motor vehicles is the use of keys which are either stolen from owners or left inside vehicles.

A Vancouver study of car crime in parking garages completed by Rondeau and Graf (1996) found that stealing from cars was three times more prevalent than the stealing of cars. Most often the culprits are habitual street criminals with drug habits, petty offenders with alcohol problems, or transients (Clarke & Goldstein, 2003). Theft from cars is more opportunistic and can be achieved quickly and with relative privacy in parking garages. The goods stolen can be easily marketed for small amounts of cash, which is often used to support drug and alcohol habits. Thieves prowl parking lots and garages for visible loot, such as purses, wallets, recreational equipment, or electronic devices.

THE FENCE

The "fence" is the broker between the thief and customer for stolen property. They convert loot into cash. Successful fences buy and sell stolen property regularly and profitably over a period of time. Their success is based on having a good reputation among car thieves or other vehicle-based criminals and the criminal community generally (Abadinsky, 1983).

As private entrepreneurs, they bargain with criminals, usually making a 30% to 50% profit of the stolen vehicle's wholesale value (Abadinsky, 1983). In some cases, the fence collects vehicles in one part of the country and resells them elsewhere in the world, such as Middle East countries, Indo-China, Russia, and the Far East.

STEALING MOTORCYCLES

A discussion about motor vehicle theft must include motorcycles. In the United States, 70 613 motorcycles were stolen in 2005. The thefts amount to a loss of over $434 million to motorcycle owners and the insurance industry (National Insurance Crime Bureau, 2005). As the popularity of ridership increases and the value of machines goes up, so does the demand for stolen motorcycles.

Because motorcycles can easily be altered, reused, modified, or have their parts and frames camouflaged, recovery rates for stolen bikes are only around 25% to 30%.

The main culprits involved in motorcycle theft are professional thieves, many of which are motorcycle gang members. Similar to chopping cars, motorcycles can be stripped down for parts or for reconstruction of a clone motorcycle. In some cases, stolen luxury motorcycles receive the same treatment as luxury cars, and are sold on the international market.

VANDALISM

The manifest realms of theft observe a high level of vandalism. Parked vehicles have their windows broken, tires punctured, paint jobs keyed, hoods dented, headlights smashed, body panels kicked in, door mirrors ripped off, and windshield wipers snapped off. Such acts happen at any time, day or night, weekday or weekend. The objective always seems to be the same: cause damage and leave a message.

Although we imagine that vandals are young people bent on thrill, they actually can be anyone. Witness a case in Sacramento where the car of an orthopedic surgeon was deeply scratched while parked at the hospital. Over the course of eleven months, his car was keyed eight different times. The surgeon countered by installing a small surveillance camera, which captured footage of a colleague vandalizing the car. Apparently, the colleague sought revenge for being asked to leave their shared medical practice. Faced with the evidence, the perpetrator entered a plea of guilty to misdemeanour vandalism (*News 10 ABC*, 2004, June 25).

Accurate statistics on vehicle vandalism are almost impossible to retrieve. Many owners do not notify the police, believing there is little they can do. Within the realm of criminal activities with which police officers have to deal, vandalism to vehicles does not rate highly. It becomes another normalized feature of car ownership in North America.

The motivation for vandalizing motor vehicles varies. A 1992 Ontario task force organized to study vandalism interviewed those who had confessed in court. Many offenders thought that vandalism was a game they could easily win because they rarely get caught and suffer the consequences. More specific reasons include teens feeling the need to fit in with a group, pleasing a friend, or building self-esteem. Some are defiant against authority or have the desire for revenge against a person, institution, or organization. For others, vandalism is a backlash to pressures experienced at home, and a cure for boredom.

The subject of vandalism is included in this book because it is a well-noted form of passive violence against innocent people. Akin to the broken window theory, vehicle vandalism is a minor crime that, if left unattended, could be the forerunner of more dangerous and serious crimes like auto theft and carjacking (Kelling & Cole, 1996).

TORCHING MOTOR VEHICLES

Revenge, jealousy, spite, crime, concealment, vandalism, excitement, and intimidation are common reasons for burning motor vehicles to the ground, through use of incendiary or bombs. Perpetrators include jilted lovers, quarreling spouses, disgruntled employees, feuding neighbours, and those feeling ethnic, racial, or religious hostilities.

Profit and insurance fraud is another key motive. Derrick's story is an example. Names, dates, location, and other identifiable information have been altered for anonymity.

Derrick, aged eighteen, admitted to police that he and his older friend, Wei, had poured gasoline into the cab of a truck. Wei then threw a propane bottle and burning piece of paper into the cab of the truck, engulfing it in flames and causing $30 000 in damage. The two arsonists admitted that they committed the crime at the request of the truck's owner, who sought to collect insurance proceeds.

Derrick had a troubled past. He barely finished grade nine, after which he was constantly between jobs. His family background was a history of dysfunction, including desertion by his father. Derrick had been put into a foster home because his mother could not manage him.

Psychological testing showed a young man of normal intelligence with chronically high levels of anger and an anti-social disposition. He was considered to be a "damaged man." Previous to the arson, Derrick had a conviction for theft over $5000.

The judge listened to the arguments and rendered a verdict. She found Derrick guilty of arson, a violent offence. She imposed six months of deferred custody, to be followed by nine months of probation.

Insurance fraud is probably the number one factor responsible for motor vehicle arson. A variety of reasons exist. A car owner hires a criminal to make his car "disappear." Such deals are commonly known in street jargon as "give ups." An owner who is behind in his lease or car payments and desperate to escape the debt collectors can torch the vehicle himself as a staged theft and burn. Other owners burn their cars because the repair bills are too high to warrant keeping it. Some owners just want the insurance money, while others want revenge. The instigators often escape punishment because the justice system has difficulty investigating and subsequently punishing these offenders. Some cities, particularly Detroit and Chicago, have an abundance of deserted lots, back alleys, and side streets that allow arsonists to operate undetected (Claxton & Hurt, 2000). Popular targets are abandoned vehicles with limited value.

Revenge by way of burning a vehicle can happen against an individual or against an institution like a government office, bank, or police department. For example, a man was accused of using an accelerant to set four Webster, New York Police Department vehicles on fire one night. The cars were torched behind the department's office. A passerby saw the fire and called 9-1-1. Quick attention allowed a staff sergeant to douse the flames with a fire extinguisher (Lavan, 2005).

IN SUMMARY

It is important to remember that episodes of car theft and vandalism constitute breaches of trust, and they constitute criminal behaviour. They are prevalent, but not as sensational as dramatic violent crimes. They touch the benchmark of our social context. Perhaps they are so taken for granted by the public and law that they are rendered invisible for serious prevention. Organized car theft has parallel practices to legitimate businesses.

Although vandalism happens routinely, it is not a high priority in crime investigation. However, criminologists often suggest that vandalism may serve as a gateway crime that leads to increasingly severe crimes like carjacking, which produces intentional violence.

ROADWAY WORKERS AS VICTIMS OF VIOLENCE

Labor is the curse of the world, and nobody
can meddle with it without becoming
proportionately brutified.

— NATHANIEL HAWTHORNE

For many people, work is a source of identity, a profession, a status. For others, it is survival in a "dog-eat-dog" workplace that is often conducive to injuries. However, it is well documented that violence in the workplace is also a serious risk (Chappell & Di Martino, 1998).

Although most discussions of workplace violence include invisible acts like threats, humiliation, bullying, or verbal abuse, we focus on violence as homicide, physical assault, or assault directed toward employees. A report by the U.S. Department of Labor (2007) stated that homicide is the second highest cause of fatal occupational injury. The United States recorded 516 workplace homicides for 2006. Canada recorded 69 workplace homicides between 2001 and 2005 (de Leseleuc, 2007).

Statistics Canada established that in 2004, nearly one in five reported physically violent incidents happened in the workplace (Statistics Canada, 2007). Three types of events dominate. One is where the perpetrator has an "illegitimate" business relationship with the workplace and enters with a criminal intent such as robbery. About 80% of workplace homicides happen this way. The second is where the perpetrators have a business relationship with the affected workplace as customers or clients (Compas, 2007) . They are dissatisfied with a service, process, or product, and respond violently. Third, colleagues may turn against one another to get even, settle a score, overcome jealousy, lash out against human resource decisions such as a promotion they did not get, or to avenge taunting by fellow workers.

Although all workers are at risk, some personnel experience higher risk of violence than others. Among them are workers who exchange money with the public, deliver passengers, goods, or services, work alone or in small groups at night, work in high-crime areas, or carry out inspection or enforcement duties (U.S. Department of Labor, 2007; Chappell & Di Martino, 1998).

Transportation- or traffic-related employees, such as taxi drivers, bus operators, truckers, bike couriers, and parking enforcement workers, bear the high risks of violence. Of all the employees who earn their living in traffic-related occupations, none are more at risk than taxi drivers, who ply city streets at all times of the night, allowing total strangers, drunk, stoned, aggressive or otherwise, into their cars and transporting them to destinations that drivers would likely not volunteer to approach in the very late hours of a Friday night.

TAXI DRIVERS

The taxi industry provides service twenty-four hours a day, seven days a week, with most drivers working twelve hours or more per day. Night driving is inevitable. Taxis are easily accessible to anyone by phone or signal at the side of the road. Cabbies drive to dispatched locations and give rides to individuals with little or no knowledge about the customers. Their shifts are fraught with danger, expressed in the statistic that in the United States, taxi drivers account for 9% of all occupational homicides, and they have sixty times the average rate of assault, keeping in mind that approximately 75% of attacks against taxi drivers go unreported (National Institute of Occupational Safety and Health, cited in Kabrick, 2004). In Canada, 16% of all workplace homicide victims between 2001 and 2006 were taxi drivers (de Leseleuc, 2007). The risks are especially high for gypsy cabs that go anywhere for a fare. Chappell and Di Martino (1998), two occupational violence researchers, estimated that taxi drivers have up to fifteen times the average exposure to occupational violence, and they have the highest rate of work-related homicide of any group (26.9% per 100 000 workers, compared with the average of 0.71). Furthermore, they are sixty times more likely than other workers to be murdered on the job and five times more likely to be murdered than police officers (Kabrick, 2001a; U.S. Department of Labor, 2000).

Because taxi drivers are independent contractors, it is nearly impossible to obtain accurate statistics on driver violence. Many drivers do not take time off to complete crime reports after an assault or wait around for a police investigation. Many cabbies in Canada and the United States are recent immigrants who do not speak fluent English and who are suspicious of authorities. For them, time is money and they cannot afford to take time off work to speak with officials whom they mistrust. Barb Kabrick (2001b), a strong champion for taxi drivers, argued that the police often do not believe them. She said the following:

> I talked to a cab driver in Kansas City who said that he no longer reports any assaults or even robberies. The first time he was assaulted and robbed, he called the police...When the officer got there, he saw that the cab was parked in a 'no parking' zone. So, the driver was arrested and the cab was towed away. (Kabrick, 2001a)

Furthermore, according to Barb Kabrick, also stated that assaulting a cab driver carries little risk because there is little chance of the perpetrator getting caught.

The Winnipeg Taxi Driver Association did a non-scientific analysis of statistics obtained from online news sources. The database included an international list of events for 255 weeks, covering January 1, 1998, to December 17, 2002. Researchers estimated that, on a worldwide scale, there is a murder rate of 1.1 drivers per week. Because of the unscientific nature of the data collection, the numbers are probably considerably understated. According to the association, two-thirds of the murders happened in the United States. All the murders have resulted from robberies and/or assaults on the job or while taxi drivers were on duty (Jha, 2001).

The high incidence of violence against taxi drivers reflects the everyday occupational behaviours that make them vulnerable. They work alone, often in the evening or late at night, in high-risk areas of the cities. They pick up young men who have been drinking alcohol, have a high level of aggression, and who may have limited funds (Occupational Safety and Health Administration, 2000; Farley, 1999).

Attacks usually come from rear-seat passengers who shoot drivers in the head, neck, or chest, or slash the driver's throat, head, or chest (Farley, 1999), which police consider one of the "most cowardly of crimes" (Calleja, 2002). For example, in December 2007, a 16-year-old girl and her 19-year-old companion sat in the back seat of a cab at 4:00 a.m. in Edmonton. The girl grabbed the head of the cab driver and held a knife against his throat, ordering him to give her his money. A struggle ensued and the driver suffered a serious neck wound (Merritt, 2007).

As a response to the high incidence of violence, some taxi companies in New York, Toronto, and other large centres have installed small cameras in their vehicles. They have been an immediate success, because, according to a Toronto detective, the more people have access to these photos, the more pairs of eyes investigators have to help identify suspects. In one case, the camera caught a robber actually slashing the throat of a cab driver (Calleja, 2002). Still, cab crime in Toronto has been reduced by more than 50% since 2001, when the bylaw requiring taxi owners to install security cameras or GPS in their cars was implemented.

To counter the rising trend in violence further, some taxi companies use a security shield, a Lexan polycarbonate plastic that is shaped to protect cabbies against attacks from the back seat. The shield covers the full width of the seat-back and follows the contour of the inside of the door pillar. It is designed to form a see-through wall between driver and passenger.

Taxi violence also happens outside the cab, when, for example, a cabbie interacts with others or makes a delivery for a customer. It happens when taxi drivers are routinely hired to deliver items like alcohol or fast food to customers. The following case study describes the brutality of an outside-of-cab incident in Alberta. Names, dates, and other identifiable information have been altered for anonymity.

On June 8 about 11:00 p.m., a taxi was dispatched to purchase and deliver an order of liquor to a residence on an Alberta First Nations reserve. When the driver arrived at the address, he was instructed to go further and stop at another house.

When he arrived, the driver took the liquor out of the car and stood beside his vehicle, waiting for someone to come pick it up from the assigned house. He wanted to deliver the alcohol, collect his money, and leave. Instead of money he received three blows to the head and face with an aluminum baseball bat. The assailant took the liquor, soft drinks, and microphone from the cab, smashed all the windows, and fled. The driver died from his injuries.

The assailant later admitted that he had made the call for an order of liquor about 9:30 p.m. He then called seven times, until about 11:15 p.m., when he saw the cabbie arrive. When the police investigated the murder, they discovered that six people had been waiting for the liquor. There was only $20 between them, not enough to pay for the alcohol, soft drinks, and taxi delivery. The Crown argued that the assailant and his girlfriend had a plan to call a cab, have liquor delivered, and then rob the driver.

The assailant was charged with culpable homicide and was subsequently found guilty of second-degree murder. He was imprisoned.

This incident is especially shocking because the murder was a premeditated plan to assault or kill the driver and rob him of the liquor. It was not an impulse action resulting from frayed nerves or a dispute over the cost of a fare.

Barb Kabrick and Candice Ball of the International Taxi Driver Safety Council are two female cabbies turned safety specialists, who recognize the potential dangers of driving cabs. Kabrick (2001a), on behalf of Ball, spoke of personal experiences with company managers who asked drivers to go home, clean up and come back to work shortly after they had been assaulted or beaten, and suffered injury and trauma. If the cabbies did not comply, the managers would charge the drivers for being absent. She reported:

> I had a knife pulled on me, a fare tried to rob me, and a couple of times I got into a scuffle with a passenger...At the company I worked for...if a driver came in bloody, he was asked if he was going home or just clean up and go back out on the job. If the answer was to go home, he was reminded that he would be charged for the time missed.

The two women offered cabbies tips on how to lessen the chance of being physically attacked. They focussed on conversational control, explaining that cabbies who manage or control the talk with customers while they are driving are less likely to be attacked. Kabrick and Ball provided the following advice for cab drivers:

> Control the conversation so you don't get the bullshit...When asked for my phone number, I always gave a business card with the dispatch number on it...When asked about my personal life, I answered briefly and asked the same question of them...If you've just picked up a creepy customer, let the dispatcher know the destination. (Kabrick, 2001a)

RACISM AND TAXI VIOLENCE

The taxi industry experiences high worker turnover in what is now largely an entry-level immigrant industry. Some people liken it to a sweatshop on wheels. Often, poorly paid drivers, many of whom are members of a visible minority, work endless hours under conditions of maximum stress. They suffer not only explicit racial conflict, but also theft of taxi service. Passengers refuse to pay, and, if threatened to do so by the cabbie, the customers may take a racist stance, yelling racial epithets at drivers.

Many people in the taxi industry believe that racism underlies much of the cabbie violence. Dispatchers routinely listen to would-be passengers telling them not to send drivers who are a specific race, skin colour, or ethnicity. However, as Jha (2001) described, in some companies 80% of the drivers come from the Middle East, Asia and East India. Hence, customer demands for drivers with preferred racial or cultural characteristics cannot be fulfilled or they go unheeded. The result may be verbal abuse and potential physical violence initiated by customers against immigrant drivers.

When racism meets physical threat, the result can be a matter of brutal violence that far exceeds statistical formulations of such acts. The following is an example. Names have been altered for anonymity.

A cab driver was helping a fare with the luggage when several young men closed in on him and started to shout racial epithets. The East Indian cabbie feared for his life. Detective McCleod, an off-duty police officer, was in the vicinity. When he attempted to intervene, the young men savagely attacked him. The cabbie called the police.

Detective McCleod suffered a fractured nose and numerous abrasions and bruises on his body, sustained from being punched and repeatedly kicked. The attending judge found the attackers guilty of assault causing bodily injury and a variety of other charges.

CABBIES AND FARE DISPUTES

The taxi business is built on trust. Riders have the reasonable expectation that all taxi drivers will get them to their destination safely and will charge fairly. Cab drivers trust that all riders will be orderly and will pay at the end of the trip.

Taxi fare disputes, however, are a trigger for violence. There is no arbitration system in place to deal with such disputes. Passengers can easily become aggressive, verbally abusive, and violent if they feel the driver has overcharged them. Often, the disputed fare is small, as in a case in Chicago in which a man, who was an AIDS activist and former health department employee, entered into a dispute with a cabbie over an $8 fare. The man got behind the wheel of the taxi and ran down the driver, resulting in a second-degree murder conviction (*Court News*, 2006, August 22).

Fare evasion is hard to prove. A rider can say he thought he had the money but forgot to bring it. So he runs from the cab. The driver is sure to pursue and make a challenge because the missed money is important for a small business like taxi driving. The driver then runs the risk of being beaten up (Smith, 2005).

By the same token, fare evasion may be the result of inflated taxi fares or a cab driver who tries to "run up" the fare by choosing an extended route for an increased fee.

CABBIES AND ILLEGAL ACTIVITIES

Driving cabs is seldom a lucrative business. To make ends meet, some cabbies procure a second income by engaging in transactions that are illegal or morally questionable. When cabbies step into the criminal world, they increase their chances of becoming victims of violence.

Two practices are evident. One is procurement of prostitution, where drivers get cash kickbacks for referring fares to prostitution businesses that front as escort services. This is illegal, a form of pimping, but some drivers see it as little more than offering advice or giving recommendations, something that should not be considered for legal sanction.

More intense and legally straightforward is the act of selling drugs from the vehicle or transporting illicit drugs from the source to the user. The following is an example. Names have been altered for anonymity.

> Cab driver Lee pleaded guilty to one count of trafficking in cocaine. He had sold .89 grams of cocaine to an undercover police officer. Before he was arrested, the cabbie threw 3.8 grams of cocaine out of the window of his car.
>
> Lee had no criminal record. He was married with four children and had spent a considerable amount of time in a southeast Asian refugee camp. He spoke little English. He was not a drug user. He was experiencing financial difficulty supporting his family. A fare he picked up several years ago introduced Lee to selling drugs from his cab.
>
> The taxi driver was found guilty of trafficking in cocaine. He received a conditional sentence of two years less a day, with conditions that included house arrest.

Vancouver, a large Canadian port city with endless opportunities for crime, has its share of taxi drivers who double as illicit drug selling middlemen. Police routinely go undercover to catch suspects. By pretending to be buyers, police officers have been driven to locations around Hastings Street, into the drug-dealing core, where drivers signal alleged dealers to approach the cab and do business with the undercover officer. Dealers then engage in drug transactions with detectives through the windows of the cabs (Howell, 2004).

Drug sales or delivery in cabs does not necessarily mean wrongdoing by the driver. Sometimes passengers use cabs when they collect and distribute drugs. If drivers take action against such passengers by refusing service, they are vulnerable to revenge attacks from drug dealers. Cabbies insist that they cannot refuse a fare simply because they think their passenger may potentially do something illegal.

BUS DRIVERS

Threat of violence is a major stressor also for bus drivers. There are frequent reports of operators being robbed and threatened at knife- or gunpoint. Carrying cash and transfers increases vulnerability. In addition, frustrated riders often vent their rage upon the drivers verbally and complain about the bad conditions in the vehicle itself or their animosity towards other riders.

Transit workers rank ninth among occupations for greatest risk of violence in Canada (LaMar et al., 1998; Olson , 1994). Like taxi drivers, they are always in contact with the public and they are exposed to violence by job functions such as handling money, dealing with frustrated and angry individuals, working in an unsheltered environment, creating waiting times for impatient passengers, enforcing fares, and dealing with complaints about service (Workers' Health and Safety Centre, 1997).

A survey was undertaken by the London Transit Operators in 2003 to establish the extent to which transit operators face physical and verbal assaults in Ontario. London is a Canadian city of 360 000, with a mass transit ridership of 16.5 million per year. Of the 320 operators who provide daily service, 232 completed the survey. The findings showed that 29.7% of respondents had been punched, grabbed, pushed, or spit on, and 41% had been verbally threatened (Gillet et al., 2003).

A researcher for the Amalgamated Transit Union replicated the London study in 2004 and 2005 at seven local offices in the cities of Halifax, Hamilton, Mississauga, Ottawa, Regina, Saskatoon, and Winnipeg. The overall return rate was rather low at 11%. However, for the total of 1468 transit operators who completed the surveys, 36% indicated they had experienced acts of physical assault and 55% of operators had experienced verbal threats. A further 16% of operators reported they had been physically assaulted with no documented correlations of verbal assault, illustrating the prevalence of the element of surprise in the assaults (Bruyere et al., 2005). The researchers defined assault as aggravated assault, sexual assault, physical gestures, kicking, pushing, biting, and/or spitting. Verbal abuse was considered in the form of rude jokes, comments, obscene remarks, insults, ridicule, swearing, shouting, or threats without weapons, causing emotional distress.

The violence against bus drivers did not go unheeded. The union, representing 8500 members of the Toronto Transit Commission advised its members to "no longer engage in fare disputes with customers" in order to reduce the risk of assaults (Amalgamated Transit Union Local 113, 2006).

Violence against transit operators, although common, has not received the priority it deserves. A description of one violent encounter between driver and passenger was aired on CBC News (2006) in Vancouver. According to the reporter, a transit driver in Coquitlam was beaten unconscious for doing his job. He had asked two young men to get off the bus for being 50 cents short for a ticket. The two riders attacked the driver, which caused the bus to crash into a parked car. One attacker was caught and charged with mischief.

In response to the beating of the Coquitlam driver, the local union demanded that more cameras be installed on buses and that drivers be removed from fare payment, because they put themselves at risk whenever they request or demand riders to pay the exact amount of money for the fare.

Violence also transpires on buses without the direct involvement of the bus driver. It can happen between passengers, as it did in Edmonton when four youths brutally beat to death a fellow passenger on a Thursday night bus ride (*CTV News*, 2006). It may also happen with someone intent on hijacking a school bus for his or her own purposes.

The following list of news stories helps to illustrate the prevalence of bus-related violence in the United States:

January 4, 2001: A bus passenger brutally beat a Metro Transit driver and dragged him off the bus in Minneapolis, Minnesota, after becoming angry at having to wait for police to help the driver deal with some women who had refused to pay their fares and refused to get off the bus. (*Star Tribune*, January 22, 2001)

January 24, 2001: Gang members shot at a group of rivals who were riding in a Durham Area Transit Authority bus in Durham, North Carolina, injuring a teenage girl and causing the bus driver to speed away with more than 20 passengers aboard. At least five bullets penetrated a side window of the bus. (*The News & Observer*, January 26, 2001)

January 30, 2001: Gunmen fleeing a robbery in Hillsdale, Missouri, fired at least one shot at a moving bus, injuring a passenger aboard the bus. (*St. Louis Post-Dispatch*, January 31, 2001)

February 4, 2001: A woman was sexually assaulted in the bathroom of a New York-bound Greyhound bus. (*Boston Herald*, February 5, 2001)

April 21, 2001: A passenger punched a Metro Transit bus driver as he was exiting the bus in Minneapolis after the bus driver asked the passenger and his friend to move their legs because they were blocking the rear exit. (*WCCO 4 News*, April 30, 2001)

August 6, 2001: A man attacked and assaulted a bus driver in Corpus Christi, Texas, when the bus driver told the man he could not give him change. (*Corpus Christi Caller-Times*, August 7, 2001)

August 14, 2001: An angry passenger sprayed pepper spray in the face of a bus driver in Pompano Beach, Florida, after complaining that the driver was not driving fast enough. The bus driver and a female passenger with asthma were taken to a nearby hospital with trouble breathing. (*South Florida Sun-Sentinel*, August 15, 2001)

August 4, 2007: The bus driver was punched in the head 10 times, then kicked in the head when he was knocked to the ground— all for simply asking the rider to see proof of fare purchase. (Soft News Canada, August 4, 2007)

December 27, 2007: There have been four attacks within four weeks on MTA buses...The latest happened early Wednesday morning in West Baltimore when a 14-year-old boy was shot as a group of teens got off the number 15 bus. Several held the rear doors open while one person fired shots inside, hitting the teen in the thigh. (*WJZ TV*, December 27, 2007)

The American Public Health Association released a bulletin in 2005 that warned the public about the increasing violence on the nation's school buses. The bulletin stated that students are increasingly inflicting verbal, physical, emotional, and sexual harm upon one another, further illustrating that violence on buses is encroaching on school buses (American Public Health Association, 2005).

TRUCKER VIOLENCE

In 2003, seventy-four immigrants were trapped in a sealed refrigerated trailer that had been abandoned in a field near Harlingen, Texas. The driver was missing. He had been paid $7500 to haul the human cargo, but the people were never unloaded. In his quest for a quick exit, the trucker had failed to turn on the trailer's refrigeration unit. The temperature inside the trailer soared to 173 degrees Fahrenheit.

The victims were desperate. All day and night, they screamed for help, banged on the sides of the trailer, clawed away the insulation, and punched out the tail-lights in a frantic effort to breathe. The next day, one of the Victoria County sheriff's deputies noted the abandoned trailer and decided to investigate. When he opened the cargo door, a stench stopped him in his tracks. Before him were seventeen dead bodies. The other passengers were writhing and convulsing. Two more died later in hospital (Rice, 2005). The victims were from Mexico, Central America, and the Dominican Republic. The main perpetrator was the trucker, who was convicted of fifty-eight counts of transporting and killing illegal immigrants (Associated Press, 2006). He had an earlier conviction for transporting thirty-eight illegal immigrants by truck.

The United States Attorney for the District of Arizona has called the smuggling of alien people into the United States a disturbing humanitarian crisis. Agents who smuggle aliens traffic in human misery (Charlton, 2003).

In 2004, over 2400 people were convicted in U.S. federal district courts under section 274 of the *Immigration and Nationality Act*, the primary statute for prosecuting smugglers of illegal immigrants (U.S. Government Accountability Office, 2005). Senator John McCain estimated that almost four million people crossed the U.S. border illegally in 2004 (McCain, personal letter, February 10, 2004). Many were transported in trucks. In Canada, many illegal immigrants come from China, South Korea, and Mexico, but unless they enter from the United States, they do not come by truck.

The trucking industry has a soft underbelly, whereby operators have the means to engage in outlaw activities that lead to violent ends. It is all too common for them to haul illegal paraphernalia like illicit drugs, alcohol, or smuggled goods.

American border patrols routinely intercept trucks that carry bundles of marijuana from Mexico to the United States. In 2006, members of the Tucson sector of the border patrol intercepted at least five different drug-trafficking operations with trucks. John Slagle (2006) encapsulated the data provided by the U.S. Border Patrol in Tucson:

DATE	CRIME	WORTH
January 27	Border patrol agents at a checkpoint discovered 124 bundles (2598 pounds) of marijuana in a semi-trailer truck.	$2.1M
January 30	Agents investigated a suspicious truck and found 81 bundles (1641 pounds) of marijuana in a hidden compartment. Driver, a naturalized citizen, was arrested.	$1.2M
February 2	Agent in helicopter spotted several vehicles driving into the United States illegally. Trucks tried to evade the helicopter and one truck crashed. Agents found 83 bundles (1938 pounds) of marijuana. Driver escaped.	$1.6M
April 12	Border patrol agents found two stolen trucks. Agents found 3835 pounds of marijuana. Drivers escaped.	$3.1M

(Slagle, 2006)

The trucker sub-culture is not far removed from violence by nature of the enterprise. As victims, truckers can be killed, assaulted, or have their trucks stolen and stripped for parts. Thieves break windows, hot-wire ignitions, and drive trucks from truck lots or truck stops to gravel pits, rock quarries, hidden countryside, or large warehouses. They strip them of valuable parts: tires, batteries, stereos, CB radios, and tail light assemblies. More sophisticated thieves will strip a truck of its electrical equipment, motor accessories, and any parts that can be sold from the back of a pickup. The parts are then peddled on the black market, often at truck stops where the trucks were originally stolen. Truckers are notified through the CB radio that someone somewhere is open for business.

Perhaps the most common act of violence is truck hijacking that involves trailer and cargo theft. Kidnapping usually happens when a driver is forced to submit to robbers and drive the truck to some designated destination. The following example illustrates a driver's confrontation with professional criminals. Names and locations have been changed for anonymity.

> In January, the driver of a semi-truck carrying $277 990 worth of electronic and computer equipment was destined for an electronics warehouse store located in Lethbridge, Alberta. The driver stopped at the side of the road to have a nap, and he was subsequently overpowered by robbers with crowbars and rifles while he was sleeping in the bunk of his truck. He was bound and left lying on the bunk while the robbers drove the vehicle down the highway. After several hours they stopped the vehicle and threw out the driver, who was wearing only sweatpants and a t-shirt. It was freezing cold outside. Luckily, the driver was able to flag down a car for help.
>
> The truck and trailer were later recovered, but the electronic and computer cargo was missing. A police investigation involving the RCMP and a local police department was initiated.
>
> The prime suspect was a local resident, who later implicated himself in a police sting operation. The RCMP staged an operation in a prominent Calgary hotel a year after the robbery and kidnapping. An undercover officer pretended to be a major organized crime leader looking for professional help. A man named Dion approached the undercover agent to apply for a job. To help make sure that Dion took the bait, the police staged a series of criminal operations organized and led by the undercover officer.
>
> When Dion met with the undercover officer, he bragged about his history in crime and highlighted his role in the truck hoist. Shortly after, the RCMP captured Dion and charged him with kidnapping, aggravated assault, and theft. Dion was subsequently found guilty on all counts, and is serving more than fourteen years in a federal penitentiary.

TRUCKERS AND ILLEGAL DRUGS

A significant risk of violence in the trucking world involves the use of illicit drugs. In July 2004, the U.S. Customs and Border Protection Agency reported that they had seized $14 million worth of marijuana in thirteen separate actions in

Arizona and Texas. In McAllen, Texas, a tractor-trailer was discovered to contain 229 bundles of marijuana weighing 5736 pounds with an estimated street value of over $4.5 million. The contraband was mixed with boxes of produce bound for Atlanta, Georgia (Slagle, 2006).

Hauling contraband often leads to further violence, including the threat of murder and destruction of trucks. The following case is an example of the interrelationship between trucks, drugs, and violence. Names and locations have been changed for anonymity.

Pedro claimed to be at risk of being killed or seriously injured if he and his family returned to Mexico. Pedro now lives in Canada, but while he lived in Mexico, he operated a small trucking business. In October 2003, he hired a new driver who subsequently introduced Pedro to people who wished to hire his truck. Pedro believed they wanted to use the truck for illegal drug business and declined the offer. A few days later, the authorities found Pedro's truck abandoned and damaged. The driver could not be located. After investigating the incident, the Mexican police informed Pedro that his truck had been used for transporting illicit drugs.

Several days later, Pedro's family began to receive threatening telephone calls and letters. Pedro did not report the threats to the Mexican police because he suspected the local officers were corrupt and part of the drug trade.

One of Pedro's friends, who also owned a truck, did agree to work for drug traffickers. After several trips, the friend changed his mind. The authorities found his dead body soon afterwards. Pedro's brother-in-law, who was also in the trucking business and was believed to be involved with heroin trafficking, had also been murdered. The violence motivated Pedro and his family to seek refuge in Canada, where he gained refugee status. The Canadian authorities agreed with Pedro's claim that if he returned to Mexico, the drug traffickers would surely kill him.

The issue of narcotics goes beyond trafficking with trucks. It also includes truckers ingesting drugs like crack or crystal meth on long trips. Each drug can create an eight-hour high. Some drivers prefer a drug named Lucille, a cocaine-like white powder that keeps them awake and in a heightened state of alertness. To counter the growing trend of such drug use by truckers, freight companies in the United States subject their drivers to random drug screens.

Statistics from roadside drug tests are difficult to attain for North America because of the legal issues surrounding the practice. The often-quoted rate of use is based on a 1995 study that showed roadside drug tests for truckers average about one in ten positive readings in the United States (Federal Highway

Administration, 1995). That parallels use with those established in other work-places, where about 12% of American workers abuse drugs, including alcohol. A study undertaken by Cooper et al. (2002) assessed 1079 Canadian truckers roadside for preliminary sobriety tests and urine specimen analysis, of which there was a 19% refusal rate. Of the 822 urine specimens, 21% tested positive for illicit prescription and/or over-the-counter drugs, and 7% tested positive for more than one drug. The high use of drugs creates major safety problems because the ingestion of certain drugs influences a driver's nervous state, the result of which can be increased aggression and road rage. It is a major headache for corporate safety managers.

Some drugs stimulate drivers (e.g., cannabis); others sedate them (e.g., sleeping pills). Still others, such as LSD, cocaine, and PCP, can cause aggression and interfere with the drivers' perceptions of the world.

CARGO THEFT AND SMUGGLING

Members of the trucking industry in the United States claim that cargo theft is a $15 billion annual industry (Jones, 2005). Large carriers have invested huge sums of money on prevention measures, such as satellite tracking devices, trailer locks and seals, and computer technology to complete background searches on truckers. But the theft continues. Some freight companies are reluctant to report trucker-related crime or prosecute thieves because it may discourage future clients from doing business with their company. Shippers are reluctant to contract with carriers whom they suspect to be targets for robbery.

Cargo theft may or may not involve truckers. Truck drivers may assist cargo thieves unwittingly through careless CB discussions about their loads and destinations or through failure to comply with company policy about stopping and securing cargo on the side of the road. Both situations create opportunities for criminals. Some drivers are directly involved. They can be bribed, releasing their loads to criminals at predefined locations. Sometimes trucking companies unwittingly employ criminals masquerading as drivers because of driver shortages and lack of criminal background checks.

Although any cargo can be stolen, the most popular commodities are designer clothing, computers and components, electronics, seafood, dry goods, fragrances, liquor, and cigarettes. But anything can be fenced. Even a trailer filled with fertilizer has been stolen and subsequently sold (Magner, 2000b).

Thieves often pick their targets at truck stops. They often pretend to be truckers as they seek out operators and chat with them about such matters as the unfairness of working for the company, unreasonable expectations held by shippers and dispatchers, or their low pay. The thieves may then offer drivers an envelope of cash in exchange for information about the loads or to get the truckers to leave their trailers conveniently unsecured. Bribes upwards of $50 000 can be offered (Magner, 2000b). The tactic is well known to authorities. Whenever investigators try to solve a cargo theft, one of the first things they check is whether the trucker is the insider. The Miami-Dade County police department's TOMCATS (Tactical Operations Multi-Agency Cargo Anti-Theft Squad) verified that at any given time, three of five Miami-area truck hijackings involved drivers who staged or otherwise fabricated their abductions (Magner, 2000b). A news brief stated, "The Hawkins County Sheriff's Department has charged a truck driver with stealing expensive mattresses and selling them" (Associated Press, 2005, December 16).

Although driver conspiracy can and does happen, the most common cause of thievery is driver carelessness. Truckers leave their rigs unlocked and unsecured at truck stops or truck-loading facilities. Criminals look for easy targets by cruising truck stop parking lots and warehouses where truckers often leave their rigs temporarily unattended to visit the washroom or chat with colleagues while waiting to unload.

Cargo theft is lucrative with a reasonably low risk of apprehension. An American law expert suggested that a cargo thief who gets caught stealing $1 million of merchandise may face three to four years in prison, while a drug dealer caught with $1 million in illicit drugs will likely receive ten to fifteen years in prison. "It is literally more profitable to highjack a cigarette delivery truck than an armored truck" (Shepherd, 1989).

Truck robbery and hijacking have a history in cigarette smuggling, which was most pronounced in the early 1990s. An interesting paradox appeared at the time. To deter Canadians from smoking in 1993, the federal government increased the tax rate per pack of cigarettes from $0.42 to $1.93. Increased provincial tax rates followed. The high taxes caused cigarette smuggling between Canada and the United States to soar (Fleenor, 2003). Trucks were the main pipelines for illegal cigarettes coming into Canada. In a short time, Canada experienced a rash of truck hijacking and cargo theft, whereupon the federal government sharply reduced the cigarette taxes in 1994 (Fleenor, 2003). The fallout is still present today. Although on a lesser scale, some truckers are still involved in cross-border cigarette smuggling, and cargo theft of cigarette cargo happens routinely. The potential for large profits is tantalizing.

Stolen vehicles and/or cargo regularly appear as news items on the Internet. For example, the Alberta Motor Transport Association publicized the following releases:

July 12, 2004: Ashton Transport has reported that a 53' Doepker step
    deck was stolen on Saturday July 10, 2004. The red and white
    deck, loaded with building products, was taken from the petro-
    pass cardlock in Fort Saskatchewan.

July 28, 2004: The unit # PL-76 was last seen Monday, July 27 at 8:00
p.m. parked in Premay Pipeline's locked yard and was noticed
missing Tuesday, July 28 at 8:00 a.m.

August 9, 2004: The AMTA has been notified that a tractor has
gone missing and unaccounted for from the Pacific Mountain
Heavyhaul yard in Calgary late Sunday evening (August 8).

Such ads, in one Canadian province in a short period of time, help illustrate the
prevalence of truck and cargo theft. Although the authorities find and recover
many of the "hoisted" trucks, just as many are never recovered.

U.S. Senator Dianne Feinstein, speaking before the Graham Commission on
Crime and Security in U.S. Seaports, February 16, 2000, stated that, according to
her sources, the American seaports are significant in the trafficking of the majority of cocaine and other illegal drug seizures in commercial cargo, measured by
weight. Drugs coming through the seaports are then transported by commercial
carriers to destinations in Canada or the American Midwest. An RCMP report
(2004) said the export of Canadian marijuana to the United States has become
a thriving industry across Canada, particularly in British Columbia, where there
is a potent hydroponically grown marijuana known as "BC bud." The report
provided several examples of drug busts on commercial trucks:

On October 16, during a routine traffic stop of a tractor-trailer in
Saskatchewan along the Trans-Canada Highway, police found 236
kilograms of marijuana hidden among its cargo. The drugs were
destined for Brampton, Ontario.

On March 16, at a weighing station in Manitoba, Transport officers
located 272 kilograms of marijuana hidden in the commercial
shipment of a tractor-trailer, which was en route to Ontario.

On December 20, at the same weighing station, another tractor
trailer was intercepted with 290 kilograms of marijuana again
destined for Ontario. (RCMP, 2004: 8)

When drivers transport illegal drugs, they seek to protect their cargo and their
lives with armaments or they have armed guards lurking around the trucks.
They are constantly prepared to engage in violence with anyone who interferes
with their cargo.

TRUCKERS PURSUING VIGILANTE JUSTICE

Motorists rarely like to follow big trucks on the highways. They obscure vision,
control the rate of speed, belch out exhaust fumes, and are general irritants.

After following a truck for a considerable distance, motorists may become irritated to the point where they take action by passing the truck whenever they can, even taking chances with approaching traffic. To avoid possible head-on crashes, motorists often re-enter the trucker's lane without giving the trucker sufficient notice. Motorists' failures to keep in their lane and to yield the right of way to trucks are two leading causes of car-truck crashes (Kostinyak et al., 2002). These motorists may become such irritants that truckers undertake their own vigilante justice. For example, a trucker who is cut off may retaliate by tailgating the other driver at high speed, leaving little space between the car's rear bumper and the truck. He may shine his high-beam headlights into the motorist's vehicle or blast his horn. The events become increasingly emotional (Rothe, unpublished personal interviews with truckers, 1995). Such truckers are examples of the most common type of vigilante, namely moralists targeting individuals whom they think are operating outside commonly considered social norms (Zimring, 2003). The target is conjured up as an immoral person who must be punished outside the law. The vigilante identifies with George Orwell's statement, "Good people sleep peacefully at night, only because rough men stand ready to do violence on their behalf."

Constant noise, tight schedules, traffic congestion, foul weather, erratic drivers, sleepiness, unfair dispatchers, and police enforcement: any or all of these frustrations are part of a trucker's day. Truckers experience stress that easily leads to anger and aggression, which can produce road rage. Any motorists who hinder the truckers' objective of arrival at his destination on time may be the recipients of hostilities. In a study on dispatchers and their role in driver safety, truckers, dispatchers, safety supervisors, and managers shared numerous accounts of truck drivers who resorted to fist fights with motorists, animated verbal exchanges, tailgating, and other threatening driving episodes over small provocations (Rothe, 1990). Few of these incidents were ever reported to the authorities.

VIOLENCE AGAINST BICYCLE COURIERS

Outfitted with spandex shorts, backpacks, and radios, bike couriers cycle down main streets or public sidewalks in cities like Vancouver, Toronto, Montreal, Los Angeles, and New York. The riders may also be sporting bandages covering gashes and scraped knees—evidence of close calls with other road users.

Being a bike courier is arguably one of the most dangerous professions on dry land (Culley, 2001). It has a high risk of injury, especially from motor vehicles. Furthermore, bike couriers operate at the whim of companies who are not safety conscious. They may "ask" couriers to take boxes on their handlebars or hold them with one hand while steering the bike with the other hand. If couriers refuse, they may be given fewer calls, or a series of low-paying calls. Some are terminated on the spot.

Typical accidents include getting "doored" in the ribs, being cut off by cars making right-hand turns, and getting broadsided or run down from behind. The Harvard Injury Control Research Center surveyed 113 cycle messengers, asking them to indicate the number and severity of injuries they had experienced in their careers. The study found that collision or the avoidance of collision with motor vehicles and pedestrians accounted for 66% of the injuries, which included bone fractures, dislocations, sprains, and strains (Dennerlein, 2003). Every nineteen hours on the job, an injury happens to a courier that requires forty-two hours off work. Unfortunately, the head researcher, a bike enthusiast, did not discriminate between accidental collisions and intentional violence.

Some couriers are responsible for promoting risk by hanging on to trucks to save energy and quicken a ride, operating on high-risk roadways, and making sudden turns without proper signalling. When the opportunities for harm are combined with intentional risks taken by bike couriers, it is easy to see how injuries result. Unfortunately, the governments in Canada and the United States do not keep statistics for on-the-job injuries for bike couriers and they do not compile research on the prevalence of intentional injury.

One common form of violence occurs when a driver intentionally hits a courier because he or she may be blocking the driver's right of way or has done something the driver thinks deserves retaliation. Sometimes, drivers attempt to hurt bike couriers because they don't like cyclists on roadways. These drivers believe that because they pay taxes for the use of the roads and the messengers do not, the latter don't deserve equal status on the road (Rothe, 2002). Culley (2001), a bike courier, detailed numerous attacks drivers unleashed on bike messengers and bike commuters. On one occasion, a messenger collided with a s u v whereupon the driver got out of his vehicle, threw coffee at the rider, and kicked the downed man, seriously injuring his ribs and spleen. The motorist then sped off.

Some members of the driving public see bike couriers as daredevils who threaten the safety of pedestrians, disrupt traffic, and do not abide by traffic laws (*National Post*, 2000). A "might is right" mentality erupts in some drivers that pushes them to discipline couriers; to teach them a lesson, which sometimes means slightly steering their cars into the bikes, pulling into the bikers' paths, or purposefully swerving into marked bike lanes.

PARKING ENFORCEMENT

Parking is part of the rhythm of driving. People consider it in terms of rights of ownership (e.g., street-side), financial cost (e.g., parking lot rental fees), time (e.g., parking meters), and location (e.g., loading zone).

Parking enforcement is a particular kind of work associated with potential violence. North American drivers can expect to be formally sanctioned for illegal parking. Parking enforcers are, so to speak, front-line monitors who are authorized to help regulate urban flow of traffic. They are granted "moral dominion" over parking spaces, decoding whether, how, and when to intervene on behalf of permit holders and other paying customers, who technically abide by local and provincial parking ordinances and laws. To enforce those rights, parking enforcement officers issue citations and/or place booting (immobilization) devices on illegally parked vehicles.

An important fact of the ticketing process is that parking enforcement officers usually do not have the right to void parking tickets once written. A supervisor or designated official must be contacted for assistance and guidance if a problem arises. Once a ticket is started, there is little chance that a driver can argue his or her way out of it, often creating frustration, anger, and retaliation.

The parking ticket has become a legal commercial commodity. More fines mean more profit for the municipality. Increased parking enforcement has become the way of doing business (Brenneman, 2004). Some cities are also maximizing the cost of parking in the downtown core in order to reduce traffic and increase bus ridership. For example, the median average rate for a monthly parking spot in Calgary's downtown is $375 per month. In Toronto it is $300. The average price for daily parking in downtown Calgary is $19 (Simons, 2007). The likely result of high prices is that more drivers will skip out of paying, and parking enforcement attendants will need to be more zealous. The fines will also be much higher. These demographic and economic changes have left parking enforcement personnel at higher risk of being confronted by drivers who take exception to receiving expensive fines. It is another kind of road rage.

A San Francisco bumper sticker reads, "Meter maids eat their young." Parking enforcers routinely experience shouts of rage, lengthy verbal abuse, spit in the face, and attempted rundowns by offended drivers. A Vancouver traffic enforcement officer described it colourfully:

> We get called names...One guy came through a window at me. He broke my window to get at me...I thought I'd heard everything until someone called me a butt plug, he reached into his grocery bag and fired a banana at me—he didn't even peel it. (O'Connor, 2004: 1)

The Toronto Police Service issued a press release in 2005 in which they publicized the assault on a traffic enforcement officer:

> On Tuesday, January 11, 2005 at approximately 1:54 p.m., a parking enforcement officer was ticketing illegally parked cars in the area of

120 Lombard Street, when a man approached and asked why he had received a ticket. Before the officer could answer, the man grabbed the officer's ticket book and threw it. He then pushed the officer in the chest, with both hands, and started walking away. The officer radioed for police to attend, and told the man to wait for police to arrive. The man spat in the officer's face, twice, and threw a cup of tea at him while the man was getting in his car to leave the scene. (Toronto Police Service, press release, 2005)

At the most severe end of the parking enforcer violence scale is homicide. In Edmonton in 2004, Mir Asghar Hussain, a parking attendant, was stabbed. He died from his injuries. The police suspect that a disgruntled motorist had confronted him. The attendant had issued four tickets at four separate downtown parking lots before he was murdered. The attacker has not yet been caught.

Although homicide is the exception, common assault on parking enforcement officers is common. The instigators are mostly young people. The Toronto Police Service has provided some interesting numbers. In Canada there were almost 33 000 youth assault cases in 1999. Four and a half percent of the assault victims were part-time, temporary, and/or full-time parking enforcement officers (Toronto Police Service, 2000).

Parking enforcement officers cannot control the conditions in the community and have little control over the individuals they encounter in their work. Training in diffusing volatile situations is usually not required as part of the job and is offered infrequently. At most, new recruits should be aware that they "sometimes deal with unpleasant, angry, or discourteous people" (Iseek, 2004).

Transportation consultants, such as Todd Litman, director of the Victoria Transport Policy Institute, used a different set of lenses to explain the problem. Parking is an economic issue. According to Litman, free parking no longer exists. It is not a driver's right. As he said, "It all boils down to the feeling that free parking is a right. We don't expect the neighbourhood grocery store to give us a free bus pass but we expect free parking. Until we change the way we think about parking, parking will always be a problem" (O'Connor, 2004: 1).

IN SUMMARY

Much of our time is spent at work, where we engage in interpersonal and social encounters with our colleagues. There is a coherence to our work activities that gives it meaning. Insofar as the workplace presents a patterned basis for the social context, designated workplaces having to do with ground transportation and traffic have, as part of their daily fare, robberies, personal degradations, altercations, and assaults of every kind, whether the worker is the victim or aggressor. Traffic-related employment is fertile ground for violence, where workers are in danger of being harmed by customers or specific interest groups, and where they have the potential to harm others.

The hazards of being a traffic-related worker are poorly understood, because there is limited data to announce the issue, and because the issue involves routine employment that, although high-risk, is not glorified in our society.

SECTION II:
THE MEDIATE AND
INTERMEDIATE ZONES

Friends may come and go, but enemies accumulate.

— THOMAS JONES

In the mediate zone, the vehicle is not the weapon, but it is part of the circumstance that contributed to a violent act. For example, a motorist is driving to a second-hand store to drop off old clothes and becomes irate when a half-ton truck tailgates him. The motorist begins to race with the other driver and forces him to pull into a parking lot. Harsh words erupt into a fistfight.

In the intermediate zone, the vehicle plays a more direct role in the violence but is still not the weapon. For example, a gang member sits in the passenger seat and aims his gun at a young man walking down the street. He shoots while the car is moving then speeds away. The victim bleeds to death.

The execution of these types of violence depends on the availability of a motor vehicle. The following chapters will explore road rage, sexual assault, police pursuits, hit and runs, drive-by shootings, and carjackings as incidents within the mediate and intermediate zones of vehicle violence.

9
VENGEFUL DRIVING AND ROAD RAGE

Revenge is a kind of wild justice, which the more man's
nature runs to the more ought law to weed it out.

— FRANCIS BACON

It is a well-known adage. Everyone should develop the capacity for self-control
in the face of frustration. Plutarch, a Graeco-Roman intellectual, wrote the following about anger:

> Anger is aroused when a person suffers a real or perceived injury.
> Usually the angered person directs his attention towards punishing
> the real or perceived offender. The feelings of anger are an
> intermingling of pain and pleasure—pain at the injury and pleasure at
> the expectation of vengeance and the overt expression of anger. (cited
> in Schimmel, 1997: 87)

Anger is the forerunner of vengeance, and few thoughts or actions arouse our
anger more than the conviction that somebody intentionally acted against our
best interests while driving a vehicle. For example, we have entered a parking
lot and are patiently waiting while another motorist exits his parking space. As
he completes his turn out, suddenly another driver pulls up from the opposite
direction and backs into the space. How dare she! Didn't she see us waiting
politely for that space? We glare, honk, and give the finger. The driver ignores
our gestures, smirking that she did a masterful job. We have just experienced
one of the top five triggers for road rage: the competition for parking space
(Harding et al., 1998).

Many of us would consider such action as an injustice or a case of one-
upmanship. The other driver taunts us into retaliation. We feel that our pride

has been wounded and an injustice has been wrought on us. So we retaliate. Fortunately, most of us have an awareness that reaches beyond the parameters of personal injustice and immediate retaliation. We abide by normative standards in many dicey social situations that we confront and in which we participate. We may be disgruntled but we continue with our lives. We abide by an assumed moral code. But others seek alternative means to combat threats by engaging in vengeful behaviour. They want to make the offending driver pay for his affront. They have angry responses to minor traffic events, such as being forced to slow down for an elderly driver, being tailgated, or being cut off by a driver who changes lanes numerous times within a city block. Such incidents can imperil a driver's sense of calm and fair play.

Anger in traffic can also be more than a response to events happening on the road. Some people are unable to deal with the original source of their anger and so they direct their hostilities to a secondary source, such as a road user. The angry driver acts out a psychodrama on the roadway in response to an annoyance, disdain, or hatred in another part of life—a form of displaced payback. An innocent, unsuspecting person receives the brunt of latent antagonism from someone who is in a bad mood over other matters. A major argument with a spouse, the loss of a job, or an intimidating experience with a bank teller can fester in our minds until it erupts onto the next road user.

Imposing anger onto other drivers is facilitated by the anonymity that gives drivers the bravado to violate other people's rights. Angry drivers who intimidate others cannot be readily identified (Hennessy & Wiesenthal, 1999). The situation becomes worse when a potential perpetrator has consumed alcohol or illicit drugs. The level of aggression increases as the degree of hesitation lessens. The following example comes from an interview undertaken for a study on traffic safety. Names and locations have been changed because of confidentiality.

> Edward was a teacher who recently graduated from university. He taught social studies and physical education. He had a quick temper. He was slightly sarcastic, but with a humorous twist. He was conscious of his moods, slight depressions, but thought them nothing out of the ordinary. His childhood had been rough. He had been tormented and endlessly criticized by his Dutch mother and stepfather for his "stupid" behaviour. Edward said, "I was never good enough. I felt that I always had to prove myself." His wife, Nancy, considered him to be intelligent and believed in his potential. Their marriage, however, was rocky.
>
> Edward drove a small truck and lived in Whistler, a tourist entertainment and ski village north of Vancouver. Whistler is situated along the Squamish Highway, also known as the infamous "Sea-to-Sky Highway."

The Squamish Highway is a predominantly two-lane road that winds steeply north with 45-degree corners and 15% grades, twisting and turning through glacier-carved peaks and mountain communities. Below are the Howe Sound fjord waters. When faced with an emergency, the driver has the option of hitting another car, tumbling into the frigid waters, or careening into jagged rock. The highway is treacherous, with boulders hanging from cliffs or the sides of ragged mountains. Rivers rush down the mountains through culverts under the road. When the rains are too heavy, the road floods and often the bridges collapse. Consequently, rocks are often scaled, surfaces are cleared from fallen rocks, boulders are blown up by explosives experts, bridges are re-built, and the highway surface is continuously repaired. Road repairs make for many traffic stoppages. To make matters worse, the area also experiences black ice, fog, and drizzle.

The highway serves as the gateway to Whistler skiing. Squamish is a Vancouver bedroom community with commuters travelling day and night. Logging trucks and eighteen-wheeler transports use the highway for hauling freight to Prince George. It's a shortcut. Tourists laze their way through the natural beauty of the valley, adding to the aggravation of local drivers.

The complex roadway was a source of stress for Edward. In his words,

> I don't mean to be an asshole, but I need my space, to relax. That drive really takes a lot out of you. All the time, and I mean always there are trucks tailgating you, driving right up your ass, and in front of you is a tourist driving a Winnebago, trudging along. Then you have the commuters. We just want to get home and relax. We want to get there, not sightsee.
>
> I hate the highway. Once you go back and forth so often it doesn't matter what the scenery is like. All you see is assholes passing around corners when, you know, look out. I just think, don't crash in front of me, okay. Don't! I don't want to scrape your body off the pavement.

When Edward and Nancy began having frequent arguments, she told him he was becoming depressed, that he was having a psychological problem, and that maybe he should see a psychologist. She believed he had a problem with women because of his shaky experiences with his mother. Edward denied it. He thought that she was taking advantage of him and that she only cared about herself.

Police records showed that Edward was never in trouble with the police. He had three speeding tickets in eight years, most of which he received when he was driving a flashy European sports car.

One Friday afternoon, around 4:00, Edward was in a hurry to leave Vancouver and get to Whistler. He wanted to get to the post office to pick up a parcel before 5:00. He had a 120-km trip. Edward was in a rush to get the parcel that day for no reason other than curiosity. There was no necessity to retrieve it. The pressure to arrive on time was purely self-imposed.

There was stop-and-go traffic up to the Squamish Highway that afternoon. Edward was on the highway, dragging behind a truck, leaving space, when a car pulled up behind him, passed, and inched in front of him, forcing Edward to lose his spot behind the logging truck. Edward boiled over. He sped up, tailgating the car in front of him, literally keeping inches of distance between bumpers. He said:

> I was totally pissed off. What the hell was he thinking? As soon as he cut in I yelled at the top of my voice, threatening him with my fist, and pointing insanely at my forehead—showing that he was a stupid idiot. I was actually shaking in rage. My mouth became dry. I had to, and I mean had to, show this bastard that he couldn't do this to me. It was personal, man, real personal.

The driver of the blue Chevrolet Impala then began yelling, making obscene gestures through the rear-view mirror. Edward hit the accelerator and tried to pass him, but the other driver sped up, leaving Edward stranded on the wrong side of the highway, facing oncoming traffic. He was approaching a train crossing and slammed on his brakes. He then moved back into the lane behind the Chevy. The fist waving continued.

Both drivers raced to the police station to lay an official complaint. They met at the front desk. The desk sergeant looked on, wondering about the sanity of the two men who stood there threatening each other. Each told their story. The officer lectured them, threatening to take legal action against both men if they did not get themselves under control. The legal action seemed severe. Edward left hastily, even more aggravated. He drove home, emotions on his sleeve.

Nancy was preparing supper when Edward stomped into the house, enraged, yelling at her about the incident. She was not hard of hearing and asked him to settle down. He couldn't. Nancy told him to lie down for a while. He didn't. He became angry that she thought that he was losing his mind. He took a bottle of beer and stomped outside, walking around the yard, talking to himself about all the things he should have said and done. He replayed the incident over and over again, and each replay brought a different dimension.

About half an hour later, Nancy asked him to go to the store for ice cream. Edward had cooled down a little, although it would have been advisable that he not drive in such a state of anxiety. He parked at the local supermarket, where he saw the blue Chevrolet on the east side of the lot. Edward took out his keys, walked beside the stranger's car, and keyed its side panels. Instead of staying to buy ice cream, Edward left immediately and bought it at a convenience store further in town.

Vengeance was his! Edward later said:

> It's not something you plan. It was there and the guy deserved it. I felt a hell of a lot better once I did it. It was a kind of closure. Now he's in for a new paint job, and that'll cost him at least a couple of hundred dollars.

Edward's story is not a special case. He felt the same way many drivers feel. His story tells how close we are to road rage. For Edward, it stopped at vandalism to the other driver's vehicle. But it was deliberate revenge.

ROAD RAGE

Extreme vengeful and angry driving is commonly referred to as "road rage," which Peter Batten and his associates (2000) defined as a situation where one driver locks onto another driver and exhibits both hostile and aggressive intent and behaviour to the second driver. An excellent definition of road rage was offered by the New York Governor's Traffic Safety Committee (2000) when it suggested that road rage happens when a driver operates a vehicle in a selfish, bold, or pushy manner, without regard to the rights or safety of the other road users.

Incidents often occur when a driver is impaired, may already have a disposition towards anger or violence, or when he feels obstructed from driving in a way to which he feels entitled. In a study of drinking and driving, we interviewed a young man who resides in northern Alberta. He confessed to being an alcoholic, angry at the world because his wife of seven years "screwed around with another man." He had become a "man with an attitude." He goes to bars to pick fights, after which he drinks beer. On numerous occasions he felt like "cracking" another car because the other driver was "a real asshole and jerk." But he didn't do this for the single reason that he just spent ninety days in jail for common assault and didn't want to be locked up in jail again. Still, as he said, he carried a feeling of "beating the crap out of a driver that pisses him off and doesn't know how to drive." The man was convinced that if he does not get his alcohol abuse under control he will once again be charged with assault while driving (Rothe, personal interview, 2003).

A fact of life is that people get angry. Hence angry drivers are not unique. They become a public problem, however, when they shed concern for common safety and use their vehicles as weapons to assault other road users. Such acts are becoming more common in Canada and the United States. People are busier. Time is a commodity. More drivers are on the roads. Drivers are getting more frustrated and feel the need to lash out.

The possibility of road rage increases as drivers feel greater social stress from alienation and isolation. These emotions may be transposed into aggression when the driver is in traffic. This transformation was clearly described in an early study by Melvin Selzer et al. (1968). After analyzing American fatal accident statistics, the researchers reported that 20% of the cases involved drivers who had been in aggressive altercations within six hours of their deaths. The researchers concluded that, in some cases, a motorist's inability to deal effectively with stress and anger seriously impaired driving performance.

Exposure to recent aggression in one's personal life substantially increases the risk of involvement in a fatal collision. Dr. Achal Bhagat, a psychiatrist for the World Health Organization, suggested that road rage is the product of a stressed-out people struggling for control through use of their vehicles (Ghosh, 2000). The car becomes a camouflage for existential angst, helplessness in an increasingly anonymous world.

Reginald Smart and Robert Mann (2002) completed a content analysis of all Canadian Press reports on road rage for 1998 to 2002. They found ninety-six articles, of which most cases occurred because of lane changes, disputes over parking spots, or rude gestures. Most of the perpetrators and victims were males (96.6%). The average age for perpetrators was 33 years old and for victims it was 34.3 years old. Serious injuries resulting from beatings with fists, bats, or clubs happened in 72.9% of the cases, and 6.8% involved deaths from shootings. Because Canada has no specific charges for road rage, 72.9% of the time the police laid criminal charges such as manslaughter, assault, or dangerous driving.

A Canadian Press survey undertaken by Leger Marketing (2001) established that of all the provinces in Canada, Alberta had the highest number of self-reported victims of road rage (23.8%), compared to Canada's average of 20.4%. The finding translates into about 4.5 million Canadians reporting that they had been victims of road rage, defined by behaviours like indecent gestures (40.5%), vulgar language or threats (27.1%), and dangerous driving (6.1%). More importantly, 4.2% of the study population, or 202 000 Canadians, reported that they had been assaulted and sustained injuries as a result of road rage, and 11.9% had their vehicles hit by aggressors. More recently, a Canadian survey of 1400 adult respondents in Ontario established that 46.6% were shouted at, cursed at, or had rude gestures directed at them in the past year. More seriously, 7.2% were threatened with personal injury or car damage (Smart et al., 2004).

The picture painted so far has not included the emotional experience of a violent confrontation. A review of media annals for cases that featured the dynamics of everyday life showed that horror stories are standard fare. For example, in Calgary, a thirty-two-year-old man began to argue with another driver over an alleged traffic violation. The man got out of his car to talk, but became hesitant when he saw two men exit the other vehicle. He decided to drive away. But the other men followed. So the man again got out of his car, armed with a snowbrush, whereupon the other driver produced a handgun and fired a shot in the man's direction. The other driver and passenger then jumped into their suv and sped off (Lay, 2004).

The website entitled *Etiquette Hell* solicits people's experiences with road rage. In one entry, a woman in Nanaimo, British Columbia described an incident that she had witnessed. The woman had slowed down for a traffic light when she saw a yellow sports car swerve onto the off ramp at a nearby exit. A pickup truck was stopped ahead at the end of a line of traffic. The sports car tapped the rear end of the truck, causing no damage. The driver of the truck, however, jumped out of the cab in a frothy rage and ran to the sports car. The driver of the sports car started to roll down his window when the truck driver began shouting obscenities, then punched the partially open window and broke it. When the sports car driver closed the window, the truck driver punched it three more times, swearing loudly. He looked as if he would escalate his attack further, so the sports car scooted away. The truck driver ran back to his vehicle and gave chase down one of the major city roads. The woman did not witness the end of the incident, but one can imagine what may have happened if the truck driver had caught the other driver (Etiquette Hell, undated).

The following story took place in Alberta. Names and locations have been altered for anonymity.

On March 3, 2004, Julio, a twenty-three-year-old man, physically assaulted Fred, aged sixty-five, in the parking lot of an Edmonton shopping centre. Julio was driving behind Fred for a while when he decided to pass him and re-enter Fred's lane. Fred was driving a white mini-van. Fred tried to keep Julio from re-entering his travel lane, making Julio upset. According to Fred, Julio was acting in an erratic manner: pumping the gas pedal, bluff charging with his car to get back into the flow of traffic in front of Fred.

Julio became disgusted with Fred's driving and followed him to a nearby parking lot, where he parked his Chevrolet directly behind Fred's mini-van and, according to Fred, Julio started to swear profusely at him. Then, "without notice or any provocation," Julio sucker punched Fred twice in the face with his fist. Fred was knocked to the pavement and suffered cuts and abrasions to his nose, mouth, and chin.

Julio was an above average student and athlete. He came from a stable home and people praised him for his strong work ethic and respect for family. Julio offered the court regret and remorse about the assault. Julio's father described how his son apologized to him about the pain he caused an older man. His former work colleague told the courts that Julio's road rage attack was "totally out of character." The probation officer, who prepared the Pre-Sentence Report, reported that in her opinion Julio realized the seriousness of his actions. He expressed embarrassment and shame throughout their interviews. She felt that Julio's involvement with the law was an isolated incident.

Because of Julio's "otherwise exemplary background," Julio's lawyer asked for a conditional discharge. The request was denied because, according to the judge, to do so would be contrary to the public interest. The fact is that a strong young man assaulted a sixty-five-year-old citizen in a classic display of road rage. Julio was sentenced to three months' imprisonment.

Julio's case illustrates how an average citizen can become enraged and lash out through the car. We cannot consider the perpetrator's transformation of social nice guy to aggressor as being unique or occasional. Thousands of aggressive drivers or motorists who have snapped and committed major violence are supposedly "good community citizens" with no histories of crime, violence, or alcohol and drug abuse. The media often reports descriptions by the perpetrator's friends and family that he is "the nicest man," "a wonderful father," or "he must have been provoked." Louis Bethesda (1997) publicized this claim after he directed a study on aggressive drivers for the American Automobile Association Foundation for Traffic Safety. The research team discovered that there were 10 037 extremely violent incidents in the United States for a period of six years between January 1, 1990, to September 1, 1996. At least 218 persons were murdered and 12 610 individuals were injured, keeping in mind that aggressive driving often results in more than one person being injured or killed (Bethesda, 1997). Of the people injured, ninety-four were children under the age of fifteen. Such incidents of road rage increase about 7% per year (New York Governor's Traffic Safety Committee, 2000).

Bethesda's landmark study further concluded that although baseball bats, crowbars, and hockey sticks are used in the assaults, the weapons of choice typically used in traffic confrontations are motor vehicles and guns (specific to the United States). In 23% of the cases, the aggressive driver used the vehicle as the weapon. Firearms also have a strong connection to road rage in the United States. David Hemenway and his team of researchers (2006) led a highly publicized survey of American households. The researchers found that motorists who have a gun in their vehicle are more likely to engage in road rage. Road rage can be a by-product of love turned sour, bad luck at the casino, a boss's tyranny, or a naturally quick temper. Bethesda's study described that at least 322 incidents of domestic problems turned to acts of violence on American roads between the years 1990 and 1996.

Peter Batten and his colleagues (2000) described what they call a "typical" case of road rage including a gun. A thirty-one-year-old male died from a gunshot (9 mm pistol) wound to his chest. His blood alcohol level was 0.06% and his blood tested positive for cocaine. A driver, whom we will call Fred, had started to hassle with Walter, the driver of another car, while each was proceeding along a two-lane highway. Walter tried to pass Fred, but Fred sped up to prevent it. Walter stomped on the gas pedal, reaching 113 km/h (70 mph) and zipped by Fred. Fred then passed Walter and forced Walter's car onto the shoulder of the road. Walter raced his engine and caught up to Fred, at which time Fred slammed on his brakes and turned slightly off the roadway. Walter hit his brakes, stopping just two feet from Fred's bumper.

Fred jumped out of his car and ran straight for Walter, who was rolling down his window. Fred cursed and yelled, punching Walter twice in the face. Walter reached into his glove compartment, withdrew a loaded revolver, aimed it, and warned Fred to back off. But Fred was out of control. He intensified his verbal and physical assault, whereby Walter, fearing for his life and safety, shot his assailant in the chest and killed him.

After reviewing the evidence, the grand jury returned an indictment of murder against Walter. The jury deliberating at the follow-up trial, however, found Walter innocent of murder, and he was subsequently released. Jury members decided that Walter was protecting himself against a driver who was enraged because of the "one-upmanship" game they had been playing in traffic.

For some, purposeful aggressive driving is a deliberate choice. For example, a commentary appeared in the *Edmonton Journal*'s Editorial section (2005, January 11) in which the writer, a pedestrian waiting at a red light, witnessed a driver backing into a major thoroughfare without looking, causing a bus and car to slam on their brakes. The writer reacted by declaring,

> I'm done being nice about it, and obeying the law; after all nobody else does. From now on, if you threaten me with your car, I won't care if it was intentionally or simply a demonstration of your incompetence, inebriation or stupidity—I will defend myself, and you'll be left with some nasty repair bills.

In other words, the writer is prepared to become one of the 33% of Canadian and 42% of American drivers who, in a 2004 unscientific Roadragers.com survey, answered that they had "gotten into confrontations with other drivers that year."

Road rage also happens between drivers and other roadway users, such as cyclists, where confrontation can easily end in death. For example, in 1999 Tom McBride was cycling east along a road when a driver coming from the south made a right turn and almost hit him. Tom swerved to avoid a collision, banged the hood of the car with his hand, and shouted obscenities. The driver of the car slowed to let Tom pass, but then accelerated to catch up with him and knocked the bike with his car. The incident sent Tom to the pavement. The car drove over the cyclist and sped away. The bicycle, however, was stuck under the car, sending sparks into the air. Tom was dead on arrival at hospital. The driver of the car turned himself in the next day. His front licence plate had been found under Tom's body (Mittelman & Mittelman, 2002).

ANGER WITHIN THE VEHICLE

Driving when we get angry within the vehicle is not the same as when we purposefully react to another driver. It does not mean driving at excessive speed, dangerous overtaking, increasing speed to stop someone from passing, tailgating, or driving without a seat belt. It does not fall within the general scope of road rage. Rather, driving a vehicle in anger because of events happening within the car suggests that drivers lose their cool and act dangerously, sometimes with a death wish.

A partner argues or is short tempered; children yell or cry; a friend teases. These are reoccurring situations that give rise to angry driving. Passengers emotionally arouse the driver, who becomes unreasonable, loses his cool, and retaliates by trying to harm or scare them. He turns to the immediate tool at hand: his car.

In one case, an Edmonton man deliberately crashed his half-ton truck into a telephone pole and a fire hydrant during an argument with his wife (McLean, 2005). The accused and his spouse, in the midst of a divorce, had been driving home from dinner when a heated argument about their sex life ensued. The man started to speed up and drive erratically, shouting at his wife that if he was "going, you're coming with me" (McLean, 2005: B1). The woman tried to jump out of the speeding truck but couldn't. They crashed. The wife suffered broken ribs and injuries to her lower back. The husband was found guilty of dangerous driving causing bodily harm.

The following is another example. Names and locations have been altered to preserve anonymity.

On a winter evening, Eric, his girlfriend (Brenda), and four friends were enjoying themselves in a Calgary bar. Shortly after midnight, Eric went to another table to talk with friends. When Brenda went to look for him, she found him in the company of another woman. An argument began between the two partners.

The argument continued while Brenda, Eric, and their friends drove to another bar. Eric was driving as Brenda escalated her accusations. When Eric stopped for a red light, Brenda berated him and began to slap him on the arm. Eric pushed her away, but she persisted. He then held her by the throat against the passenger window. Eric had lost his temper. He angrily stepped out of the car, went around the passenger side, and began yelling and pounding on the car door, which Brenda had locked out of fear.

A few minutes later, Eric briefly composed himself. He returned to the vehicle and began to proceed through the intersection. Brenda started to complain about the way Eric was driving. She suddenly put the gearshift into the "park" position while the car was moving. Eric shifted back into drive and stepped on the accelerator. He was speeding up and driving more erratically, at which point, Brenda ordered Eric to stop because he was scaring her friends.

Eric sped up even more. He lost control of the car and collided head-on with a concrete retaining wall. Brenda suffered a fractured humerus and a laceration above the left eyebrow line. The other passengers suffered broken joints (legs, feet, and arm), torn ligaments, cuts, and bruises. Eric was more fortunate than the others, suffering only minor injuries.

Eric was charged with dangerous driving causing bodily harm. However, because Brenda introduced the first physical contact, and put the car in park while the car was in motion, she tempered the moral blameworthiness of Eric's acts.

Eric showed no concern in court for the injuries sustained by the other passengers. The judge criticized Eric's physical assault on Brenda when he grabbed her by the throat and tried to choke her. The judge imposed a sentence of eighteen months to be served in the community, subject to Eric's compliance with a conditional sentence order. Eric was fined $800 for the assault and ordered to pay the victims $100 each. He was prohibited from driving for two years.

VENGEANCE AS A FORM OF VIGILANTISM

It sometimes happens, especially in the United States, that local citizens attack drivers because they crashed and hurt people in the community. Although this crime has not been reported in Canada's major cities, vigilante crime is becoming a more common form of violence in suburbs of large American urban centres.

The *Chicago Tribune* reported that in 2000, the city of Chicago had a vigilante crime rate of 627 murders per 100 000 citizens (*Chicago Tribune*, 2003). Chicago also has the dubious honour of being the lead city for auto crash vigilantism.

The following story illustrates this type of confrontation. In Chicago, six men walked to a crash site and pulled two men, Jack Moore, sixty-two, and Anthony Stuckey, forty-nine, from a rented van on the city's South Side. The two victims cried for mercy, but to no avail. The group of six men beat the driver and passenger to death with bricks and pieces of asphalt. They were exacting vengeance for three women in the neighbourhood who had been run over by the van. The women had been sitting on the front stoop when the van drove into them after skidding through a stop sign and weaving past an obstacle course of cars and trees. The women were seriously injured, but survived (*Jet*, 2002).

In some cases, citizens believe that the police are not enforcing the law as strictly in poor, dominantly black, or minority communities as they do in more upscale parts of the city. As a result, these citizens decide to become the final arbiter of justice. They take control in a violent way. Their actions represent an issue of class privilege and its after-effects.

Similar concerns are noted elsewhere in the world. For example, teenagers in Dublin, Ireland, were routinely stealing cars and crashing them. Parents were afraid that these joyriders, who travelled in excess of 120 mph, would hit their children. The parents warned city administrators that if the police failed to take more concerted action, they were prepared to deal with the matter as vigilantes (O'Keefe, 2002). They would take the law into their own hands and threaten teens they believed had something to do with the thefts. The parents considered their actions to be preventative measures for greater community safety.

Disenfranchised people who feel that the police force is not protecting their rights take on the essence of empowered citizen. They take action because of what they perceive to be impotent local law enforcement and the potential corrupt bureaucracy of a government service. They become the citizen-police officers, or worker-patriot. Vigilantism, however, poses a concrete threat to the fragile boundaries of self, community, and law.

IN SUMMARY

Each day we experience a measure of anger which, if allowed to fester, can become a hidden desire for revenge. This desire can prompt a sudden fit of rage, which can lead to high-risk driving that hurts other drivers (Schimmel, 1997).

Road rage is violent, rampant, and costly. Angry driving, which may lead to road rage, is common, and may be the result of systemic issues, engineering faults, driver errors, or passengers provoking drivers. They all create serious damage and often result in mortality, morbidity, or damaged mental health.

SEXUAL ASSAULT

The greatest trick the devil ever performed was
convincing the world he didn't exist.

— AL PACINO

Systematic male dominance—patriarchy—is a condition in which men control
and violate women. Although many changes about gender equality have taken
place, our society's dominant ideology still reflects male sexual dominance over
females. Many people still assume that men have greater power than women.
Such power is woven within all our practices and ideas. It is exercised in relationships, groups, and social practices. The emphasis on male superiority, dominance, physical strength, and male honour forms a patriarchal system that helps
perpetuate conflict and violence.

Males are more likely to perpetuate violence against women partly because,
in the male culture, power and control reproduce themselves in the high schools,
sports clubs, pubs, and many of our revered institutions. For example, to legiti-
mize sexual assault, the myth commonly invoked is that women like "rough sex"
or "no means yes," and if women report assault to the authorities it is because
they "cry wolf" when things don't go their way. Such myths are held firmly in
many people's minds and still appear in court decisions.

SEXUAL ASSAULT

Violence against women takes many forms, including battering, sexual harass-
ment, and rape. Sexual assault is a form of unwanted sexual activity that includes fondling, touching, and/or penetration that is forced upon another person
where that person does not give consent, gives consent as a result of intimidation or fraud, or is legally deemed incapable of giving consent because of youth

or temporary/permanent incapacity (Krug et al., 2002). Although sexual assault happens among men and women, it occurs most frequently between men and women. Between 1999 and 2004, 84% of Canadians who reported being sexually assaulted in the twelve months previous to the survey were women. Only 16% were men (Statistics Canada, 2004).

The term "rape," typically used in many countries, is no longer the legal term in Canada because it fails to include all forms of sexual violence. Sexual assault is the legal term that refers to non-consensual sexual touching or intercourse achieved through physical force, threat, intimidation, and/or coercion. It takes a variety of forms, such as forced sexual touching, fondling, oral sex, vaginal or anal penetration, flashing, or voyeurism (Mathews, 1995).

In 1999, 23 872 sexual assaults (total of all types) were reported to the police in Canada. This translates into a rate of seventy-eight sexual assaults per 100 000 people, a number that is consistent with the statistics for 2004 (Statistics Canada, 2000; Statistics Canada, 2006). Given that this figure represents only approximately 6% of the sexual assaults that occur each year, we take note that sexual assault is highly prevalent in Canada. The motor vehicle often plays a significant role in these cases. For example, a breakdown of sexual assault by location showed that 25% happened in motor vehicles, 24% took place in the victim's home, 21% occurred in a public place, 20% happened in the perpetrator's home, and 10% were instigated in someone else's home (Ontario Women's Directorate, 1995).

It is important to debunk the myth that sexual assault is an act of sexual release or pleasure, motivated by sexual desire. It is an act of power and control, intended to hurt and humiliate the victim. The following case graphically illustrates the intensity of the violence. Two convicts who had escaped from a state prison captured a young couple and drove them to an isolated area. They repeatedly raped the woman and then severely beat the couple and locked them in their car's trunk (Hazelwood et al., 1992). The rapists then set the car on fire and left the couple to burn. According to the special investigator of the case, these men were not sexual sadists; they did not remain at the brutal scene until the suffering ended, which sexual sadists would have.

Sexual assault can happen at any time, anywhere, often in ordinary, seemingly safe places. Women in vehicle-related locations like parking lots can experience it. An example of such a case happened in Minneapolis. It was about 1:30 a.m. when a twenty-year-old woman was warming up her car after work in a parking lot. A man pushed her face into the passenger seat, got into the driver's seat, and drove away. As he was driving, he took $400 from her wallet, and then pulled into a parking lot on Portland Avenue. The man sexually assaulted the victim and eventually let her go (Mayron, 2003).

Often, a rapist will sexually assault a victim repeatedly. The power game is extended and becomes an horrific, drawn-out affair for the victim. The following case illustrates the severity of such violence when it includes a motor vehicle. Names and locations have been altered for anonymity.

It was early afternoon in a small western Saskatchewan town when Jody, a resident for ten years, decided to go for a walk near her home. She headed for the local ATM machine to withdraw some money. She was making her way across a street towards an alley that led to her house, when she noticed a half-ton truck driving by. The truck, showing Alberta licence plates, stopped a short distance down the road. Because the town had many Alberta visitors, Jody paid no attention. She kept walking down the lane.

Mike, the driver (a twenty-six-year-old man), turned around and headed towards Jody, abruptly stopping beside her. He got out of the truck, pointed a loaded rifle at her head, and demanded that she get into the truck or he would kill her. Mike then pushed her into the driver's side of the truck and forced her to lie down on the floor. He threw an old blanket over her, and demanded that she stay very still.

Mike sped out of town on a gravel road, eventually veering into a farmer's field. He stopped the truck and grabbed his rifle. After handcuffing Jody's hands behind her, Mike led her to the back of the vehicle. He attempted to rape her but couldn't get an erection. Frustrated, he forced her back into the vehicle, swearing profusely, and drove on a few miles. He stopped again, and this time he raped Jody.

Mike forced Jody back into the truck. He sat with his victim for a period of time, waiting for dusk. When darkness approached, Mike again pushed Jody to the floor of the truck, threw a blanket over her, then drove for some distance on the highway. Jody asked him to stop so that she could go to the bathroom. Mike pulled off the highway and allowed Jody to relieve herself. She wanted to run but was too terrified. Mike then raped her again.

They got back into the truck and drove to Regina. Mike told Jody that he rented a house here. Jody peered out the passenger window and noticed several road signs.

It was dark and late at night when Mike handcuffed Jody's hands behind her back and put duct tape over her mouth. He guided her to the third floor of the house, where he fondled her, then tied her hands and left ankle to a bed frame. He fell asleep in a chair beside the bed.

As dawn approached, Jody told Mike that her wrists hurt because the cuffs were too tight. Mike took out the key and unlocked them. He then lay on the couch beside her, telling her of his need to have her like him. Jody refused to answer. She lay quietly, feigning sleep, praying that help would soon come. Mike cuffed Jody's hands again. After the extended silence, Mike told Jody that he was going to take a shower.

While Mike was in the shower, Jody managed to wriggle her hands free from the cuffs. She ran out of the house into the path of an oncoming mini-van, forcing the driver to stop. The driver took her to the nearest police station. She was taken immediately to the hospital for treatment.

The mini-van driver showed the police where he picked up Jody. At 10:00 p.m., the police surrounded the house and advised Mike to come out without any weapons. Mike exited the house and was arrested. When the police executed their search warrant of the truck and house, they found a pair of handcuffs, duct tape, Jody's underwear, her sunglasses, a .303 rifle, and three .303-calibre bullets.

A forensic psychological assessment determined that Mike had a delusional disorder of the persecutory type. For the past few years he had paranoid delusions that he has been harassed by his former army sergeant, which resulted in harm to his health and an inability to function sexually. Mike believed that the sergeant was stalking him, booby trapping his house, and poisoning his food.

Mike told the police he thought that once he had sex with a unknown girl, he would gain confidence, causing his stalker to cease and desist. He would be free.

The judge heard all the facts from forensic psychologists, victim, prosecution, and defence. Mike was found guilty of sexual assault and kidnapping. He was sentenced to fifteen years in prison.

The half-ton truck played a vital role in the rapist's actions. He planned for the event by stocking his truck with a blanket, handcuffs, and duct tape. He carried spare fuel in a jerry-can to avoid being spotted at a gas station. Although the plans called for sexual exploitation of an innocent victim, there was little evidence produced in court that sexual fulfillment or pleasure was the driving force. His intent was to control through violence.

Motor vehicles are frequently used in sexual assaults. They are used to confine the victim or, when sexual assaults are inflicted elsewhere, vehicles are used as a place in which to initiate the assaults. Women accept rides from friends or strangers who drive them to their homes or to other destinations where sexual assaults are executed.

In one case, two women were considering accepting a ride from a man that they had just met at a celebration, when he pulled out a knife and forced them into his truck. Three more men joined the group. Once on the highway, the driver pulled into a field to allow the men to urinate. When the truck stopped, one man wielded the knife and forced the first woman to take off her clothes. The men raped and beat her in succession. The second woman screamed for the men to stop, and she was subsequently raped. The men fled the scene. The two women ran a mile to the nearest farmhouse and called the police (WorldNet Daily Exclusive, 2006, September 10).

A woman may also be trapped in her own vehicle as a potential rapist stalks her when she enters her car, drives to her destination, and exits without attending to danger signs around her. Closely related is the issue of a potential rapist forcing his way into a woman's unoccupied car, laying low on the floor in the back, and forcing himself on her when she enters the vehicle and prepares to sit in the driver's seat.

In another example, a woman saw a truck fill her rear-view mirror and decided to speed up to get away from it, whereupon the trucker floored the accelerator to close the gap. The woman saw an exit ramp coming up and decided to get off the freeway and try to lose the trucker in the nearby town. But the truck kept coming. As she was driving through the town, she ran a yellow light. The trucker continued to follow and charged through a red light, trying to stay on her tail. Becoming desperate, the woman pulled into a gas station, nearly hysterical. The truck followed and pulled along beside her. The trucker got out quickly, ran towards the woman's car, pulled open the back door, and yanked out the man who was hiding in the back seat (Myer, 2006). The trucker became a hero.

Women should take measures to protect themselves from sexual attacks. They should always park their vehicles in highly visible, well-lit areas, and keep their eyes open for suspicious activity nearby. They should check their cars before they enter because someone could be crouching in the back seat. They should always have their keys ready to unlock the car door, enter quickly, and lock the door. They should never leave house keys attached to car keys at service stations or parking lots.

If her car breaks down, a woman should raise the hood of the vehicle or attach a handkerchief to the door handle, and stay in the car with the doors locked. When someone approaches to help, she should roll the window down slightly and ask the person to call for assistance. If a woman witnesses another car broken down at the side of the road, she is advised not to stop for the stranded motorist. Instead, she should use her cell phone or drive to the nearest phone booth and call the police for assistance. Finally, if a woman thinks that she is being followed into her driveway, she is advised to stay in her vehicle with the window locked and sound the horn to get the attention of neighbours or scare the other driver off.

Some of the women most vulnerable to sexual assault are sex-trade workers, because of the belief among abusers that the police pay less attention to them than to other women. As was sarcastically pronounced by the Prostitute's Collective of Victoria, raping a prostitute is like stealing a car left in the middle of the street with its doors unlocked and the key in the ignition (Matheson, undated).

Much of the sex trade revolves around the automobile. Men seeking prostitutes for sex (johns) drive around looking at women who stand invitingly on the roadside. The automobile becomes the means for initial contact, solicitation, and negotiation of the sexual act. It is also a natural facility for the sexual event. Hence, the motor vehicle can be one of the most opportune venues for sexual assault on sex-trade workers. Nova Scotia's Justice Minister Michael Baker called for changes to Nova Scotia's *Motor Vehicle Act* that would allow for bylaws giving police officers the power to seize the vehicle of anyone suspected of picking up a prostitute (Canadian Press, 2000). Similar ordinances have been passed by other jurisdictions in Canada, such as Manitoba and Alberta, and large American cities, such as New York, Los Angeles, and Oakland. In Nova Scotia, however, the legislation has not yet been enacted.

Evidence suggests that sexual assault is a frequent event experienced by street prostitutes. Melissa Farley and Howard Barkan (1998) completed a ground-breaking survey of Canadian prostitutes. They concluded that 82% of the adults working in prostitution reported that they had been physically assaulted, 83% had been threatened with a weapon, and 68% had been raped while working as a sex-trade worker. Eighty-four percent of the prostitutes researched experienced current or past homelessness. Their sexual activities happened most frequently in vehicles. A more recent study by Roberto Valera, Robin Sawyer, and Glenn Schiraldi (2000) reported that 44% of the prostitutes sampled had been raped.

The following descriptions were included in a "Bad Client List" produced by the Sex Professionals of Canada (SPOC). Each incident demonstrates the range of vehicle use for violence against sex-trade workers.

Assault: May Have a Weapon

Friday, May 26, 2006

Date picked up pro on the street and drove to an alley...He got into the back of his van and took his clothes off...Date didn't want to use a condom, he was also drunk and started to argue with her. He grabbed the pro by her hair...then bashed her head into the side of his van...He then grabbed her throat and started choking her...Pro...pulled him to the ground and kicked him...Pro found the door release and managed to get it open and jump out of the car. She grabbed his pants so that he couldn't chase after her.

Assault/Abduction

End of summer 2005

After picking up pro, date stole her cell phone and locked her inside of his car. He then proceeded to drive north...where he raped and sodomized the pro before bringing her back downtown and dropping her off without any payment.

Assault

Monday, May 30, 2005

A male has been attacking pro's. He negotiates for sex, gets pro into a truck and then chokes them and doesn't pay.

(Sex Professionals of Canada [SPOC], 2006)

These incidents were specific to Toronto. Similar postings are offered in other Canadian cities. They candidly illustrate that it is not uncommon for prostitutes to be raped at knifepoint, thrown from cars, and severely beaten in clients' vehicles. Although community organizations like SPOC and Project KARE encourage sex-trade workers to provide details of violence at work, the majority of incidents remain unreported because the complainants fear that the police will identify them as prostitutes. The incidents that are reported are often not deemed high priority by individual police officers. For example, an unnamed community in southern California closed all rape reports made by prostitutes and drug addicts and placed them in a file stamped NHI, meaning "No Human Involved" (Fairstein, 1993). At the same time, the Oakland police closed more than 200 allegations of sexual assault reported by prostitutes and drug addicts without a single interview or follow-up investigation. The cases were simply "unfounded"—police jargon for saying that no crime ever occurred (Fairstein, 1993).

In Canada in 2007, however, Robert Pickton, the serial killer whose victims included prostitutes from Vancouver, was found guilty of second-degree murder in an extended court case. Prior to the case, the police were criticized for not doing enough to find the missing women. As a result of the Pickton case, the assault and murder of prostitutes has become a national issue. Sue Davis, a co-ordinator for the Prostitution Alternatives Counselling and Education Society (PACE), reported that police have become more responsive to the complaints of sex-trade workers: "I see a total change in the way police are handling the situation. They take reports when sex-trade workers are assaulted now" (CBC News, 2007).

Canadian and American men and women date in an informal way. Couples go out for an evening to the movies, the theatre, or a concert. They share drinks at a bar or just hang out. The time spent together is defined according to a shared sense of trust that safety and respect for each other is valued and maintained.

The assumed trust can be misplaced. Contrary to popular belief, most rapes do not occur in a park where a stranger jumps out of the bushes to attack a lone jogger at sunset. Rape usually happens by men who know their victims, who have dated them previously, and are supposedly friends. That is why date rape is also referred to as "acquaintance rape."

A review of the FBI Uniform Crime Reports shows that there were an estimated 93 934 rapes in the United States in 2005. Of these, 8% occurred when the victim was going to work, school, or somewhere else. Twelve percent happened somewhere away from buildings, and 18% occurred in places like vehicles. More importantly, 65% of all victims were known by the offender; many were teenagers on dates (U.S. Department of Justice, 2006).

Date rape is forced, unwanted sex with a person that the victim knows. Teens between the ages of sixteen to nineteen are the prime target group. They experience 26% of all rapes (U.S. Department of Justice, 2006). This statistic is probably low. In their benchmark study on date rape victims, Mary Koss et al. (1988) reported that only about 2% of all date rape incidents are reported to the police. Several reasons account for the low number of reports. One is self-blame. Victims often have an overpowering sense of guilt about not having seen a sexual assault coming before it was too late. Another is familiarity. Teen girls are reluctant to report sexual assaults because they know the young men well enough to have gone on a date with them. And there is shame. Teens do not want parents or friends to know that they placed themselves in a risky situation, such as sitting in a parked car with a young man late at night.

Date rape is an act of violence that can happen in automobiles. Although it is often spontaneous, many such rapes are planned, sometimes days or hours in advance. It also happens in a moment of passion, where the man and woman "make out" or "neck" in the car, after which the man demands sex and the woman refuses. If the woman has not set precise sexual limits and communicated them to the man before entering the car, she could easily find herself the victim of an attack.

A drug commonly used in date rapes is called Rohypnol, an illegal substance also known on the streets as roachies, La Roche, rope, rophies, roofies, ruffies, R-2, rib, Mexican Valium, or the "forget me pill." It is an inexpensive, potent tranquilizer that can be bought illegally for about $5 per pill. The drug is about ten times as strong as Valium. Because it is a small pill, virtually tasteless, and easily dissolvable, it can be dropped into drinks, whether in a glass or bottle.

Victims of Rohypnol experience severe dizziness, headaches, slow response, and lower inhibitions. They may have difficulty moving and display similar effects to "feeling drunk." When it is consumed with alcohol, the drug quickly lowers women's inhibitions, facilitating potential sexual conquest. Police departments in most major cities have compared notes about the drug and find certain commonalities. Young women wake in party houses, strange apartments, or in the back seats of cars, naked with clothes lying about, surrounded by strangers.

When a woman sips an infected drink, she appears extremely intoxicated, with slurred speech, no co-ordination, swaying, and bloodshot eyes, but no odour of alcohol. She becomes so disoriented that her mind is not likely to be working normally when a sexual attack is taking place. She doesn't scream, because she is in a daze, semi-conscious, or in a dream-like trance. She experiences memory blackouts and feels nauseous the day after ingestion. A woman under the influence of Rohypnol will drive a car erratically and if noticed by the police, she is likely to be charged for impaired driving.

Rape-prevention literature suggests women carefully monitor the amount of alcohol they drink, watch the glass of wine or bottle of beer they are drinking, and be careful with whom they enter a car.

IN SUMMARY

It has often been said, and with justification, that sexual assault is the fastest growing violent crime in Canada and the United States. Few attacks are random, and those that occur outside the home most often happen after women accept rides from men they either do not know or know only slightly.

Aggravated sexual assaults vary as offenders and circumstances vary. But one thing appears to be consistent: the use of a motor vehicle to complete the assault. Sexual assaults often happen in vehicles, or a woman may be stalked in a car, or she may be abducted and transported to a specific location where she is harmed. The motor vehicle is such a vital component of sexual assault that forensic psychologists characterize it as an essential component for helping to profile murderers and rapists of sex-trade workers.

For example, Project KARE, an RCMP-based investigational unit, was set up in 2003 to solve the murder of over twenty prostitutes within the vicinity of Edmonton. The police suspect a serial murderer. To help catch the killer, the RCMP behavioural science team offered a news release in which they provided five of the killer's characteristics. Three of the five clues feature the vehicle:

» The person or persons responsible drives a truck, van, or a sport utility vehicle as opposed to a car, and that he is comfortable driving in rural areas.

» That the vehicle will be suitably maintained and likely has a
   significant amount of mileage. This does not necessarily mean
   that it is exceptionally clean but that it is a reliable vehicle. The
   vehicle may be used for work and outdoor activities such as
   hunting, fishing or farming.
» The person or persons responsible may have periodically cleaned
   the interior and exterior of his vehicle, perhaps at times that are
   unusual for this particular individual.

(RCMP News Release, 2005, June 17)

11
THE POLICE AS
PURSUERS AND VICTIMS

Good people do not need laws to tell them to
act responsibly, while bad people will find a
way around the laws.

— PLATO

We usually assume that law and order go together: the police enforce laws and make demands in order to create or maintain social order. Not surprisingly, we share an absolutist view of the police as agents who act for the good of the community. When we observe a police officer chasing a suspect down the street, our observation propels our belief in good over bad. We assume that the police officer is the good person while the one being chased is a bad person; at least, he has done something bad enough to be chased by the police.

The police officer intervenes on our behalf to maintain a sense of safety and justice. Yet police officers may create circumstances that are unsafe and violent. Policing of our roads can easily result in violence to the police officers, the suspects, or innocent bystanders. Nowhere is this clearer than in police pursuits.

POLICE PURSUITS

The objective of police pursuits is to apprehend suspect drivers whose offence may range from being involved in illegal parking, speeding, running a red light or stop sign, stealing a vehicle, stealing gas, or selling illegal drugs. Once suspects recognize imminent police apprehension, they jump into vehicles and flee the scene. The police pursue as their primary duty to stop suspects and uphold justice.

Although police officers take the oath to help keep public safety, sometimes they jeopardize that safety, and innocent bystanders may get caught in the middle. A police chase often ends when the suspect wraps the car around a pole, misses a turn at high speed, or collides with other vehicles, killing or injuring an unsuspecting third party.

Although car chases typically end in disaster, they are considered to be appropriate policing strategy in the United States. In 2000, the American Supreme Court ruled that a driver who flees from the police merely at the sight of them is suspicious enough for the police to chase, stop, and search the person. According to Chief Justice William Rehnquist, nervous, evasive behaviour translates to reasonable suspicion and justification for a stop. Flight is the consummate act of evasion (CNN, 2000).

Police work is largely based on the belief that an officer should be on guard at all times, scanning the roadway for possible violators. Their suspicion converts a livable world into one fraught with danger and hostility, where nothing is as it seems (Crank, 2004). Suspicion provides the police with means to decide on action, such as pursuing drivers. Once suspects are identified, the police can escalate the action by giving chase.

The police chase may also happen because of sheer cynicism. There is a shared feeling among some police officers that too often people get away with doing bad things. When a particular driver is spotted, the officer uses her own discretion to give pursuit, recognizing that she will not tolerate an illegal driving action or the suspicious nature of a driver. At the start of the pursuit, the target symbolically represents all people who break the law (Neiderhoffer, 1967).

In her speech on September 30, 2000, Shirley Heafey, the chair of the RCMP Complaint Commission articulated the violent nature of the police chase and the use of the cruiser as a weapon:

> As Peace Officers, when you envision yourself in that position where
> you have to make a decision one day to perhaps take a human life,
> you don't often think about it being through a vehicle, but let's face it,
> you're driving around a big bullet, and it can kill. I never figured that
> I'd ever be involved in a situation as a police officer, contributing to
> someone's death in a chase. (Heafey, 2000: 2)

Although the speeding police cruiser may be like a "big bullet," some police departments in Canada still do not have standard operating procedures that bind officers to standards of police pursuits. Hence, some police behaviour broadly reflects the "cultural right" to apprehend a bad driver at all costs. Officers are basically left to their own discretion for dealings they have with unpredictable driver behaviour.

The Supreme Court of the United States has before it a case entitled *Scott v. Harris* that addresses the issue. In short, it states: "If the practice is rare because it's so risky to public safety, does its use when there might be non-lethal alter-natives make it 'unreasonable'? Especially when the chase is set off by a small traffic violation as it was in *Scott v. Harris*?" (Solomon, 2007). When hundreds of people die annually in high-speed police pursuits in the United States, does it make sense to put innocent drivers and pedestrians at risk to stop a common offender who can be arrested more safely at work or at home the next day?

Policing the streets carries a certain amount of situational uncertainty, which requires common sense and some bravado. Police chases are a form of impro-visation, whereby officers take action to adjust to unknown and unpredictable observations and encounters. The selection of a particular action depends on the way in which an encounter between a police officer and driver unfolds, the behaviour of the driver, the real or perceived seriousness of the infraction, the need to control the situation, the potential threat to the officer or bystander(s), traffic flow and road safety, the attitude of the officer in charge, and available backup (Crank, 2004).

Although literature on police culture provides a general description of fac-tors at play before a police chase, precise data on police pursuits are difficult to determine. One reason is that police officers or their agencies sometimes deter-mine that a crash occurred right after a pursuit was "terminated," hence they do not necessarily define the crash as having been pursuit-related (Hills, 2002). Police officers may have slowed down and the suspect sped up and crashed, creating a situation whereby the officers who investigate the scene interpret the crash as not having resulted from the pursuit. Agencies can determine if a pursuit-related crash occurred by replaying tapes of radio transmissions dur-ing the pursuit, or later in an accident reconstruction investigation. However, the investigative process may be subjective, because the superior officers who investigate the reports are sensitive to the thought processes of officers involved in pursuits. Some Canadian police forces, like the Edmonton Police Service, have pursuit review boards that evaluate the pursuit events and the decisions that were made by the pursuit officers.

Although statistics on police pursuit-related crashes and deaths are difficult to find, American researchers have proposed that police pursuits result in just over 350 deaths per year (Hills, 2002). But the number of pursuits fluctuates per year. The NHTSA (2000) reported that 314 people were killed during pursuits in 1998. Of this total, 2 were police officers and 198 were individuals being chased. The remaining 114 were either occupants of unrelated vehicles or pedestrians. The total was higher than in each of the four previous years.

The U.S. Fatality Analysis Reporting System database is a benchmark from which many criminologists work. The database showed that 200 or more sus-pects, over 100 bystanders, and 10 or less police officers died in police chases between 1994 and 1998 (FARS, 2000). The number increased to 365 deaths nationwide for 2003 (FARS, 2004). Although variations appear, still we may conclude that there is a consistent level of mortality caused by high-speed police pursuits. But we must view these statistics with healthy skepticism, because there is no mandatory reporting system in place that tracks pursuit fatalities. The rule of thumb is that only 90% of American states report pursuit fatality data. If all the states reported fatalities in a consistent and reliable way, the rate would likely increase dramatically (Van Blaricom, 1998).

Similar default data exist in Canada. Towards the end of 2000, the RCMP did not share recent comprehensive data on high-speed pursuits. The most recent and comprehensive national RCMP data is for the period from 1991 to 1995. During that five-year period, there were 4232 hazardous pursuits in the country, of which 587 resulted in injuries and 19 in deaths (Heafey, 2000).

Data for British Columbia showed 3991 pursuits that resulted in 818 injuries and 23 deaths between the years 1990 and 1998. In Ontario, data from non-RCMP forces indicate that between 1991 and 1997, there were 10 421 pursuits, which resulted in 2415 injuries and 33 deaths (Heafey, 2000). For these two provinces alone, there have been over 14 412 pursuits, 2845 injuries, and 46 deaths in the span of eight years.

The numbers would look even more alarming if the remaining seven provinces were included in the database. There were 892 police pursuits in major Canadian cities in 2003. Edmonton led the country. Officers pursued 232 vehicles during that year, compared with 176 in Toronto, 142 in Montreal, 98 in Vancouver, and 70 in Calgary (Cormier, 2005). Two reasons were offered. One was that Edmonton had a significant increase in car thefts and the other is that Edmonton was the fastest growing city in Canada at that time (CBC News, 2004).

When we look at the charges laid after pursuits—for example in Ontario—the data indicate that 35.8% of the charges laid are for theft/possession; and 32.4% are for Criminal Code traffic violations, not including the most serious offence of impaired driving (8.5%). In contrast, serious violent offences (including homicide and weapons offences) involved only 2.8% of pursuits (Heafey, 2000).

The numbers, although descriptive and not conclusive, do present an issue. Whereas a considerable number of Canadians nationwide are injured or die in police pursuits, whether as innocent bystanders, suspects (drivers and/or passengers), or police officers, some officers still engage in pursuits for what appear to be low-priority traffic behaviours or criminal suspicions. Most chases last only seconds or minutes and typically end in safe stops. But those that flee for extended periods of time at high speed often produce violent ends. Researchers funded by NHTSA interviewed a sample of police-pursuit suspects in the United States. They found that almost 70% of the interviewees would have slowed down if police had terminated the pursuit or even backed off a short distance (Hills, 2002). Still, a strong societal principle is that no one should expect to flee from police without consequences. To refuse to stop for the police is against the law. Corporal Justin Thompson told a group of new recruits in Arkansas that, in his experience, suspects in most pursuits are fleeing because of outstanding warrants against them, they are driving a stolen vehicle, they are intoxicated, or they are in possession of narcotics (Thompson, 2005).

The following case shows that bad things can happen even when the police slow down their pursuit. Names and other identifiable information have been altered for anonymity.

It was about 4:00 Saturday afternoon, when Tommy, driving a blue 1990 Honda Prelude, ran a red light in Calgary. He had a friend riding with him, a sixteen-year-old boy. Two officers on routine patrol gave chase. Tommy wasn't about to be caught. He made a sudden left turn off the main street and roared through a residential area. The police were on his tail. One of the officers called for backup. Two more police cars were dispatched to the area.

Tommy tore through a stop sign, keeping one eye directly in front and one eye in the rear-view mirror. There was no time to look left or right. He reached speeds of eighty to a hundred kilometres per hour through a number of intersections.

Larry, driving a 2002 Toyota Camry, was taking his three friends to the nearby grocery store. He was going east when he entered the intersection because he had the right of way.

Immediately from his right came a flying blue machine. It didn't slow down or stop as Larry assumed it would. Larry couldn't stop in time. His Camry struck the right side of the Prelude, causing it to trip violently into a curb. It was t-boned, which caused it to become airborne, flying roof first into an aging pine tree. Amazingly, the Prelude landed on its wheels. The Camry spun out of control, struck a stop sign, and came to rest against a light pole on the northwest corner of the intersection.

Emergency services appeared quickly, using hydraulic cutters to remove Tommy and his passenger from the Prelude. Tommy was pronounced dead at the hospital. His passenger was dead at the scene with massive cranial trauma. In the Camry, Larry's passenger in the front seat had died instantly of catastrophic head injuries.

The resulting police investigation established that the Prelude had been stolen. Yet the police had given chase because Tommy had run a red light, not because he was driving a stolen vehicle. The first set of pursuing officers reported that they had slowed down their chase because of the danger. When the second cruiser came up another street, however, Tommy had panicked. His attempt to outrun his pursuers ended with three deaths.

The impulse to flee created a panic situation. Although the offending driver (a teen) may not have wanted to evade the police initially, flight quickly became his priority when a police cruiser challenged him to stop. The challenge was met with a counter challenge. The young driver sought to escape, regardless of the odds.

Technology can decrease pursuit risks. Officers can deploy spiked strips in the path of a fleeing suspect. The strips create a controlled loss of air (not a blow-out) from the suspect's tires. Once the violator crosses the strips, the deploying officer quickly pulls them from the roadway to allow pursuing police vehicles to pass. Some police departments are also testing a radar warning system that sends a signal to any motorist who has a radar detector that a police pursuit is approaching. It allows motorists to pull over to the side of the road or otherwise get out of the way. This strategy is of little use to Albertans, however, because radar detectors are illegal in their province.

Technological innovations in the planning and implementation stages include an ultrasonic device that shoots a burst of microwave energy at a fleeing suspect. This causes the vehicle's electronic system to fail and the car is immediately disabled (Hills, 1999). Experts are studying a similar technology in which a robot-like cart jettisons from the front of the primary police-pursuit vehicle. The cart then attempts to overtake the fleeing vehicle and electronically "zaps" the engine out of service. Researchers are also testing radio-technological devices (similar to stolen-car tracking systems) that electronically disable a fleeing vehicle. These innovations have not yet been marketed to North American police forces.

Agencies have used helicopters with good results in pursuits in different American cities. The bird's-eye view from above, versatility, and range of the helicopter allows ground officers to decrease the use of high-speed pursuits and potentially increase apprehension rates (Alpert, 1998). With a helicopter observing the suspect, pursuit vehicles can slow down to reduce the risk of high speed in heavily populated areas. Unfortunately, the purchase of a helicopter is costly and use of the strategy is selective. Future partnering between police detachments located within greater metropolitan regions may corral the financial resources needed to have a helicopter at the ready.

In Surrey, England, officials tackled the police-pursuit problem in the mid-1990s. The 1995–1996 Annual Report of the Police Complaint Authority of Surrey recommended that the police formally use the Tactical Pursuit and Containment (TPAC) method of dealing with vehicle pursuits, which allows fleeing vehicles to be brought safely to a stop without the need for the traditional high-speed pursuit. Similar to the American use of spiked strips, TPAC encourages use of devices that can be laid across the road to deflate a vehicle's tires and bring it to a controlled stop. It also endorses using several police cars working together to halt a speeding vehicle gradually and safely. Surrey police officers are required to participate in a five-day course to learn the TPAC techniques.

In North America, people do not have to live in fear of being potential police targets, but they should keep a wary eye on their roadway environment so that they do not become bystander victims of police pursuits. If a speeding police car hits a vehicle parked on the side of the street, the parked vehicle is little more than a sidebar to the police's main objective of chasing and apprehending their foe. A review of court complaints show that owners of the vehicles damaged during a police chase are usually unsuccessful in getting reimbursed for their losses.

POLICE PURSUITS AS REALITY TV

Television reality shows such as *cops* and *Real Stories of the Highway Patrol* emphasize sensational car chases that usually end in horrific crashes. The episodes are chosen for their dramatic effect and leave even the most moderate viewer's heart pounding. The shows almost always conclude with the police being in control of the situation. Few episodes show the police in a critical light, an understandable situation since the production of the television shows depend on police co-operation.

VIOLENCE AGAINST THE POLICE

Rap music, especially gangsta rap, can be angry, raw, and violent, and it can be a platform for the presentation of ideas by the powerless against the powerful. Gangsta rap often refers to external sources of social problems plaguing minority groups, and a key problem often identified is oppression by the police. The organic message is to confront the police. The lyrics are perilously close to Malcolm X's challenge for young people to stop singing and start swinging. The idea is illustrated on the cover of a CD entitled *Fuck tha Police*: in a mock court scene, Ice Cube, MC Ren, and Eazy-E put "the police department" on trial. Some of the lyrics on the CD express a desire to commit violence against police officers.

Amir Crump, a rapper who calls himself Trajik, led a rap group called the Desert Mobb. Armed with a knock-off AK-47, Crump fired more than forty shots at police officers when they responded to a call that he was beating his girlfriend. One officer was killed, and another was sent to the hospital (*News 3*, Las Vegas, 2006, March 10).

Policing is a perilous life, made even harder by images of defiance through ghetto songs. The police stand in the way of bad people doing bad things. Officers operate in a dark world of law breaking, where they are often targets.

The FBI routinely collects information from law enforcement agencies throughout the United States. In 2004, American police agencies employed 499 396 officers. Of those officers, 59 373 reported that they were assaulted while performing their duties, establishing a rate of 11.9 assaults per 100 officers. Of those assaults, 27.9% of the assaults resulted in injuries (U.S. Department of Justice, 2004).

The most common assaults are physical, with weapons like fists, bats, or other blunt instruments. Guns are prominent. Motor vehicles are also routinely used to attack police officers. Traffic-related circumstances and sites are common bases for assaults. Eleven percent of the assaults reported to the FBI happened when police officers were conducting traffic pursuits or stops (U.S. Department of Justice, 2004). Motor vehicles are often the weapons aimed at the targets; they comprised part of the 14.5% of weapons referred to by the FBI as "other" types of dangerous weapons.

Suspects attempt to assault police officers by purposefully hitting them with their vehicles, whether they ram police cruisers with officers inside (referred to in the United States as "battery on a police officer") or they attempt to run down police officers while they are outside their vehicles.

Violence against the police can take on many forms: ambush, stand-off, self-defence. In traffic it mostly happens at the spur of the moment when a motorist is cited for a traffic offence, or when a driver is stopped for a breach of traffic laws but is suspected of other crimes, such as breaking and entering or car theft. The following case is an example of this type of violence. Names and other identifiable information have been changed for anonymity.

Phil, a forty-year-old carpenter, was driving his Ford Taurus down a main street at 3:00 a.m. Saturday morning, when he was stopped at a random police Checkstop. A police officer decided to check the vehicle licence plate before engaging the driver. He found that the licence plate was registered to a rental company for a Chevrolet Impala. The officer approached Phil and asked him to produce his vehicle registration, insurance, and operator's licence. Phil was unable to do so. The police officer asked Phil to turn off his car. Phil reached down, pretending to do so, but instead he prepared to flee. The officer noticed Phil's reaction and reached into the car to shut off the engine.

In the ensuing struggle, the officer's arm became entangled in the driver's seat belt. Phil sped off, dragging the police officer by his right hand. The officer and Phil punched at each other while the car was speeding and zigzagging all over the road. The officer was dragged for four blocks before he broke free and fell to the pavement. Phil continued his escape. Luckily the police officer suffered only minor injuries.

The officer ran back to his car, alerted the dispatcher, and a police pursuit was initiated. Phil was stopped with the use of a spike belt. As Phil screeched to a stop, he crashed into a parked vehicle. Emergency personnel had to extract him from the wreck. Inside his car were stolen licence plates, jewellery, a screwdriver, pliers, and binoculars—tools for breaking and entering. Phil was charged for criminal negligence and received a sentence of five years in prison.

Numerous court cases reveal a consistent pattern of suspects who were found guilty of criminal negligence causing bodily harm to a police officer, and who cared little about killing or injuring a police officer. Some applauded themselves for having engaged the police in such a deadly manner. Some aggressions were more aggravated than others.

In the following case, the perpetrator decided to harm a police officer in an attempt to escape capture for another misdemeanour. Names and other identifiable information have been changed for anonymity.

Constable Miles was on a routine patrol, alone in an unmarked car just a few kilometres outside of Lethbridge, Alberta. In the early hours of the morning, she noticed Randolph in a Dodge Ram truck on the side of the road in a nearby city subdivision. She left her police cruiser to investigate.

She approached Randolph and asked for documentation. She told him to stay in the car and wait for her while she used the police computer in her cruiser. The computer check revealed there was an apprehension warrant against Randolph for a parole violation. (He had two months remaining on his parole after spending two years in prison for a number of offences, including possession of marijuana for the purpose of trafficking.)

While Constable Miles was reading the computer screen, her car suddenly jolted forward. She was thrown to the side. Randolph had rammed his car into the passenger side of the cruiser. He backed up and rammed her again. He pushed the police car about fifteen metres into a ditch. Constable Miles began to panic, trying to open the driver-side door. She was convinced that Randolph was trying to kill her.

She felt pain; her body was at an awkward angle, positioned between the ground and the opened car door. She got out and ran to the nearby bush, hoping the shrubs would give her cover. She then ran back to the police car, believing it would provide her with better protection. Randolph was roaring his engine, ready to ram the police cruiser again. Constable Miles drew her revolver and fired at least five shots. Randolph sped away from the scene.

Randolph was arrested at home the same evening. He was later convicted and sentenced to sixteen months in prison. He received two years in lieu of time already spent in jail waiting for his trial.

Constable Miles spent three days in hospital with severe pain. A psychiatrist later diagnosed her as having a severe case of post-traumatic stress disorder.

At times, police officers are the primary targets of violence. A driver decides to hurt or kill a police officer as a form of power, or as a dangerous act against a symbol of authority.

Violence against the police with a motor vehicle is a fairly recent phenomenon, but by no means a rare occurrence. Bethesda (1997) reported that, from 1990 to 1996 in the United States, 221 drivers purposefully used their vehicles to attack police officers. They aimed to kill. Forty-eight of the 221 police officers attacked died at the hands of drivers. The remaining officers were injured, some severely.

It is difficult to obtain more recent statistics in the United States or Canada. However, Edmonton police received a great deal of media attention in 2003 because of the rash of police attacks in that year. Six incidents were reported in one month. One possible reason was the increased use of drugs. Another was the copycat factor. One person takes a run at the police and others imitate or duplicate it (Weber, 2003).

Battering a police officer with a vehicle often leads to a police pursuit. After a driver makes a run at an officer, he flees. The officer gets into her cruiser and pursues. In the process, she is likely to radio other officers, who join the pursuit.

IN SUMMARY

It is a truism that police work is hazardous to officers and members of the public. Police officers need to anticipate that a routine traffic stop can become an unpredictable and violent event. A driver with a guilty conscience may harm the officer and instigate one of the most intense encounters between the public and the police: the high-speed vehicle pursuit.

The majority of police chases are short in duration, but many of the high-speed pursuits end in tragedy for the officer, suspect, and/or innocent bystander. Although rules and regulations about police pursuits have been invoked in many parts of Canada, more can be done to bring fleeing vehicles to a halt without a traditional high-speed chase.

HIT AND RUN

Character calls forth character.

— JOHANN WOLFGANG VON GOETHE

It is bad enough when someone smashes into your car when you pop into a convenience store for milk, or when you park your car on the street for the evening. But when the driver takes off, leaving behind all responsibility, we suffer a further loss. In the scope of things, however, a hit and run of a parked vehicle is low hurt compared with a hit and run involving the injury or death of drivers, passengers, cyclists, or pedestrians.

Each year, hundreds of thousands of people worldwide become victims of hit-and-run crashes. To leave the site of an accident, and, worse, to leave another person badly wounded or dead, is a serious, violent incident that is common in the annals of policing and the history of traffic violence. It happens often and for numerous reasons. The following is an example. Names and other identifiable information have been altered for anonymity.

Jill was a nineteen-year-old student who usually rode her bike to the University of British Columbia in Vancouver. Early one morning, she left to go to her history class and then visit her grandfather.

Jill did not see the half-ton truck that struck her, either before or after the collision. She thought the vehicle came from her left, travelling south, but she was unsure. She remembered landing on the hood of the truck, striking and breaking the windshield. The truck was exceeding the speed limit. The next thing she recalled was regaining consciousness by the side of the road near the southwest corner. The truck did not stop. There were no witnesses.

Jill had excruciating back pain. With a great deal of difficulty, she hobbled back home with her bike by her side. She called her grandfather, who drove her to the hospital. The doctor diagnosed her injury as a compression fracture of one of her thoracic vertebrae. She was in the hospital for two weeks.

The following day, Jill's grandfather went to the Vancouver police department to report the crash as a hit and run. The police made no further inquiry with Jill. It was a nearly impossible crime to solve, mainly because Jill could not remember the exact time or location of the hit and run; she had a degree of retrograde amnesia. The result: Jill, in horrific pain, had to fight to get her insurance company (a Crown corporation) to pay costs. She was successful, but the law did not touch the driver.

INCIDENCE OF HIT AND RUN

The American Insurance Information Institute (2006) reported that, nationally, 11 of every 100 traffic collisions are hit and runs. From January to September 2006, approximately 1153 people were killed by hit-and-run drivers in the United States, and another 78 453 were injured. In Canada, about 9% of all accidents reported to the police were hit and run. The general breakdown is that of these, 4% involved pedestrians, 21% moving vehicles, 74% parked cars, and 1% other property, such as houses and yards. Umesh Shankar's (2003) research report for NHTSA found that 18% of pedestrian deaths involve hit-and-run crashes. Nearly one in five pedestrians killed on America's roadways is a victim. Of the 4881 pedestrians killed in 2006, 974 died in hit and runs (FARS, 2006). Furthermore, vulnerable populations, such as young children and senior citizens, are especially susceptible to becoming victims of fatal crashes because they are more often pedestrians.

THE OFFENDERS

An important question to ask is why drivers leave the scene of a collision. One reason is that drivers have outstanding warrants for their arrests. Two, they have been driving under the influence of alcohol or drugs and do not want to be charged with a criminal offence. Three, they are not covered by auto insurance. Four, they have an invalid or suspended driver's licence, or they don't have proper registration for the vehicle. Five, they are driving a stolen vehicle. Six, some don't understand the law, especially if they are young teens or recent immigrants. Seven, others simply panic; they fear being arrested.

Many famous American politicians have been found guilty of killing people in hit and runs. For example, Tennessee Senator Carl Koella, Jr. killed Terry Barnard in 1996. Pennsylvania State Representative Thomas Druce killed

Kenneth Cains in 1999. Although ex-senator Bob Torricelli's hit-and-run case did not kill a victim, it does stand out for the deceit the case entailed. The incident happened when the ex-senator and his wife backed into another car at the market. According to the newspaper item, a witness saw Torricelli get out of his car, inspect the damage, and drive away. Torricelli told the *Trenton Times* that he assumed at the time that the other car was not damaged because the impact occurred at a very low speed. He also asserted the other vehicle was parked illegally and its owner should have been ticketed. Finally, he claimed that his ex-wife was driving the car. The judge did not believe him and found Torricelli guilty of leaving the scene of an accident (Associated Press, 2004).

Famous victims are former N F L linebacker Jamie Fields, who was killed when a motorist ran a red light and slammed into the driver's side of Fields's car. The driver fled on foot. Keven A. Conner, known to his fans as Dino of the music group H-Town, was killed when he and his fiancée were struck and killed by a hit-and-run driver in Houston, Texas (Deadly Roads, undated).

In 2003, Dwayne Goodrich, a Dallas Cowboy football player, was charged with two counts of manslaughter for killing two people and injuring two others. The police reported that Goodrich's B M W clipped a tractor-trailer rig on Interstate 35 in North Dallas. While three Good Samaritans tried to rescue the trucker from his burning rig, Goodrich raced through the crash scene at an estimated 177 kilometres an hour. As he tried to swerve between the disabled vehicles, he struck the three rescuers and killed two of them. The third rescuer escaped death but suffered a broken leg and other minor injuries (Richards, 2003).

The football player fled the scene in his car. When the police caught up with him, he surrendered. Officers found tissue and hair underneath weather stripping near the windshield and near the right headlight. Fragments of glass with blood were collected from the right dashboard. Goodrich was charged with two counts of manslaughter and three counts of failure to stop and render aid, as well as aggravated assault and running stop signs. He was sentenced to seven and a half years in prison plus three additional five-year concurrent terms. He was also fined $20 000 (N B C, 2006).

Although rationalizations abound regarding the psychological and social factors that influence drivers to flee after a crash, it can and does happen to people least likely to be suspected. One of those was Bishop Thomas O'Brien, head of the Phoenix Roman Catholic Diocese. He became the first Roman Catholic bishop in American history to be convicted of a felony. He was on his way home from celebrating Mass when he hit a pedestrian, leaving a giant spider-web crack in the windshield. He drove three kilometres to his house and parked his Buick in his garage while the victim lay in the street (Wagner, 2003). Arizona prosecutors claimed that the bishop did not call the police the following day and that he tried to have his windshield quickly repaired, knowing that the police were looking for the car. Jurors found him guilty. O'Brien would likely not have been charged if he had stopped, waited for the police, and helped the victim (CNN, 2003). Shortly after being arrested, O'Brien resigned his office.

The concept of unintended consequences may help us understand why people leave the scene. Measures that are implemented to improve traffic safety often create destructive results. For example, the cost of car insurance is based on risk. Drivers who are deemed to be high-risk will pay exorbitant insurance rates, some approaching $10 000 per year for a vehicle worth $2000. Often, high-risk drivers cannot afford the costly premiums, or they are unwilling to pay. So they drive illegally without vehicle insurance. If, or when, they become involved in a crash, they are unlikely to remain at the site to be questioned and possibly charged by the police. Their tendency is to make a run for it, leaving desperate victims lying on the road. Similarly, drivers who have suspended or revoked licences because of previous bad driving may also flee their moral and legal responsibilities to avoid being apprehended by the police.

Unlike premeditated murder, the driver seldom knows the victim. It happens by blind chance or coincidence. Often there are no witnesses to the event. The pressure is on the police to find the guilty party, often with few leads. It is a difficult task especially for minor hit-and-run accidents like dinged fenders, sideswipes, bumper hits, or rear-end collisions with parked cars. Nearly every police department in the world has specifically assigned police officers whose sole responsibility is to maintain a case load of hit-and-run accidents, locate and apprehend suspects, and file cases with the courts.

Hit-and-run offences are not reserved for the "typical criminal." Rather, they can be an outcome of possibilities for many. Everyone has the capacity to do wrong, not thinking of the consequences of the action or recognizing the impact their act has on others. It is a test of character, not unlike that of Plato's story about the magic ring of Gyges. Anyone who puts on the ring becomes completely invisible. Herein lays the test. If a person could become invisible, or if in some other way her actions could be an absolute secret, what would she do? Would she behave differently? If, as in the case of injuring a pedestrian with a car, the driver were removed from possible punishment, censure, or retaliation, would she stop and wait for the police for the sake of doing the right thing?

People panic. And in their panic, they engage in irrational, unpredictable behaviours. The following is an extreme example. In Fort Worth, Texas in 2001, Chante Mallard, a twenty-five-year-old nurse's aid, had been drinking and taking Ecstasy when she struck a homeless man with her car. She drove to her house and parked in the garage with the man still lodged in her windshield. He was still alive but Mallard did not call the police or try to get medical help. He died a few hours later. The next evening, her boyfriend and his cousin removed the body and left it in a park, where it was discovered the next day.

Several months later, acting on a tip, the police searched Mallard's property and found the bloodstained, dented car and a burned passenger seat in the backyard. Mallard received a fifty-year sentence for murder plus ten years for tampering with evidence. Her boyfriend was sentenced to ten years in prison for tampering with evidence, and his cousin was sentenced to nine years (Associated Press, 2003). It is believed that the man would have lived if he had been given prompt medical attention (Fox News, 2003).

The Mallard case illustrates that when people commit a hit-and-run offence, they can slip into breaking a series of other laws, such as tampering with evidence. In some cases, the hit and run turns into charges of manslaughter or even murder.

Hit and runs get the attention of the public especially when the victims are children. Thirteen-year-old Dara Toeun was walking to school in San Jose, California, when a car slammed into her. Instead of stopping, the driver took off and left the girl in the street with a broken hip, arm, and leg. Unusual? Not really! Of the 4881 pedestrians killed in the United States in 2005, 974 (20%) died in hit and runs (NHTSA, cited in Vertanian, 2006).

A disturbing hit-and-run incident occurred in Morley, Alberta in 2006. A 16-year-old girl was walking along the Trans-Canada Highway one Sunday morning when "she was struck by one vehicle and then hit by several more as her body lay on the road. Nobody stopped" (Canadian Press, 2006: A8).

> Grieving family members ask how anybody driving could possibly be unaware they had hit something, and if they did know, not stop. These drivers, including the one who fatally struck the girl, must have known they hit something. It's hard to believe the driver who caused her death didn't stop. (Canadian Press, 2006: A8)

Domestic animals, especially dogs, are often hit by drivers who leave rather than help the animal or attempt to find the owners. For many people, the moral obligation of caring for the wounded ends with human beings. Unless for insurance purposes, drivers seldom report incidents involving dogs or other large domesticated animals. There are few statistics on this topic, other than self-report questionnaires, few of which are published.

IN SUMMARY

Whatever the cause, hit and run is an act of violence in response to fear. The act comes after the fact of a crash. A driver hurts or kills someone, then flees. Although the original crash may have been little more than an error in judgement, the fleeing turns it into a violent and illegal act.

13
GANG VIOLENCE AND
DRIVE-BY SHOOTINGS

The majority of murderers and notorious thieves began
as children who have been abandoned, and the true
seminary of crime must be sought for upon each public
square and/or each crossroad of our towns, whether they
be small or large, in those flocks of pillaging street urchins,
who like bands of sparrows, associate together, at first
for marauding, and then for theft, because of a lack of
education and food in their homes.

— GABRIEL TARDE, 1912

Drive-by shootings, originally used as hit-and-run tactics by Japanese soldiers
during World War II, have become one of the main offensive tactics for gangs
(Klein, 1971). They are mobile attack forays that involve shooting a firearm from
a moving vehicle (Howell, 1999). Whereas gangs in the 1960s and 1970s engaged
in "rumbles" and "gang fights" to establish status and turf rights, today they
engage in drive-by shootings for similar goals.

Rumbles and gang fights were cumbersome adventures that required the
use of fists, clubs, chains, knives, baseball bats, and other hand-held weapons.
Combatants proceeded by foot to the battle site with little means for quick escape should the police enter the fray (Miller, 1982). In modern times, the drive-by
is a hit-and-run tactic where members of one gang drive a vehicle into a rival
gang's area and shoot a targeted person. Extremely violent drive-by shootings
have become part of western popular culture, as expressed in hip hop or rap
lyrics. A stand-out incident in hip hop history was the murder of rapper and
song writer Tupac Shakur, who was shot four times in a Las Vegas drive-by
shooting.

Drive-bys have become the signature of gangs, who have proliferated in numbers all over the world. Los Angeles recorded 6327 drive-by shooting incidents between 1989 and 1993; 9035 people were shot, of which 590 died. Forty-seven percent of the people shot at, and 23% of the homicide victims, were innocent bystanders (Hutson et al., 1996). Lewis Yablonsky (1962), a professor of criminology at California State University, estimated that only about 50% of gang-related murders hit the actual target. The rest of the bullets spray and hit innocent bystanders. (Yablonsky's estimates are still used by criminologists today.) Many of the gang-related drive-by shootings take place near shopping malls or plazas, fast food restaurants, bars, nightclubs, targeted apartment buildings, carwashes, and gas stations, where large numbers of people congregate.

Numerous newspaper articles pay witness to the innocent bystander as victim. Here are a couple of examples.

> LOS ANGELES—A drive-by shooting critically wounded an 18-month-old girl in a car seat and a man who was standing outside the vehicle.
>
> The girl's mother, Rebekah Harris, was dropping off the man at an intersection Sunday night when a car pulled up and about 10 shots were fired, said police Detective Sal LaBarbera.
>
> The little girl, who was in the back seat of the vehicle, was hit in the face, LaBarbera said. Harris and another child, a 4-year-old boy, were not hurt.
>
> The man, Hollis Roberts, 25, was in critical but stable condition with wounds to the chest and leg, LaBarbera said. (Associated Press, 2007)

*

> Two teenagers were arrested in the drive-by killing of an 11-year-old girl...The girl was an innocent bystander to a street dispute involving a neighborhood turf war. She and some friends were outside her home trying to get relief from the heat at the open hydrant on a hot day. Investigators believe the girl was shot in the head after friends of her 17-year-old brother exchanged angry words with another group of young men. Sometime later—with the girl, her brother and his friends gathered outside her home—the second group of men drove by in a dark sedan and started shooting. (Newsday, 2006)

A groundbreaking research paper on drive-by shootings appeared in the *New England Journal of Medicine* in 1994. The authors, Range Hutson, Deirdre Anglin, and Michael J. Pratts, focussed on children and adolescent involvement in Los Angeles drive-by shootings in 1991. The researchers tabulated 1548 drive-by shootings involving violent street gangs: 583 of the incidents (38%) involved children and adolescents less than eighteen years of age. In these incidents, 677 children and adolescents were shot at. Of the 677 victims, 36 died from their injuries. Among the injuries inflicted in drive-by shootings, 359 (84%) occurred on city streets; 50 (12%) occurred when gang members shot into a car while it was being driven, stopped at a traffic light, or parked; and 14 (3%) occurred when gang members shot into homes (Hutson et al., 1994). Although the statistics pertain to Los Angeles, where drive-by shootings are endemic, the researchers proposed that this type of violence transcends the California borders and has become a "national disaster." Unfortunately, there is no national data on the prevalence of drive-by shootings, those who commit them, those who are killed and injured as a result of them, the types of firearms used, where they take place, or at what times they most often occur (Violence Policy Center, 2007).

Essentially, a drive-by shooting requires two technological devices: the car and the gun. Since the 1970s, for reasons not clear, gang members decided to combine them and create the now popular drive-by shooting (Miller, 1982). It is widely used to settle accounts between gangs or between members of the same gang.

In one case, members of a gang named Piru were hanging out in front of a liquor store in Los Angeles. Some Crips, another street gang, pulled up to the guys and asked, "What's up, Blood?" The Piru gang members refused the invitation to talk and turned away, whereupon the Crips started firing shots at them. Three Piru members were killed. The Crips escaped easily. They were never caught (Sanders, 1994).

But the score was evened when, on a Saturday afternoon, a member of the Crips was sitting against a wall and a car drove up. The Crip turned his head nonchalantly to look at who it was and then slowly turned his head back. At this point, a bullet grazed his head. The victim ran to a friend's house, noting that the shooter was wearing red, the colour of the Piru. Revenge was being meted out (Sanders, 1994).

The motor vehicle ensures that the violent encounters are kept brief, a rapid-fire raid. Drive up to the target, shoot, and roar off. The weapon of choice in the United States is a 9-millimetre semi-automatic handgun, with magazines that can hold fifteen or more bullets without reloading. The use of such weapons with large-capacity magazines increases the risk of injury and death to rival gangs and innocent bystanders (Hutson et al., 1994). But it does not stop here. The semi-automatic handgun is often replaced by an even more potent killing machine: the submachine gun or AK-47 assault rifle, each of which can shoot quick rounds in fractions of a second.

Another advantage that drive-by shootings have over other means of violence is they are camouflaged. A car driving down a city street is a common sight, unworthy of special notice. Since about 75% of drive-by shootings in the

United States happen in the evening or at night (between 7:00 p.m. and 7:00 a.m.), identifying a car as belonging to a rival gang is fraught with problems (Violence Policy Center, 2007). An innocuous-looking vehicle stops, shots ring out, and the shooters mingle with traffic once again.

Gang-related drive-by shootings are also becoming increasingly frequent in major Canadian cities. In one case in Toronto, a twenty-six-year-old man was struck in the upper chest and backside in a volley of gunfire during a drive-by shooting at a strip plaza at about 5:00 p.m. "I heard four or five shots and saw a dark vehicle like a Suburban pull out of the parking lot, drive on the wrong side of the road, and then turn onto Church Street," said a witness, who was on his balcony. Across the street, the victim was lying sprawled beside his black Mercedes sports car when officers arrived. At least two suspects were in the vehicle that fled the scene (Stancu, 2005).

A string of drive-by shootings occurred in Edmonton in the late 1990s and early 2000s. In the fourth shooting that happened in August 1999, an eighteen-year-old was killed in a drive-by shooting at a busy intersection (CBC Newsworld, 1999, August 21). Police suspected that the killing was part of the escalating warfare between Asian gangs fighting for Edmonton's drug trade and defending their turf. Such a suspicion brings with it the public health warning that innocent people are likely to die because the police are not optimistic about halting gang warfare. One of the problems is that victims and targeted individuals often refuse to co-operate with the police because they fear for their safety. (CBC Newsworld, 1999, August 21).

The drive-by shootings in Edmonton have continued. In September 2006, a woman was killed and two men were injured in a triple drive-by shooting. It was considered to be gang payback (Farrell, 2006). Six weeks later, three men were shot dead in a triple homicide in a downtown lounge. The police considered this incident also to be payback.

Drive-by shootings have long been a centrepiece of criminal activity in Toronto, Montreal, and British Columbia's Lower Mainland. The following is an abbreviated case. Names and other identifiable information have been altered for anonymity.

In the early evening of April 19, 2004, four fifteen-year-old friends (Nina, Kim, Lee, and Dat) were walking towards the centre of the city. A car drove up to within a few feet of the four friends. Two 9-millimetre handguns were extended from the passenger side of the vehicle and shots were fired at Dat. A total of six bullets from two different guns hit Dat's body. Two bullets became lodged in his spinal column. One shot grazed his skull and caused some brain damage. A handful of bullets entered into the remaining parts of his body. Dat became a paraplegic, paralyzed from just above the waist down. The shooting lasted only five seconds.

The driver fled the scene, but Nina had a good look at the assailants. It was Ding and his younger brother, both in their early teens. Earlier in the year, Dat was assaulted and badly beaten by Ding.

The day after the shooting, the police set up a surveillance of Ding's home. When the suspect was leaving his mother's house in the same vehicle from the previous day, the police immediately forced the vehicle to stop. Ding was driving, and his passenger was a young man named Bim. They were both arrested. Upon their arrest, a 9-millimetre handgun dropped from Bim's waistband, but it was not one of the guns used to shoot Dat.

When the case appeared before the judge, the charge of attempted murder against Ding was dismissed. The judge considered the identification evidence too frail, since the witnesses and victim had only a few seconds to identify the accused. Furthermore, there were many inconsistencies in Dat's testimony. While dismissing the case, the judge said that he had strong suspicions that Ding was involved in the shooting, but that was not enough for a conviction.

The case illustrates how the perpetrator can escape conviction because the act happened so quickly. This is especially true at night when it is difficult to identify licence plates and faces.

There are also many occasions when a gunman in a motor vehicle shoots at a residence. The purpose for the shots may be intentional harm to someone in a house, or it may be a warning that worse is yet to come if the targeted individual does not change his behaviour. The home is usually known to the shooter, and it usually has gang-related or gang-known residents. For example, one night, several shots were fired into a house in Surrey, British Columbia, around 1:00 a.m. Three people were in the house but nobody was injured (Carrigg, 2005). Around the same time, an Abbotsford home was targeted in a drive-by shooting. Police were called after a resident heard several shots fired. Two vehicles parked in front of a home on the block were shot at and police found several shell casings close by. No one was injured in the shooting, which police believe targeted residents in the affected home.

There are several reasons the probability of getting caught and prosecuted for a drive-by shooting is low. Witnesses are afraid to give details about the shooting for fear that they will be the next targets. A second reason is that most drive-by shootings happen at night. The shooting takes place in a few seconds, and the killers have an immediate escape. The third reason is American-specific.

Once a drive-by hit on a gang member has occurred, those close to the victim try to pin the event as the murder of an innocent man or woman. Staging the event this way is important because of the money the American federal government provides for drive-by victims. Whereas innocent people who die from drive-by shootings are compensated financially, a dead gang member's family does not qualify for the compensation (Ramos, 1998). So applicants must make sure that gang victims look like innocent targets. In some cases, local newspapers are called and reporters are told that the corpse is an "innocent victim of a drive-by shooting," not a gang member who received a hit.

With gang-initiated drive-by shootings, there is the distinct possibility of innocent people being killed. The spray of bullets can hit unintended targets, or sometimes an innocent victim is mistakenly targeted. Such a case happened in Long Island when a fourteen-year-old boy was shot while riding his bicycle. Prosecutors believe he was mistaken for a member of a rival gang because he was dressed in blue (*Nation*, 2004).

Many kinds of gangs roam in American cities, the most common of which are violent youth gangs. Gang-related homicides are usually more chaotic and involve more participants, and the attacks are usually more out in the open than are non-gang murders (Maxson et al., 1985). Furthermore, there is some evidence to show that in some cities, such as Los Angeles, gang homicides more often involve cars than non-gang murders (Klein & Maxson, 1989; Violence Policy Center, 2007).

The United States has become the central breeding ground for many different kinds of gangs, namely racial or ethnic gangs (e.g., Black, First Nations, Latino, Asian), street gangs (e.g., Crips, Bloods), prison gangs, and motorcycle gangs (e.g., Hell's Angels, Satan's Choice), among others. They all have different beliefs and codes of honour, manifestos, and mission statements. They represent their unique identification and affiliation through symbolic dress such as ball caps, leather, and sports clothing. They often mark their territory by graffiti that warns rival gangs to stay away and serves as a kind of "street newspaper." Tattoos usually represent icons of violence or the gang logo.

Gangs in Canada appear to be an emerging phenomenon, as opposed to the chronic problem in the United States. Historically, street gangs have been predominantly active in major urban centres, particularly Vancouver, Toronto, and Montreal. However, they are increasingly expanding into other cities, such as Edmonton, Calgary, and Winnipeg. In the western provinces, ethnic gangs are largely composed of young men from India, Asia, and eastern Europe. Aboriginal-based gangs are particularly active in Calgary, Edmonton, Regina, Saskatoon, and Winnipeg. Some of these gangs have also been observed in more rural areas as well as on First Nations reserves in Hobbema and Saddle Lake. Their primary criminal activity is street-level drug trafficking with drugs obtained from other crime groups, such as Asian-based networks or the Hell's Angels. The rivalries among various Aboriginal-based street gangs can occasionally erupt into violence (Criminal Intelligence Service Canada, 2005).

Many of the street gangs operating in Ontario were initially formed from singular ethnic groups, but they are now increasingly multi-ethnic. In Quebec, the main street gangs are Caribbean-based, although other ethnic-based gangs, such as the Vietnamese and Russians, are increasingly emerging (Criminal Intelligence Service Canada, 2006).

Most of the gangs' rituals or membership ceremonies require new members to commit felonies like car theft, armed robbery, drive-by shooting, or stabbing. Further initiation rites often take place when the recruit stands defenceless before flailing fists and boots, suffering the beating of his life at the hands of incumbents (Decker, 1996). Violence becomes the fundamentalist virtue. When a gang member decides to retire from the gang, a serious beating again befalls him. Violence is the heartbeat of a gang.

Certain gangs want specific automobiles that symbolize their pride, reputation, identity, ideals, and significance. Asian gangs embrace compact import cars like the Honda Civic and Accord, Acura Integra, Mitsubishi Eclipse, and the Toyota Supra and MR2, and modify them into compact hot rods for the street racing "tuner" scene. "Tuners" are car enthusiasts who spend tens of thousands of dollars to modify their vehicles for maximum performance and style. Other gangs prefer luxury vehicles like Cadillac Escalades, GMC Envoys, and Jaguars.

MOTORCYCLE DRIVE-BY SHOOTINGS

Unlike with street gangs, where the vehicle is a primary platform for violence, motorcycle gangs are more likely to use their vehicle as a symbol of defiance and violence.

The American-based Hell's Angels is one of the most prominent and powerful motorcycle gangs in the world. The modern version of biker gangs really started in 1948, when the first Hell's Angels motorcycle club was formed in Berdoo, California. World War II veterans would sit low in the saddles and roar their motorcycles in town, forcing townsfolk to look up and say, "There goes one of those Hell's Angels" (Barger, 2002). Their bikes were stripped of fenders, turn indicators, front brakes, and all parts deemed too big, heavy, ugly, or not absolutely essential to the basic function of the motorcycle. These dissenters and rebels have since transformed themselves into violent criminal gangs, the most notorious of which are the Hell's Angels (Allender, 2001).

The emergence of the Angels spawned rival gangs like the Pagans, Banditos, Satan's Choice, and the Outlaws, formed in parts of the United States where the Hell's Angels have not yet settled. Here, these gangs (like the Hell's Angels) set up criminal organizations that supplied prostitution, contract violence, drug peddling, extortion, racketeering, and protection for organized crime. The police have tried to crack the foundation of these gangs, only to meet with stiff resistance. There is a strong bond among members that sustains an "us versus them" view of the world, helping to freeze law officials outside the circle of members.

Similar to Asian street gangs, the Hell's Angels have a powerful and unshakeable relationship with their vehicles: Harley-Davidson motorcycles, commonly referred to as "choppers" or "hogs." Chopped up or customized Harley-Davidson motorcycles are the American freedom machine, symbols of confidence and raw power. The sight of choppers being driven by leather-clad Hell's Angels—with their low lines, large front tires and headlights, smaller tear-drop fuel tanks, extended narrowed and raked front forks, high handlebars, custom-built exhaust pipes, and roaring four-stroke engines—elicits feelings of awe and fear from passers-by, magnified when the Hell's Angels ride in large numbers.

Although motorcycle gang members literally travel nowhere without their choppers, when it is time to settle conflicts, they are more likely to depend on traditional drive-by shootings. The motorcycle is too inconvenient to use as a shooting platform for one rider. A passenger needs to be the trigger man. Hence, gangs shoot at each other from cars, aiming at known drivers, pedestrians, or clubhouses. Still, there are occasions when drive-by shootings from motorcycles do happen with deadly force. CBC radio reported that a Montreal man, sitting in the passenger seat of a car, was killed in a drive-by shooting on a Wednesday afternoon. Two men on a motorcycle pulled alongside the car and opened fire on the vehicle. Typical of drive-by shootings, the victim was not a random innocent bystander. According to the police, the shooting was possibly a settling of accounts (*CBC News*, 2006, August 31). It was likely payback delivered at the hands of a motorcycle gang.

IN SUMMARY

The involvement of gangs in drive-by shootings has become lethal fare in major American and Canadian cities. Fierce competition and ambition among different gangs leads to settling of personal accounts in public locations. Cars have become key instruments in the perpetuation of gang violence: they serve as the platform for the shootings and the means of escape.

CARJACKING AND KIDNAPPING

Being kidnapped and held for ransom never
worries the poor man.

— *The Bible:* Proverbs 13: 7–8

Many writers in criminology talk about polarity in crime. They describe how anti-crime programs or technological innovations help prevent one crime, only to open the door for another more severe and violent crime.

This concern is certainly relevant to motor vehicle violence. To help reduce car theft, we have crude prevention instruments like steering wheel clubs and sophisticated technology like the satellite Global Positioning System (GPS). While these have become effective means to reduce incidents of car theft and break-ins, they have become the raison d'etre for carjacking. Until recently, a criminal intent on stealing a vehicle would do so with stealth. The owner was preoccupied elsewhere while the car was quietly hoisted. With the introduction of technology such as GPS in new cars, however, the criminal is now more likely to partake in physical violence to get the car, substantially raising the possibility of extreme violence against the owner or driver.

CARJACKING

Carjacking is typically a brutal form of motor vehicle theft, synonymous with violent acts like rape, aggravated assault, and murder. Carjackers use extraordinarily cruel means to force motor vehicles away from their owners. The random nature of the crime, bravado of the carjackers, and display of sadism have caused substantial fear among the general public and concern among law enforcement agencies.

True to the polarity effect, carjacking can be an unintended outcome of foiled car theft. Anti-theft devices like mechanical barriers, alarms, vehicle-tracking technology, electronic immobilizers, and hidden kill switches have stacked the odds against successful thefts of stationary or parked vehicles. To compensate for the higher risk of being caught, criminals began stealing vehicles with people still in them. The motor is running, the tracking devices can be knocked off, alarms are no threat, and motor kills used by the police are not likely to be used with human shields in the car. The issue is not that a car can easily be stolen this way, but that the thief is left with a serious mess of having witnesses in the car after the theft. Brutal methods are often used to help solve this problem.

In the United States in 2006, the motor vehicle theft rate per 100 000 people was 398.4 (Insurance Information Institute, 2008). Carjacking crimes, which occur most frequently in urban areas, account for approximately 3% of all motor vehicle thefts. About 43% occur on major business streets, at intersections with stoplights, roadsides, or vehicle line-ups near freeway on-ramps that are used as escape routes. Another 20% happen in parking lots or at momentary stops near convenience stores, hotels, valet parking, restaurants, gas stations, and office buildings. Some of the consistent findings are that firearms and sometimes knives are commonly used, resulting in about 25% of the injuries to victims. Of further interest is the majority of all carjacking heists happen within five miles of the victim's home or that of a friend or neighbour (U.S. Department of Justice, 1999).

Carjacking is more likely a crime of easy opportunity than of pre-planned strategy. Carjackers need a vehicle immediately. They usually are fleeing from the police or other person or group. Carjacked vehicles can serve as get-away cars for robbers, drug dealers, or kidnappers seeking a ransom (CNN Interactive, 1998). Carjackers usually catch drivers by surprise, or they persuade drivers to give them entry. The innocent driver acquiesces to the demands or persuasions and becomes a victim. It happens quickly; most carjacking episodes take only fifteen to thirty seconds. The resulting drama, however, may last for hours or days. Such was the case for an Alberta man who was a thirty-five-year-old paraplegic confined to a wheelchair. Names and other identifiable information in the following story have been altered for anonymity.

One Friday night, the man went to the local convenience store to purchase a few items. While he was there, a twenty-year-old hitchhiker befriended him, chatting about Calgary and his need to get to Banff for a family emergency. While the man paid for his purchases, he considered the hitchhiker's offer of beer and money in exchange for a ride to Banff. He decided to accept the offer.

The hitchhiker and his sixteen-year-old friend hopped into the man's modified 1994 Mercury Montcalm. Their 120-kilometre trip began. The two passengers made conversation, drank alcohol, and snorted cocaine during the ride. The driver had no fear, thinking the two transients were a couple of fun-loving pranksters. When the car reached Banff, however, the two passengers demanded that the driver continue to Lake Louise. The driver refused because he wanted to head back to Calgary. One passenger pressed a gun to the driver's head, threatening to shoot him if he did not obey. The driver did as he was told.

It was early Saturday morning when, en route to Lake Louise, the two men told the driver to stop so that they could take a bathroom break. When he stopped, one of them dragged the driver out of the car with a gun to his head and dumped him on the shoulder of the road. The other passenger threw the man's wheelchair into the ditch before getting back into the car and speeding off. The driver lost not only his car to the two transients but also his medical supplies and cell phone.

About 5:00 a.m., the driver dragged himself upright and flagged down a motorist, who gave him a ride to the Banff RCMP detachment. He was treated for minor injuries at the hospital and was released shortly after.

The two hitchhikers were caught just over the Alberta-British Columbia border around 7:00 a.m. that day. They had crashed the car into a ditch one kilometre out of Lake Louise and hitched a short ride into British Columbia. The police arrested both men shortly after they had passed out in the lobby of a lodge.

One passenger was charged with robbery, assault, and firearms offences. His accomplice was charged with unlawful use of an imitation firearm, robbery, and assault with a weapon (Zickefoose, 2005).

Carjacking is synonymous with extreme violence. Drivers are thrown out of the car, stuffed on the floor, or dumped into the trunk and terrorized later. An example from Carling, Wyoming illustrates the severity of the act. Frank Klein was visiting his sister in Cheyenne when two men approached him and asked for a ride to their car, which they said needed a jump start. Klein was a Good Samaritan and consented freely. Once in his compact Chevrolet, the men took out their knives and forced Klein to head west. When the group reached Utah, the men bound Klein with duct tape and put him into the trunk. Twice, the car-jackers pulled him from the trunk, beat him, and stabbed him. The second time they slit his throat, then dumped him back into the trunk. One last time, they pulled him from the trunk and kicked him into a snow-filled ravine, where he remained motionless until the two assailants left. They thought he was dead. Klein, however, scratched and crawled his way back to the highway. A snowplow operator picked him up and took him to the nearest hospital (Associated Press, 1998).

Although carjacking usually includes violence, at times it is little more than a means to an end: someone's fast ride. In Seattle, a criminal had just robbed a bank and was looking for a quick getaway. He ran up to a forty-year-old woman driving a Jetta with her two toddlers in the back. Brandishing a gun, he demanded she give him the car. She refused to leave her children with him. He forced himself inside and drove with the woman and children to a residential neighbourhood. There, he quickly stopped the car, wiped his fingerprints off the steering wheel, and walked away. According to the mother, "As bank robbers go, I guess you could consider him nice. He was very polite" (Koch, 2000).

Some criminologists suggest that carjacking is a crime against the most vulnerable people in the community—children and senior citizens. In Montreal, four men jumped an elderly woman with a walker from behind while she was getting out of her vehicle. They grabbed her keys and stabbed her several times then fled in her car. The four suspects ranged between the ages of sixteen and twenty-four (*CBC News*, 2005).

Wealthy people can be targeted for carjacking. In a case in Arlington, Texas, a woman driving a Mercedes attracted a criminal's attention by leaving Gucci designer boots, a purse, and three pairs of shoes in the back seat of the car, in full view (Crime Reports, 2000).

Equally horrific is the collateral suffering and death resulting from carjacking. In Kansas City, a six-year-old child was waiting in the car while his mother dashed into a sandwich shop for a brief moment. A carjacker jumped behind the wheel and tried to shove the boy outside. The young boy became entangled in his seat belt. He tried to undo himself while his mother came running out of the shop to help. The carjacker sped off, but the boy remained caught outside the rear door. The driver was stopped on Interstate 70 when motorists in two trucks and a car surrounded him at a stoplight. They wrestled the man to the ground and roped his legs, waiting for the police to come. The little boy died. The carjacker was charged with second-degree murder, child abuse, robbery, and kidnapping. The distraught mother told authorities that the man himself should be dragged at high speed as punishment (Associated Press, 2000).

A deviation of the typical carjacking is the "bump and rob," which, according to Toronto police, is a relatively new crime in Canada. A car, usually with a driver and at least one passenger, rear-ends or bumps another in traffic. When the victim gets out to check damage and exchange information, an accomplice jumps into the victim's car and drives off. Eighty-seven incidents of this type were reported in the Toronto area in 1999.

Schuyler and Lynn Sigel, corporate lawyers in Toronto, were involved in one of eighty-seven Canadian cases of carjacking and trunk entrapment in 1999. Three young men rammed the rear bumper of their Mercedes in the affluent Rosedale area (Gadd, 2000). When Mr. Sigel stepped out to investigate the bump, two thugs jumped him, punching him repeatedly and spraying Mace in his face. The third culprit tackled Ms Sigel, punching and spraying her with Mace after she slipped and fell on the ice. After the group entered an underground garage, they bound and gagged the Sigels and threw them into the trunk. They tortured Mr. Sigel to learn where he lived. After Mr. Sigel told them the location, they broke his jaw with a pistol butt. Later, at the Sigels's apartment block, the building superintendent became suspicious when he saw the young men smoking marijuana. He immediately summoned the police.

According to the lawyer representing the youngest of the three carjackers/kidnappers, one of the young men involved in the incident had experienced abuse and times of homelessness. The lawyer said that an increase in violence (such as carjacking) by people who have nothing against people who have everything is inevitable (Gadd, 2000).

KIDNAPPING AND TRUNKS

As many of the examples in this chapter have shown, carjacking often becomes kidnapping. The Court of Appeals in Indiana wrote that carjacking involves a person's knowingly or intentionally taking a motor vehicle from another person, or from the presence of another person, by using or threatening the use of force on any person, or by putting any person in fear. There is no confinement of the victim. Kidnapping, however, includes a person's knowingly or intentionally removing another person from one place to another by fraud, enticement, force, or threat of force, or while hijacking a vehicle. The kidnapper uses force or threats to keep the occupant inside the vehicle against his or her will (Court of Appeals of Indiana, 1999, February 16). An essential point is that kidnapping is a form of vehicular violence in and of itself.

Violent criminals often use car trunks as "prisons on wheels." It is estimated that between 20% and 25% of the people locked alive inside the trunks of cars die of hypothermia and asphyxiation. Vehicles parked in direct sunlight can reach internal temperatures of 131°F to 172°F, even after only fifteen minutes in direct sun. APB News (1999) reported the case of a sixteen-year-old boy who had been abducted and placed in the trunk of his car for approximately five hours in the Florida summer heat. The temperature inside the trunk climbed to 140°F. Although the boy survived, he had suffered severe brain damage and was in a deep coma for two weeks. In another incident, a teenage girl died after being stuffed into the trunk of her car; the temperature in the trunk had reached 175°F (APB News, 1999).

The following case illustrates that being stuffed into a trunk can be a predecessor to further events. Names and locations have been altered to preserve anonymity.

Floyd was a powder keg. His common-law wife, Faye, believed that although he had a troubled and dark past, love and care would make him a more sensitive human being.

Floyd always became angry over the smallest things. He once broke Faye's collarbone, for which he was charged with assault. Another time, he trashed their home, destroying Faye's personal possessions.

One day, Faye was staying at her mother's house when Floyd called her to meet and discuss their marriage. He suggested dinner, and Faye agreed.

They met in a neighbourhood restaurant, ate, and talked. While they were leaving, Floyd flipped out. He grabbed Faye's arm, pulled her into his Chrysler sedan, and drove to his house. He pushed her into the house, threw her onto the bed, and climbed on top of her. Faye could barely breathe. In a rage, Floyd repeatedly yelled, "You're dead!"

Floyd then bound and gagged Faye and forced her out of the house. He threw her into the trunk of his car and sped off. She struggled to loosen her hands and remove her gag. She felt Floyd drive over extremely rough terrain. Although she had now freed herself of the rope, there was little she could do. The constant tossing and bouncing about in the trunk caused numerous bruises to her arms and legs. Her head hit the top of the trunk, so she bent down in a fetal position, trying to protect herself the best she could.

Suddenly, the car stopped. Floyd let Faye out in a farmer's field. She looked about hopelessly; there was no escape. He picked her up and forced her to undress and get into the rear seat, where he raped her.

When Floyd started driving again, he repeatedly told Faye, "You're going to die. You did me in." Later he was chanting, "This is it, I'm a dead man, they're going to lock me up for this and throw away the keys." On the floor of the car, Faye noticed a bread knife that was taken from their home. She was horrified. Was he intending to use it on her?

Floyd threw Faye into the trunk again and then drove off. Later, after he had calmed down a bit, he stopped the car and brought her back into the front seat and turned on the heater. Most of her clothes were in shreds and it was mid-November on the prairies.

Floyd's bizarre driving over the hard plains damaged the car's engine. The motor was blown. Floyd decided to walk down the road to find help, leaving Faye unbound in the car in the middle of a huge field. He returned with a taxi, took her home, then turned himself over to the police.

Floyd was given eleven years for kidnapping and six more for sexual assault to be served concurrently. Faye's emotional scars did not go away. She moved to another province to be closer to her sister and to find some peace.

In another example, Janette Fennell and her family were ordered at gunpoint to get into their car trunk without their baby. They were driven to a remote area, robbed, and abandoned. The Fennells were frantic about the safety of their infant son. In desperation, they tore apart the trunk's interior and found a buried cable, which they used to free themselves. They drove to a phone to call the police. Fortunately, the baby was already at the police station. He was fine (McLoughlin & Fennell, 2000). Of interest here is the local police recorded the Fennell entrapment as a robbery, not as vehicle-related violence.

Fennell became a woman with a mission. She worked overtime to create public awareness of intentional trunk entrapment and an advocate for intervention. She turned to sources such as newspapers, direct interaction with victims, court records, Internet sites, and criminal justice proceedings to create a database on intentional trunk entrapment. By May 2000, she had documented 931 incidents of trunk entrapment involving 1082 worldwide victims in the last quarter century (McLoughlin & Fennell, 2000). The database became her platform for lobbying car makers to include automatic or manual release handles inside trunks.

Intentional entrapment can occur as part of a carjacking, robbery, ATM holdup, ransom request, homicide, burglary, rape, kidnapping, assault, child abduction, prank, joyride, or a combination of the above. In the absence of a federal database or surveillance system in either Canada or the United States, the incidence of trunk entrapment is probably vastly understated.

However, the prevalence and seriousness of kidnappings by trunk entrapment—and successful lobbying by Janette Fennell—have led automakers to implement safety devices. All major car manufacturers now have release mechanisms in their new cars. Ford and Toyota have T-shaped handles that glow inside the trunk as a standard feature on their new car models. General Motors has developed a heat detection system that automatically opens the trunk if anyone is inside and the car is parked.

POLITICALLY MOTIVATED KIDNAPPING

In Canada, the most famous politically motivated kidnappings that directly involved a vehicle were those during Quebec's 1970 October Crisis, when two prominent government officials were kidnapped and held in cars.

Armed kidnappers forced British Trade Commissioner James Cross into a taxi as he left for work. He was later released. On October 10, 1970, kidnappers with machine guns pulled up to Quebec Labour Minister Pierre Laporte's house and shoved him into the back seat of their car. On October 17, his body was found in the trunk of another car. He had been strangled.

The Front de Libération du Québec (FLQ), a Quebec-based terrorist group, claimed that they had kidnapped the two statesmen in order to draw attention to the social injustice of the country. The group had demanded a ransom of $500 000, the release of seventeen political prisoners, dropped charges for six more interned individuals, and the broadcast and publication of the FLQ Manifesto. As a result of the dangers posed by the FLQ, Prime Minister Pierre Trudeau invoked the *War Measures Act*, giving the police extensive powers.

The motor vehicle was instrumental in this crisis, and it is still a primary tool for politically motivated kidnapping throughout the world.

SEXUALLY MOTIVATED KIDNAPPING

Sexual assault victims have been studied more intensively than any other kind of crime victims, to improve understanding of the nature of the suffering inflicted on them. The crime is rarely defined as kidnapping for sexual purposes. The charge is almost always sexual assault, a charge much more severe than kidnapping.

Sexually motivated kidnapping is closely related to sexual assault. A woman is physically forced or vocally coerced into a motor vehicle, and subsequently she is sexually assaulted. Once inside the car, the rapist feels it is more advantageous or safe to inflict the violence. In a series of incidents in Vancouver, a man dubbed the "bicycle rapist" sexually assaulted at least six women. His modus operandi was to select a woman, crash his bicycle into her car, feign injury, and beseech her to drive him home. Once alone with the victim in the car, he would force her at gunpoint to drive to a desolate area where he would rape and rob her. The women who were attacked were dubbed the "Good Samaritan" victims (Crowley, cited in Karmen, 1994).

IN SUMMARY

Statistics about carjacking and kidnapping are flawed because of differences in, or lack of definition of, the crimes. For example, the incidences of carjacking are understated. Although carjacking is a formally defined crime in the United States, it has no legal standing in Canada. Yet there is sufficient evidence to show that the dangers of this type of violence is present and deserves discussion. Carjacking happens to victims who are unwittingly in the wrong place at the wrong time. Kidnapping stands as a singular act of violence or an accompanying act after a carjacking, and has become a highly visible element of vehicle violence.

SECTION III:
THE IMMEDIATE ZONE

The bitterest tragic element in life to be
derived from an intellectual source is the
belief in a brute Fate or Destiny.

— RALPH WALDO EMERSON

In the immediate zone, the automobile is used to make direct contact with a victim. The perpetrator chooses the motor vehicle as a weapon and aims it directly at him or herself or another person for some socio-psychological or financial purpose.

The events leading up to the act of violence are like scripts for a dramatic work (Goffman, 1959). They involve persons bent on revenge (e.g., ex-spouses); suffering from mental anguish like depression or schizophrenia (e.g., suicidal persons); seeking to be recognized (e.g., gang members); or seeking monetary gain (e.g., hitmen). The aggressors act upon defined motives and intents.

The following chapters will explore suicide, car bombs, and homicide as incidents within the immediate zone of vehicle violence.

15
SUICIDE

When you gaze long into the abyss, the abyss
also gazes into you.

— FRIEDRICH NIETZSCHE

"There is only one truly serious philosophical problem," wrote Albert Camus, "and
that is suicide." Suicide is nothing new. Sara Goldsmith et al. (2002) provided
accounts of suicides beginning in the year 1293.

Many cultures consider suicide to be a morally reprehensible act. Others,
however, have traditions that sanction the practice. For them, suicide is an act
of faith, commitment to a cause or unselfish statement of plight, or it is an act
of heroic martyrdom. Islamic extremists seek entrance to heaven when they
die from an act of self-destruction, usually accompanied by the death of others,
through bombs strapped on their bodies. Buddhists have set themselves ablaze
to make political statements in Asia. In Japan, citizens consider suicide a culturally appropriate response to disgrace and dishonour (Sakuta, 1995).

In North America, suicide is unsanctioned. For some, it is the ultimate in
narcissism, whereby persons who have killed themselves leave messages with
which no one can argue. For others, it is the final stage of despair and hopelessness. Their written words become their final communication. People close to the
victims suffer emotionally, socially, economically, and/or physically. Often, the
victim expresses sorrow for causing distress to the survivors, yet sometimes it
is the victim's intent to make friends, family members, or lovers feel guilt—a
form of payback.

Suicide has surpassed motor vehicle crashes in mortality rates. When the
two are combined—for example, when a driver takes his life by means of carbon
monoxide poisoning, running into a wall, hurtling down a ravine, or colliding
with a transport truck—the rate of death becomes nothing short of astonishing.

The car is the weapon that kills instantly, or it is the facilitator of death when, for example, the driver shoots himself in a parked motor vehicle.

VEHICULAR SUICIDE

Suicide by vehicle is like a deep, dark secret hidden in the closet. Precious little has been written about it, yet it happens routinely. Vehicular suicide is not a Dodge Intrepid mysteriously bursting into flames as a final act of contrition. It is not a passenger falling out of an unlocked Ford Explorer. Rather, it entails drivers who take their life while operating their cars or trucks. The movie *Pollock*, about the infamous, hard-drinking, abstract expressionist painter, Jackson Pollock, is an example of the impact of vehicular suicide. The painter's artistic passion came to a sudden end when, in a downward spiral, he created a sensational crash where he, his young mistress, and her friend died violently. He raced his car at speeds where he could no longer control the curves, steered into a thicket of trees, and forever cheated the world of his future creations.

Purposeful death by automobile holds potential benefits for a suicidal driver. It offers special concealment of the act. The crash may appear to be the product of driver error, which falls under the public health umbrella of unintentional death or injury. It lessens the likelihood of detection. Second, vehicular suicide allows troubled individuals an opportunity to protect their families from disgrace and to ensure payment of life insurance. If the case is assessed as an "accident," the victim has cleared the family name of the suicide stigma. Finally, vehicular suicide is practical. It is easily accessible, frequently used, and recognized as a routine crash in a mode of transportation with inherent risks. It is an ideal instrument for self-destruction.

In some cases, suicide in the car occurs only because previous strategies did not work. Some suicide participants will first stab or shoot themselves. Unable to complete their act through these means, they step into the car and drive away, looking for a bridge abutment, a tree, or a semi-trailer truck to hit.

AVAILABILITY OF LETHAL METHOD

As described in earlier chapters, motor vehicles are extensions of people's selves. Vehicles are always at arm's reach; they are waiting on streets, in garages, ready for our next move. It is not surprising that their accessibility can easily be translated into violent goals.

Ronald Clarke and David Lester (1989) documented the availability of lethal method for suicide. The authors described how the availability of handguns in different American states over time was related to the firearm suicide rate. They found that, over a ten-year period, the states that allowed and promoted the use of handguns had accelerating rates of suicide by handgun compared to those states that did not promote easy access to such weapons. Unfortunately, it is nearly impossible to reduce access to motor vehicles but, as described later in the chapter, some technological changes have reduced the ease with which people can take their lives with a vehicle.

There are no accurate, comprehensive statistics on completed suicides in the world, and official records do not reveal the extent of suicide by automobile (Peck & Warner, 1995; Schneidman, 1968). Suicides in some regions of the world are classified as accidental or culturally determined actions. For example, an elderly woman with a chronic disease in a rural part of Asia may step in front of a fast-moving truck so that she is no longer a burden on her family. She may also be making a statement that her siblings have not cared for her sufficiently. Officials may certify death as much through religious, social, community, and insurance claim pressures as through tangible medical observations and tests. For example, a coroner may be reluctant to classify a death in a car crash as suicide if the survivors are members of a large family and are left destitute. Finally, the determination of suicide requires the establishment of intent to die, which is an ambiguous term and a difficult job. What we do know, however, is that countries with higher numbers of cars per capita have higher suicide rates from car exhausts (Lester, 1994).

INHERENT HAZARDS

Driving is a high-risk action. The possibility of a crash looms whenever we step into a vehicle. Even people who do not own vehicles use some form of public transit. Heavy use, unreliable driver behaviour, the presence of impaired driving, variations of extreme weather conditions, variable and dangerous road conditions, and high-risk roadway designs such as intersections all contribute to a daily menu of risk and danger.

We routinely hear about drivers who were involved in car crashes, were injured, or died. Car crashes are no longer a sensational venue for death. Speakers at traffic safety conferences often announce to the audience that one in five people will be injured in a vehicle collision in their lifetime. In effect, we expect to become involved in a car crash at some time in our lives. As a result, suicide by motor vehicle is a short extension of a statistical probability.

When a crash occurs, the investigators are charged with finding cause. The possibility of suicide is part of that assessment. A list of common factors helps investigators to make that assessment:

» history of psychiatric hospitalization or therapy
» previous suicide attempts

- » suicide note, or previous mention of suicide plans
- » single-vehicle collision into the middle of a fixed object
- » accelerator pedal mark on shoe
- » no skid marks
- » a witnessed acceleration into oncoming traffic
- » simultaneous other suicide methods used, such as an overdose of drugs

Because of the social implications, the investigators lean towards caution before announcing a suicide.

The following is an example of suicide involving a vehicle. Names and other identifiable information have been altered for anonymity.

In the early afternoon, Jane was driving a small Hyundai on a two-lane highway in southern Saskatchewan. Although it was raining lightly, visibility was good. Jane crossed the centre line, however, and sideswiped a semi-trailer truck. She died immediately on impact.

Jane was not wearing a seat belt and held a tube of toothpaste in her hand. On the front seat, there were vials containing 5 mg and 7.5 mg of Imovane (a sleeping pill) and 50 mg of Sertraline (an antidepressant).

A diary and loose pages of writing were recovered in her vehicle. Here she had documented her desire to end her life by driving into a semi-trailer. She had feelings of loneliness, having recently ended a love relationship. For the last two weeks of her life, the desire to kill herself had been incessant. Her diary expressed the following thoughts and emotions:

- » a sense of pointlessness
- » fear of the future
- » an inability to do anything right
- » tiredness of being isolated, alone, and without family
- » sadness at not being able to keep a relationship with Sarah

A letter, not mailed, was also found in the car. In it, the forty-year-old woman expressed her unhappy memories as a child: her mother's cancer diagnosis; her discovery that her father was physically abusing her mother; and her own experiences with sexual abuse. She wrote, "Facing the sexual abuse I experienced is a part of soldiering on—it is not easy or pleasant, but an important part of healing. My path lies in remembering and forgiving."

Interviewed after the suicide, one of Jane's friends, Elaine, said that the woman had been depressed since she was eight years old; her mental state was not the result of her recent breakup with Sarah. During the last month before her suicide, Jane had explicitly contemplated her own death. The day before she drove into the truck, Jane had been agitated and contemplative. She talked with Elaine about different ways of killing oneself, including driving into a semi, hanging, and overdosing on pills.

Jane did as she had planned. Driving at about ninety km/h, she crossed the centre lane twice. The trucker pulled over to the shoulder of the road as far as he could go into the gravel to avoid the crash. Jane swerved a second time, straight into the truck's fuel tank. This time, she hit the truck, which went off the road, jackknifed, and plunged into the ditch. Jane's car flew into the air and rolled a number of times.

PSYCHIATRIC CLUES

Psychiatrists are an important source of information about people's ideation of suicide involving vehicles. As early as 1935, Professor Karl Menninger wrote that automobile crashes often occur under circumstances suspiciously indicative of unconscious intent. His patients frequently confessed that they had fantasies of driving their cars off cliffs or into trees or power poles. These violent incidents were fantasized as accidents. In one example, a middle-aged man who suffered from depression was severely injured in an horrific car crash. When he greeted his doctor after this disaster, his first words were, "Now I have paid for everything" (Menninger, 1935).

Dr. Hamburger (1969), a psychiatrist working for the National Institute of Mental Health in Denver, Colorado, reported the cases of six patients who had idealized suicide as an escape. In one case, Mr. Beta was a well-groomed, forty-five-year-old, unemployed family man. His business had failed, and he was facing bankruptcy. Mr. Beta confronted the problems with self-degradation, referring to himself as a loser who let his family down. Dr. Hamburger reported that Mr. Beta did not hallucinate or describe any illusions. He was mentally sharp and had a good memory and perception. Yet he thought himself worthless and analyzed his situation as hopeless.

Mr. Beta made no secret about his desire to commit suicide; his wife knew of it. When questioned about the mode of suicide he was contemplating, he appeared to have thought it through. He would drive his car off the road at high speed, which would eliminate any ugly stigma for his family and would grant financial recompense to his family through his insurance policy. As well, death would be quick. After undergoing psychotherapy, Mr. Beta reversed his suicidal tendencies.

A study by Melvin Selzer and Charles Payne (1962) noted that psychiatric patients who had attempted suicide or had persistent suicidal thoughts had twice the number of traffic accidents as did patients who did not have suicidal ideation. Based on matched groups of suicidal and non-suicidal alcoholics, seventeen suicidal alcoholics had sixty-three car crashes, while fourteen non-suicidal alcoholic patients had sixteen accidents.

Today, psychiatric disorders like mood disorders and psychoses have been primary topics of investigation for suicide. The studies usually profile the victims and analyze the means of suicide like motor vehicles. The most prominent motor vehicle-related method is by auto exhaust (Lesage & McPhil, 2005).

VEHICLE EXHAUST

Suicide from vehicle exhaust is a prevalent mode of self-death, particularly among twenty- to fifty-year-old North American males (Goldsmith et al., 2002). It is also prevalent in Japan where it occurred in about 5% of all suicides in 2002 (Ahira & Ahira, 2003). Car exhaust fumes are often used for "Shin-ju," (double suicide), a practice reserved for lovers or for entire families (Tsunenari et al., 1985).

A Finnish team of researchers determined a relationship between the number of people who own automobiles and the number who commit suicide by carbon monoxide. As car ownership increases, so do suicide attempts (Ohberg et al., 1995). In a study by David Lester (1990) of the twenty-eight nations from which data were available, those with more cars per capita had higher suicide rates from gas emissions. These countries did not have lower rates from other means of suicide.

When emission controls became a North American standard, the use of car exhaust for suicide declined (an unintended outcome). In contrast, England did not introduce emission control technology until many years later. The use of car exhaust for suicide grew rapidly, in line with the increase in car ownership (Clarke & Lester, 1989; Lester & Abe, 1989). These observations are still relevant today as car manufacturers increasingly cut carbon monoxide emissions.

The culprit—carbon monoxide—is a colourless, odourless, and tasteless gas produced from the incomplete combustion of organic fuels. The human brain and heart are susceptible to the toxin because they depend on oxygen to function. People who inhale carbon monoxide experience myocardial infarction. As the gas enters the bloodstream, the victim gets a headache, feels drowsy, loses consciousness, and dies. If the poisoning is not fatal, the person may experience confusion, disorientation, incontinence, amnesia, short-term memory loss, and/or muteness (Routley, 1998).

Although our discussion is focussed on the North American scene, the following example from Germany is a hallmark study of the chronology of events leading to a man's suicide from inhaling vehicle exhaust (Flanagan et al., 1978).

A serviceman had become deeply involved in an affair with a young woman. Around midnight one night, he decided to end his life because she wanted to stop the relationship. He had become highly emotional, a cocktail of depression, agitation, anger, and fear. A visit to a friend's house ended at 1:00 a.m. when he left abruptly, telling his buddy that he was going to end it all. His friend didn't take the threat seriously.

As dawn broke, a game warden found the serviceman dead in his car near the local forest. He was sitting upright in the driver's seat, and the engine was still running. He had attached a rubber hose to the exhaust and passed it through the rear window of the Mark II Austin. The open end of the pipe where the carbon monoxide passes was carefully located in the centre of the rear seat. For whatever reason, the man had placed a tape recorder on the front passenger seat and turned it on. A suicide note and a will were found in his jacket pocket.

The tape recorder played for sixty minutes. No spoken words were recorded, only a variety of sounds, such as the engine starting, breathing, and movement. The tape provided medical professionals with evidence for the survival time that might be expected in exhaust suicides before the popularization of catalytic converters. The survival time was about 20 minutes (Flanagan et al., 1978).

COPYCAT SUICIDES

In his essay, "Monkey" in his book *Influence*, Robert Cialdini (1993) suggested there were increases in vehicular "accidents" following well-publicized suicides. He referred to the phenomenon as "hidden instances of imitative suicide." People use the actions of others as models to decide how they themselves should behave under similar circumstances.

The source for the copycat attempts can be the media (Bollen & Phillips, 1981). Cases of suicide increase dramatically in the geographic areas where a suicide is most publicized. David Phillips, an American sociologist, was the first to call this pattern of media-induced imitative suicides the "Werther Effect" (Phillips, 1977). He described how the number of suicides in the United States jumped 12% in the month after Marilyn Monroe was found dead beside a bottle of sleeping pills. More specific to vehicular suicide, Phillips concluded, "Suicide rates, motor vehicle fatality statistics and non-fatal accidents all rose immediately following the transmission of fictional televised suicide stories in 1977" (Phillips, 1979: 1350).

In California, Bollen and Phillips (1981) researched the relationship between published stories of suicides and whether the stories affected suicide rates. Three days after vehicular suicide articles were publicized in the media, there was a 31% increase in California motor vehicle fatalities. The study was replicated in Detroit. The increase in motor vehicle fatalities ranged from 35%

to 40%. In both studies, the most striking result is the third-day peak in motor vehicle fatalities.

CHILD SUICIDES

Children are the most vulnerable group of people to be mistreated by adults and can be at high risk for suicide. In the United States in 2004, teen suicide was the third leading cause of death among children, after accidental death and homicide. In 2002, despite declines among all age groups nationwide, the suicide rate for adolescents between the ages of fifteen and nineteen increased by 6%; the suicide rate for children between the ages of ten and fourteen increased by more than 100% over the previous two years (Center for Disease Control, 2002).

In Canada, suicide is the second highest cause of death for youth aged ten to twenty-four. The rate for the year 2000 was 10.8 per 100 000 youth (Wasserman et al., 2005). Many more teens attempt it. Aboriginal youth are particularly at risk. In 1995, the Royal Commission on Aboriginal Peoples in Canada reported that the rate of suicide among Aboriginal youth was five to six times higher than the Canadian average. This statistic is still relevant today.

Children's suicide may take the form of a pedestrian traffic accident where the child, intent on self-harm, bolts in front of a car, bus, or truck. Unfortunately, we can never be sure whether the child's impulsiveness was a simple miscalculation or an intentional act. All children act impulsively at times. They have difficulty judging speed, spatial relations, distance, and velocity, and often dart into traffic without recognizing the danger (McComas et al., 2002). But some young children take their own lives (Moyle Information Services for Law Enforcement, undated). Studies have shown that getting run over by a vehicle is a frequent cause of death for children aged ten and older in the United States and Canada (National Adolescent Health Information Center, 2006). Some appear to be suicides, but there are no unequivocal statistics.

Risk factors for child suicide and attempted suicide include social and educational disadvantage; childhood and family adversity, such as family violence, family arguments, not living with both parents, low level of parental support, frequent geographical moving, exposure to sexual abuse, psychopathology; and exposure to stressful life events and circumstances (Beautrais, 2003; Pelkonen & Marttunen, 2003). Although suicidal behaviour in young people often appears to be a consequence of adverse life, there are many events whereby causes are unexplained. The child is a successful student, has a proven friendship circle, is loved by parents, and enjoys the advantages of a comfortable lifestyle. Such a child falls within the spell of depression, situational loneliness, or a sense of momentary hopelessness. This child is more difficult to characterize.

The causes of young child suicides are almost impossible to determine because, as adults, we are reluctant to believe that a six-year-old child would do such a thing. We believe that young children are incapable of understanding permanent death and suicidal acts that lead to death. We do not think that young children have the power of imagining a suicide beyond some ideation that may start around the age of nine. We are reluctant to accept that children can be so unhappy or can experience a level of despair and depression that paves the road to self-inflicted death. Death certificates seldom list child deaths as suicide.

The literature or lack of literature on child suicides illustrates that there has been little reliable research into the subject. There have been few recorded suicides for children under the age of fourteen. Yet, some child psychiatrists have discovered the presence of factors such as schizophrenia that suggest suicidal behaviour in children as young as five years old.

Studies have been undertaken to determine how many children do consider suicide, or think or talk about it. Cynthia Pfeffer's (1989) study, still quoted by researchers today, concluded that of normal children aged nine to fourteen years old, 11.9% had some suicidal ideation, or they expressed behaviour commonly associated with suicide. The students' answers suggest that parents can precipitate self-harm by forcing unrealistically high expectations on their children. When the children suggested or reported pre-suicidal thoughts to their parents, their mothers or fathers distorted their thoughts as being nonsense or an active imagination. Parents wouldn't, or couldn't, believe their children.

PEDESTRIAN SUICIDES

Each year some pedestrians attempt to kill themselves by placing themselves directly in the path of an oncoming vehicle, often a truck or bus. Because the episode is so complex, it is almost impossible to determine with any level of accuracy the number of pedestrian-induced suicides. When pedestrians are killed in Canada, investigators typically attend to the driver causality, because of our policy that the pedestrians have the right of way. To investigate a situation as a possible suicide is not a common strategy.

One group of pedestrians who may participate in pedestrian-based suicide is senior citizens. Their potential chronic pain and medical conditions, loneliness, despair, and limited access to other methods of suicide make walking in front of moving vehicles during poor or limited visibility a simple and morbidly effective strategy. Again, no definitive statistics can be reported.

Like all suicide attempts, there is no distinct marker as to who engages in pedestrian-initiated suicide and who does not. It can be an unemployed postal worker, an ailing senior, or a police officer. Gary Born, a former Colorado state trooper, was sentenced to two years for repeatedly sexually assaulting an eight-year-old family member. In addition to his prison term, the former police officer received twenty years' probation and a fine of $3100 (Denver Channel, 2002). The state trooper was killed in an auto-pedestrian accident two weeks later. Investigators found suicide notes left behind.

KABC TV (2004) reported a case where a murderer committed suicide by stepping in front of a semi-trailer truck. An associate professor of psychology at California State University in Los Angeles was found decapitated in her kitchen. The suspect, whom the newscast did not mention by name, took off in his car, removed all his clothing, left all his belongings in the car, and walked directly in front of a semi-trailer truck on southbound Interstate 15. The man died instantly, about thirty minutes before the woman's body was discovered.

Although big rigs are common vehicles for suicide attempts, transit buses and commuter trains are also chosen. In all cases, victims-to-be step in front of a large, oncoming, fast-moving vehicle, or they lay, often drug-induced, on the tracks, waiting for the next train, which will likely arrive within a short time.

SUICIDE IDEATION

The term "suicide ideation" refers to thoughts someone has of ending their life. It is the first phase of suicide, typically followed by a plan and the physical attempt. For some people, suicide ideation includes the use of the car. As part of an earlier case study, we observed a group of recidivist impaired drivers who were in a program to regain their driver's licences. A self-defined alcoholic told others in the group, "It's common for me to be driving and checking out the poles beside the road, thinking which one has my name on it. I am thinking of an exit." His life reflected a common pattern for potential suicide. The man felt guilt about his history, experienced total despair and failure, and he possessed an ongoing existential angst about the worst that can happen in his life rather than seeking happiness, success, and optimism. He continuously sabotaged his potential for success. Part of that sabotage was thoughts of suicide with his car.

Conservative estimates indicate that there are approximately 3000 suicide ideators per 100 000 population in the United States each year, of which 14 complete their suicides (Kessler et al., 2005). Suicide ideation appears to peak at the age of sixteen. Canada's numbers, as presented in a large Ontario research study, are lower for fifteen-year-olds by about 10%, and they are equal to the United States for seventeen- and eighteen-year-olds (Canadian Association of Mental Health, 2003).

Suicide researchers generally agree that suicidal ideation is one of the best predictors of a completed suicide. A case control study by Lawrence Lam and associates (2004) concluded that there is a relationship between suicide ideation and car crashes. The researchers wrote that risk of involvement in an injury crash is significantly increased for drivers who have current or previous suicidal ideation when compared to drivers without suicidal thoughts.

POLICE-ASSISTED SUICIDE

Police officers are sometimes unwillingly used in suicide attempts. In one example, a man slowly drove into a police station parking lot and deliberately rammed two patrol cars, then slowly drove away. Then he drove to a gas station and purposefully hit the fuel pumps head on. He returned to the police station and crashed into another cruiser, all the while yelling and begging that the officers shoot him to death. He was Roman Catholic, afraid to take his own life, so he wanted the police to do it for him. The police charged him with aggravated assault, resisting arrest, hindering apprehension, and criminal mischief. A psychiatric evaluation was undertaken (Donnelly, 2000).

In another case, a New York state police officer pulled over nineteen-year-old gambler, Moshe Pergament, who was spotted driving erratically. As the officer exited his patrol vehicle, Pergament got out of his car and approached the police officer with what appeared to be a revolver. Despite the officer's repeated requests for him to drop the weapon, Pergament continued to advance. Faced with the prospect of his own death, the officer fired three times, killing Pergament. Only later did the officer learn that the weapon was a toy gun (*New York Times*, 1997, November 16).

"Suicide by cops" happens in many scenarios. A would-be suicide victim may initiate a bank robbery with an unloaded, inoperable, or toy weapon in the hope that the police will shoot him. A physical assault on a police officer can also lead to a deadly response by the officer. In another scenario, a would-be suicide victim initiates a high-speed pursuit then turns toward the police cruiser to cause a deadly crash.

Police in Canada have a set of rules that they are expected to follow if they believe that a suspect is suicidal and coaxing for a police response. Officers are "not to shoot at a moving vehicle unless there is an immediate need to protect the life of a person." The policy states, "Should the police officer have reasonable and probable grounds to believe the driver of the pursued vehicle is suicidal, he shall consider terminating the pursuit and engage an alternative solution" (Alberta Solicitor General, 1990).

Police estimates in the United States suggest that as many as 10% of those killed by police officers had intended to die at the hands of the police (Brown, 1998). The person who commits suicide by cop has, by definition, transformed himself from being a victim to becoming a perpetrator.

Police-assisted suicide research is limited because of the onus on proof and conclusiveness of the findings. However, researchers at the Los Angeles Sheriff's Department (LASD) did analyze this form of suicide by developing variables they thought were relevant to police-assisted suicides. They examined 437 officer-involved shootings investigated by LASD from 1987 to 1997. Their results indicated that suicide by cop accounted for about 11% of the total shootings (Hutson et al., 1998). One of the important findings from the study is that the most easily recognized catalyst for police-assisted suicide was the dissolution of a relationship: a breakup with a girlfriend or a divorce. Unable to commit suicide themselves, the perpetrators looked to the police to emancipate them and set out to execute a plan that would culminate in their death (Dingsdale, 1998).

IN SUMMARY

When suicideologists speak of suicide prevention, they have traditionally focussed on interventions designed to reduce criminal motivation. However, suicide is not simply a matter of motivation; it is also a matter of situational opportunity and wavering thoughts of despair and hopelessness.

For some people, the motor vehicle is there to fulfill a death wish. Suicide attempts with a vehicle most often involve would-be victims inhaling exhaust fumes, staging sensational crashes, setting fire to their vehicles and themselves, and running, jumping, or standing in front of large, fast-moving vehicles like semi-trailer trucks, buses, or commuter trains. The opportunity theory suggests that the increase in the numbers of vehicles available and being driven increases the likelihood of those vehicles being used for suicides.

16
CAR BOMBS

It is not such a big leap from leaflets to bombs.

— ANNA MARIA TREMONTI,
The Fifth Estate, 2002

Eleven-year-old Daniel Desrochers was pedalling his bicycle down Adam Street. As he rode past a curbside SUV, a bomb planted in the vehicle exploded. Four days later, Daniel died after being in a deep coma. This brutal act did not happen on the other side of the world. It happened in Montreal. The Quebec-based Hell's Angels were waging a war against their rivals, the Rock Machine. Car bombings had become a standard means of combat for the two groups.

Although car bombings happen more routinely in parts of the world such as the Middle East or Asia, they do comprise a formidable type of roadway violence in North America. Car bombings have the potential to kill hundreds, if not thousands, of people in one blast.

There are no statistics specific to car bombs, but the U.S. Bureau of Alcohol, Tobacco, Firearm and Explosives (ATF, 2004) reported that between 2002 and 2004, they received 700 reports of bombing incidents each year. These may or may not include car bombs. Nineteen people were injured, and five were killed. In addition, seventy-four actual incendiary incidents injured a further ten people and killed one.

Similar statistics are available on reported incidents involving the criminal use of explosives in Canada. But they do not feature car bombs, and they are not exhaustive. Researchers can never be sure that all the actual incidents were reported to the Canadian Bomb Data Centre. Nevertheless, some relevant numbers do show bombing incidents or explosives statistics. The Canadian Bomb Data Centre (2007a) reported that in 2006 there were 194 bomb incidents, 75 of which occurred in British Columbia. An additional 8 occurrences were defined as attempted bombings, and 31 involved hoax devices. These numbers are not specific to vehicle bombs (2007b).

When we first began research for this book, vehicular bombings were a grow-ing concern around the world and within Canada. Since 2000, the problem of bombers using motor vehicles has increased. Car bombings, whether triggered remotely or by a suicide bomber, are often vehicular-based acts of terrorism steeped in historical hatreds, religious zealousy, disenchantment, or despair. In many cases, they are revenge tactics or counter measures to earlier events. In other cases, they are attempts at extortion, suicide, or murder.

CAR BOMBS AND TERRORISM

The most frequent reason for car bombings is terrorism, the unlawful use of fear and force to achieve political, economic, or social aims. It is a growing in-ternational problem witnessed, in part, by the new terrorist groups that have sprung up all over the world during the last twenty years. The terrorist threat includes the United States and Canada, where both governments are attempt-ing to deal with the causes, actions, and results of terrorist strikes.

Terrorism is meant to terrify, as in the Latin stem, *terrere*, or "to cause to tremble" (Juergensmeyer, 2000). It is an assault on civil order, and is usually politically motivated whereby dissidents or enemies of a state deploy systematic acts of destruction aimed at altering or maintaining power relations. Although government and the military personnel are often the targets, innocent civilians are usually harmed.

Certain psychological, social, economic, metaphysical, or spiritual conditions foster terrorism (Reich, 1990). Because people have easy access to different parts of the world through air travel and computer technology, a rebellion, revolution, or internal conflict in one country can easily be exported to another country. Hatred no longer has geographic barriers. Canada is inherently vulnerable to acts of terrorism. Incidents associated with conflicts abroad and transferred to the Canadian environment are termed "homeland issues," and underlie the major concerns about terrorism affecting Canada today (Canadian Security Intelligence Service [CSIS], 2005). For example, Sikh groups who want to carve out an independent Sikh state called Khalistan (Land of the Pure) from Indian territory are suspected of having militant cells in Vancouver, among other inter-national sites. These cells are suspected of participating in violent acts against Hindu Canadians living in British Columbia. In 1985, when Air India Flight 182, which started its journey in Montreal, was blown up mid-flight to London, some Canadian Sikh leaders were key suspects.

Some religious zealots intent on gaining power or influence have turned to terrorism. Osama bin Laden is the most well known leader of terrorist ideology today, with his followers from Al-Quaeda ("the Base"). He is believed to be at the centre of an international coalition of Islamic radicals, having forged alliances with like-minded fundamentalist groups such as Egypt's Al-Jihad, Iran's Hezbollah, Sudan's National Islamic Front, and jihad groups in Yemen, Saudi Arabia, Somalia, and Indonesia. Suspected cells are operating in the United States and Canada.

Terrorism usually involves spectacular feats; that is why, in part, it attracts the young, whose thirst for notoriety places them on the vanguard of action. Vehicle bombs are a particularly attractive mode of violence for terrorists, partly because of high casualties and indiscriminate targeting, and partly because of ease of manufacture, delivery, capacity, and lethality. Internet sites provide instructions on how to build, place, and detonate bombs. A parked car on the side of a main street can be deceivingly benign.

Islamic terrorists made the front page on February 26, 1993, when they drove a rented van loaded with explosives into the parking lot under Tower One of the World Trade Center in New York City. There, they detonated the car bomb. The explosion killed 6 people and injured 1042 others. The infrastructure of the building and the subway tunnels were damaged, and smoke reached the top of the 110-storey building in minutes. The Joint Terrorist Task Force eventually brought twenty-two Islamic fundamentalist conspirators to trial for the incident. The court proceedings revealed that the accused had extensive plans to use terrorism to wreak havoc in the United States. The 1993 attack was the precursor to the destruction of the World Trade Center on September 11, 2001 by Islamic terrorists.

"Domestic terrorists" have also sprung up in parts of the United States in the form of local militias and right-wing organizations, bringing with them serious threats of car bombings. The most destructive car bombing in North America happened in Oklahoma City, when a rented van containing explosives was detonated in front of the Alfred P. Murrah Federal Building on April 19, 1995. The explosion killed 168 people and injured more than 500 others. Timothy McVeigh was one of the men convicted of the bombing, for which he was later executed. He was a leader of the "True Believers." This domestic terrorist group is part of the American far right, which includes armed covert groups such as neo-Nazis, tax haters, skinheads, white supremacists, the church of the Aryan Nation, survivalists, and Christian Identity adherents (Haught, 1995). These groups profess patriotism, and their leaders include fundamentalist preachers, utopians, gun dealers, and gun ownership advocates.

The "True Believers" are at the far fringe of the "militia" movement. It is a paramilitary group that supports the right-to-bear-arms policy in the United States. McVeigh's act was revenge against the American government for its part in the siege of the Branch Davidian compound in Waco, Texas in 1993. ATF and

FBI agents had stormed the compound and killed almost 100 men, women, and children. The federal agents were serving a search warrant issued on the suspicion that the group was stockpiling automatic weapons. McVeigh interpreted the Waco siege as evidence of a federal plan to take away citizens' rights to own guns (Haught, 1995). He and his colleagues constructed a fuel-and-fertilizer vehicle bomb and detonated it in Oklahoma City on the second anniversary of the Waco tragedy, achieving a symbolic date for retribution against the federal government for all militia members.

THE VEHICLE AS CONTAINER BOMB

The Oklahoma City bomb was a homemade van bomb. The vehicle was used as a container in which materials were stored that, when ignited, blew up the van in a blast powerful enough to destroy large buildings. The van in effect became a bomb, with butane bottles for enhanced blast effect and a blasting cap to set it off. In other instances, a vehicle is packed with traditional explosives to maximize the number of deaths upon impact or detonation, as in the near-simultaneous bombings of American embassies in Nairobi, Kenya, and Tanzania on August 7, 1998. More than 260 people died as the result of these truck-bomb explosions.

Car bombs don't just go off. They are detonated, rigged to explode by pressure, pressure-release, motion (pull, push, tilt), shift in velocity or acceleration, braking, or electrical, chemical, thermal, and barometric activating systems. Some bombers prefer to install a timing device to fire the bomb at a time when it is known that the target person will be in or near the vehicle. Common places for locating bombs are in the engine compartment, the passenger compartment, the trunk, underneath the vehicle or the outer bodywork, or near the gas tank. Bombs planted in the engine area are often wired to the ignition coil or starter to blast when the driver turns on the ignition. However, a bomb can also be wired to detonate when a light is switched on, a horn is blasted, the windshield washer button is pressed, the brake pedals are pushed, or the radio is turned on.

Bombs planted in the outer bodywork or underneath the vehicle can be triggered by any moving part that can be closed by compression or pressure release. Inside the passenger compartment, a bomb can be triggered by a pressure switch or mat placed under a seat, seat cover, or carpet. Switches can be connected to any moving part in the interior, such as the glove box, cigarette lighter, ashtray, door, window handles, mirrors, switches, dials, or pedals.

A number of factors enable car bombings to be used successfully in major North American buildings. Rising land costs in the downtown core of cities, and the visual blight created by above-ground parking lots, has stimulated the construction of underground parking in garages beneath large buildings. A bomb placed against a support pillar can cause everything above it to collapse like a pack of concrete cards (Monday & Stubblefield, 1997). The blast's thermal effect can ignite leaking fumes from the gas tanks of crushed vehicles. In a glass-skinned tower, every window can become a grenade, showering victims with shards of glass. The final outcome of a building explosion is difficult to prevent and control.

PERSONAL AGENDAS

Car bombs are not solely the work of terrorists who are trying to undermine democracy. Some troubled individuals have made their own car bombs to achieve personal ends. For example, in Nashville in July 2004, an suv exploded in a parking lot at the Gaylord Opryland Resort and Convention Center. The man inside the vehicle died (Joyner, 2004). The police believe the bomb was homemade, and the motive was likely suicide. In another incident, a woman whose husband tried to blow up a police station with a car bomb explained to the Grand Rapids media, "He's not a bad guy. He just wanted his voice heard." (KFMB TV, 2005).

Because car bombs are widely recognized for their ease of use and potential for destruction, some malcontents will threaten to use a bomb. In Toronto, a man displeased with the charges for a taxi ride threatened the cabbie with a bomb. The police arrived on the scene and sealed off the area on Bloor Street West. Officials tried but failed to communicate with the suspect for nearly two hours, creating a stand-off. Finally, a team of four officers fired tear gas into the car. The man was taken to hospital and later faced a string of charges (Song, 2006).

In the following example, the would-be bomber had a general grievance against society. Names and other identifiable information have been altered for anonymity.

Konrad, who was employed by an Alberta municipality, told a colleague, Brent, that he felt nervous and had thought about getting an animal and blowing it up to help him calm down. He pulled a gym bag from his car and showed Brent a litre-sized jar with wires extending from it. The jar was three-quarters full of a yellow liquid. Brent thought it was a bomb.

The next day, Konrad did not show up for work. Brent notified the police, who took the matter seriously and went to Konrad's residence. His apartment was in a state of disarray, with PVC pipes, electrical components, wires, and transistors lying on the living room floor and kitchen table. Because the police felt the matter needed more investigation, they sought and obtained an official search warrant.

When the officers carefully analyzed the residence, they found numerous electrical component systems, parts, and an electronic technician-type workbench, complete with tools and diagnostic equipment. Beside the workbench was literature on procedures for constructing and preparing explosive devices. There was also general literature on Timothy McVeigh's Oklahoma bombing and the Waco armed stand-off.

When the police checked Konrad's vehicle, they found a bomb in the form of bottles containing unstable chemicals, and a duffle bag full of other chemicals. The chemicals found in the vehicle could on their own, or in combination, form highly explosive substances.

The police considered the materials to be a bomb that, if detonated, would have destroyed the vehicle, killed the person who activated the device, and would have caused mass destruction. The municipality's emergency response department for dangerous goods helped dismantle the unstable bomb.

Konrad was arrested. A search into his history revealed that he had been charged five years earlier for bringing a gun to work, intending to shoot a co-worker. Konrad had admitted to having a continued preoccupation with death. He thought that society was rife with injustice and corruption, which he wanted to avenge.

Bomb-making instructions are easily available on the Internet. Supplying this information is not illegal; freedom of speech allows people to correspond about illegal matters without necessarily participating in them, except in cases of child pornography. There is also a jurisdictional problem, because the information on how to develop a bomb can originate in one part of the world and be received in another.

ORGANIZED CRIME

Car bombs have become a signature of some organized crime groups. Their targets tend to be rival gangs. For example, in Chicago in 1994, the Outlaws detonated a stolen car next to a clubhouse owned by the Hell's Henchmen. The car was packed with an estimated 100 pounds of a military-grade plastic explosive (National Crime Research Center, undated).

In another case, David Leisure was convicted in 1987 for planting the car bomb that killed underworld boss James Michaels Sr. in 1980. Michaels was the reputed head of St. Louis's Syrian crime faction (Bell, 1999). The Leisure syndicate had wanted control over the Laborers Local 110. Leisure had crawled beneath Michaels's parked car and planted a remote-controlled bomb. When Michaels unlocked the car and sat down, it blew up.

HITMEN

Hitmen are murderers for hire. Although they usually work for organized crime syndicates or rich citizens to eliminate enemies or competition, they are also hired by jealous lovers or spouses who are intent on revenge. A preferred method to fulfill a "kill" contract is to booby-trap cars with bombs. The case of Christopher "Snakebite" Madison is an example of a successful hired killer working with minimum personal risk (Eikel, 2000). Over the span of two years, Chicago experienced a rash of serious vehicular explosions that claimed more than fifty lives. The explosions originated from cheap, foreign-made, sub-compact cars, which detonated during rush hour. An organized crime informant told police that a hired killer named Madison had been charging $50 000 a job to pack a small car with explosives and steer it by remote control to blast a marked victim. Innocent bystanders were killed too.

Another example in the American annals of sensational crimes was the St. Valentine's Day massacre. Men hired by Al Capone drove a Cadillac touring sedan into the garage of George Moran, a ruthless competitor in America's bootlegging enterprise. The Cadillac served as a Trojan Horse, in which Capone's hired killers hid before they killed the seven men in the garage. As it turned out, Moran was not on the scene.

IN SUMMARY

Although car bombings are not common hazards in North America, they can be a formidable source of urban insecurity. A car loaded with explosives is a stealth weapon of surprising power and destructive efficiency. Car bombs are also anonymous; they leave minimal forensic evidence.

Although international terrorists create the fear, domestic terrorists are most likely to use car bombs in North America. Militias or other right-wing cultist organizations may plant bombs in vehicles in the name of defending their belief systems. Motorcycle gangs like the Hell's Angels, Rock Machine, and the Outlaws have also taken their disputes to the streets and used car bombs to settle scores. Professional killers use vehicles booby-trapped with bombs to blow up their targets. In all cases, the motor vehicle becomes the means of executing the desire to cause maximum harm.

HOMICIDE

One must never set up a murder. They must happen unexpectedly, as in life.

— ALFRED HITCHCOCK

Many theories are devoted to explaining how the motor vehicle is involved in violence. Much of that violence results in aggravated assault, and some in murder.

Criminologists tell us that the risk of murder is greater for urban residents than for suburbanites or rural dwellers. Furthermore, most of the people murdered in North America are males, and their slayers are other males. Most of the time, slayers of women are also males (Karmen, 1994).

Statistics Canada (2007) reported that there were 605 homicides in 2006, which is 10% lower than in 2005. The national homicide rate is 1.85 homicides per 100 000 people. Researchers have concluded that Canada's national homicide rate has declined since the mid-1970s, when it was about 3.0. A different picture has emerged in the United States, where the homicide rate rose 1.8% in 2007 after hitting a two-decade low in 2004 (U.S. Department of Justice, 2007).

In the United States, the dominant areas for homicides are cities with a population of over one million. The city of New Orleans has the highest murder rate, which registered 72.6 homicides per 100 000 citizens. Next are the cities of Gary, Indiana at 48.3 and Detroit, Michigan at 27.1 (U.S. Department of Justice, 2007).

A closer look at the provincial and city rates in Canada shows that the four highest murder rates are in the west. Saskatchewan reports the highest homicide rate at 4.1 per 100 000 people. The city of Regina has the highest rate of all cities in Canada, with 4.5 homicides per 100 000 people, followed by Edmonton at 3.68 and Toronto at 1.83 (Statistics Canada, 2007).

A consistent trend has been noted for the last ten years. On the average, 33% of the murder victims in Canada were killed by a family member, and approximately 20% were killed by a spouse or a former spouse. Another 20% of the victims were killed by casual acquaintances, and 14% of those murdered were slain by partners in crime. These situations are shared in the United States and other parts of the world (Stillwell, 2004).

TYPES OF HOMICIDE

In Canada, homicide is the killing of one human being by another. Culpable homicide suggests that a person has caused the death of another person by means of a defined criminal act or criminal negligence. The person committing the homicide is blameworthy, accountable, and responsible for the death. It includes such acts of violence as murder, manslaughter, and infanticide.

First-degree murder is a culpable homicide that is planned and deliberate. Second-degree murder is murder that is not deliberately planned. It may occur in "the heat of passion" where the killer acts out intense fear, rage, anger, or terror.

Voluntary manslaughter is a culpable homicide where the murder is intentional, but the intention to cause the death did not occur before the act began. For example, a fight begins without an intention to kill, but during the fight, one of the brawlers decides to kill the other.

Involuntary manslaughter is the unlawful killing of a human being without intent. It could happen from recklessness or negligence. For example, a drunk driver negligently causes the death of a passenger. The absence of intent is the essential difference between voluntary and involuntary manslaughter.

In the United States, first-degree murder is defined as an unlawful killing that is both willful and premeditated where the murderer plans to "lie in wait" for the victim. The legal concept known as the "felony murder rule" is usually invoked whereby a person commits first-degree murder if any death (even an accidental one) results from the commission of certain violent felonies like arson, burglary, kidnapping, rape, or robbery.

Second-degree murder in the United States is ordinarily defined as an intentional killing that is neither premeditated nor planned nor committed in a heat of passion. A killing caused by dangerous conduct or the offender's obvious lack of concern for human life is also considered second-degree murder. Second-degree murder may best be viewed as the middle ground between first-degree murder and voluntary manslaughter, the latter of which is commonly defined as an intentional killing in which the offender had no prior intent to kill, such as a killing that occurs in a heat of passion.

Most murder victims die at the hands of someone they know. The murders are usually the result of passion and heated arguments—styles of interaction reserved for people who know each other, who share interests, money, property, and affection, and who experience broken expectations and shattered dreams (Daly & Wilson, 1988).

Witness the following account that involved a misguided attempt at suicide. A U.S. district judge sentenced a man in Phoenix, Arizona to ten years in prison for voluntary manslaughter in the death of his girlfriend. The man was driving a vehicle while intoxicated. He was angry, upset, and depressed while driving and told his passenger (his girlfriend) that he wanted to kill himself. He said, "Here comes a car" and "I'm just going to hit it," then he did hit it head on. His girlfriend died at the scene. She left behind two children (Office of the U.S. Attorney, District of Arizona, 2007).

Strangers seldom quarrel with each other. Intentional violent death is usually direct, first person, oriented toward the immediate target, or it is transferred when the killer strikes out at another person instead of the person who is the object of disdain. It can be a measure of vengeance, remorse, filicide, or fratricide, among others.

A famous case of filicide is the one involving Susan Smith in 1994. On a mild October night in Union, South Carolina, Susan had been driving around the countryside with her two young sons, trying to come to terms with a broken romance with her boyfriend, Tom Findlay.

In despair, because of her impending divorce from her husband and the breakup with her boyfriend, she decided to take extreme action. She got out of her Mazda Protégé and released the emergency brake. The car rolled into the lake with her two children asleep and strapped into their child seats inside. After Susan stared at the sinking car for a few moments, she ran to a nearby house for help. When the police arrived, Susan lied, telling the officers that a man had carjacked her and kidnapped the children. The police closely monitored the highways, and they decided to search the lake.

In the meantime, investigators were becoming suspicious of Susan, trying to break down her story. The police interviews lasted for nine days. Finally, under strong interrogation and dramatic talk between Susan and the sheriff, the woman began to cry uncontrollably and presented a written confession. Susan told the police where the car was located and that her children were likely drowned (Pergament, 1999). Susan was convicted of two counts of first-degree murder and sentenced to life in prison with the chance of parole in thirty years. In her confession, she wrote that she did not want to live anymore and that she originally wanted to kill herself along with her two sons (*Herald Journal*, 1994).

At the last moment, however, she had saved herself but allowed her sons to die. Prosecutors suggested that Susan Smith wanted the children dead so that her estranged boyfriend, who did not want children, would love her again.

ROAD RAGE AND MURDER

Road rage may be the determining factor in some murders. Drivers and/or passengers get into an argument and take action against one another, sometimes ending in second-degree murder or the lesser charge of voluntary manslaughter. Such an event happened in Edmonton, when a fifteen-year-old boy was charged with second-degree murder for deliberately running down a twenty-two-year-old man (Loyie, 2006). The victim, David, was out with two friends when, on their way home, the three stopped at a red light. A silver Cadillac with several young people inside pulled up alongside. Some bantering and swearing ensued between the two groups. When David and his friends turned off the main street to go home, they noticed the Cadillac had stopped a little way down the street. David walked towards the car to see what the group's intentions were. The Cadillac sped up and aimed directly at David. He was killed instantly.

American statistics show that within a span of six years (1990 to 1996), there were at least twenty-two cases of aggressive drivers who had intentionally aimed their vehicles into crowds of people (Bethesda, 1997). Anthony Brooks of Massachusetts was such a person. He was charged with attempted murder when he became impatient and angry at an outdoor New Year's celebration in Boston. He ploughed his car into the crowd, injuring twenty-one people (Bethesda, 1997). In another case, a twenty-nine-year-old man created a half hour of chaos in San Francisco when he purposefully sped up and down ten blocks—sometimes the wrong way—picking off people in crosswalks and on sidewalks. The driver was booked on fourteen counts of attempted murder and one count of first-degree murder. One witness reported that it all started when the suspect's SUV approached a red light as a woman was crossing the street; the driver let her walk in front and then hit his accelerator and knocked her down (Buchanan et al., 2006).

KILLING AS TRANSFERENCE

"Transference" refers to redirection of feelings we have about our significant others. Although transference is quite common, it can become a pathological issue when it is acted upon in personal or socially harmful contexts (Jung, 1957). A classic case often quoted is that of the killer Caroll Cole. While his father was away fighting in World War II, Cole's mother engaged in extra-marital affairs and forced the boy to watch. She beat Cole to stop him from telling his father.

Cole later murdered many women whom he considered "loose," particularly those who reminded him of his mother.

Transference, at the most elementary level, suggests a person who has experienced great emotional turmoil and applies those feelings to someone else, whether that is a friend, colleague, or stranger. When it comes to driving, the target of transfer is other drivers or pedestrians, and the outlet for that emotion is the vehicle.

An example is the case of children being killed by a Cadillac Eldorado at the Childhood Learning Center playground in Costa Mesa, California in 2001. Two young children were crushed beneath the car, and four other children were injured. Once stopped, the driver, Steven Allen Abrams, sat dazed behind the steering wheel, staring into space, silent. He was an unkempt-looking thirty-nine-year-old who had slammed his Cadillac through a chain-link fence and raced around the playground. "I was going to execute these children because they were innocent," Abrams told the police (*Los Angeles Times*, 2001a).

At the police press conference, the officer in charge explained that Abrams linked the daycare facility to a failed romantic relationship he had with a married woman who had filed a restraining order against him. When questioned further, he said he had thought about killing other people, especially police officers and firefighters. But he decided to kill children, symbolized by innocence, to illustrate his sour love life. According to a police officer at the scene, Abrams also associated the daycare with the neighbourhood in which he used to live (*Saskatoon StarPhoenix*, 1999).

The jury convicted Abrams on two counts of murder, five counts of attempted murder, and two counts of attempted voluntary manslaughter. The jury decided that he was sane at the time of the murders. The judge sentenced Abrams to a concurrent term of twenty-five years and four months, and ordered him to pay $12 000 in restitution for the children's funerals (*Los Angeles Times*, 2001b).

SETTLING THE SCORE

Revenge is one of the oldest human desires, consisting primarily of a desire to retaliate against someone in response to perceived wrongdoing. It has a high probability of causing psychological and physical pain to appease a perceived injustice. Philosopher Martha Nussbaum (1999) wrote that revenge is a standard feature of our social context. It begins with people being vulnerable and victim to the actions of others. When they are violated, they violate in return:

> And to right the balance truly, the retribution must be exactly, strictly proportional to the original encroachment. It differs from the original act only in the sequence of time and in the fact that it is response

rather than original act—a fact frequently obscured if there is a long sequence of acts and counteracts. (157–58)

Motor vehicles are often used as a weapon for revenge. Typically, alcohol is consumed before committing the vengeful act. The following case study shows that the mix of alcohol, anger, and an accessible vehicle can form an explosive cocktail. Names and locations have been changed to preserve anonymity.

Dick and Harry were friends who lived in a northern Saskatchewan mining town. One evening, Dick picked Harry up in his half-ton truck to go play snooker. They parked their vehicle at the local tavern at 9:00 p.m. and entered the bar. They found a table near the pool table. The two men played billiards while drinking numerous beers followed by a couple of shooters.

Al, a stranger, asked if he and his buddy, Pete, could challenge the two friends to the next game. Dick and Harry agreed.

More drinks were consumed, and the four played for fun. As the evening progressed, however, the games became increasingly tense. All players were starting to feel the alcohol. Dick and Harry won some money, the result of which was Al and Pete had to keep playing so that they could win back their losses. Winning was no longer a choice, but a must.

It was 2:30 a.m. when the bartender asked the four to stop playing for the night. It was closing time. Al and Pete were upset, thinking that they had been hustled. They put their cues back on the racks, however, and returned to their table.

Just as Dick and Harry were walking out the door, Al and Pete decided to leave too. On their way out, they picked up another friend, named Don. The three men exited behind Dick and Harry.

On the way to the parking lot, Dick said some uncomplimentary things to Don, who took offence and confronted Dick. Pete, Al, and Harry stood aside. They wanted nothing to do with the altercation, which appeared to be little more than verbal sparring. But soon the jostling turned to shoving and a physical fight. Dick and Don began to wrestle. Dick had Don in a headlock and forced him to the ground. Don jumped up and backed off. For all intents the two men had parted. Dick, however, kept making derogatory remarks as Don ran to his company truck and started it up.

Don drove through the parking lot at about twenty km/h. He was heading towards Dick, who was jeering him on, waving his hands above his head mockingly, telling him to stop. Don became irate, stepped on the gas, hit Dick head on, then stopped immediately. Dick ended up on the hood with his face against the windshield. Don backed up quickly. Dick fell backwards and his jacket got caught on the bumper. Don dragged Dick for about forty feet before Dick got loose. He was lying flat on his back, bleeding profusely.

Don stopped the truck, Al jumped in, and they drove off. Harry ran back into the bar to call an ambulance. Another bar patron performed mouth-to-mouth resuscitation on Dick, but to no avail. Dick was pronounced dead at 5:20 a.m.

The police caught up to Don and Al later that morning. Neither man tried to flee when the officers confronted them. Although Don was originally charged with first-degree murder, he was found guilty of a reduced charge of voluntary manslaughter. Al was charged for being an accessory to the crime.

When vehicles are used for murderous revenge, the vehicle becomes the extension of emotional eruption.

MURDER-SUICIDE

A study entitled "The Untold Story of Murder Suicide in the United States" by the Violence Policy Center in 2002 indicated that murder-suicides are usually random acts of violence. They are most common in families and partnerships where 90% of the time, men kill their mates and then shoot themselves afterwards. All major murder-suicide studies in the United States completed since 1950 have shown that firearms are by far the most common method of committing homicide, with the offender choosing the firearm for suicide as well. Published estimates are that 80% to 94% of murder-suicide cases involve firearms, but many other weapons make up the remaining percentage. One of those weapons is the motor vehicle. Although 76% of murder-suicides occurred in the home, most of the remaining murder-suicides occurred in motor vehicles (Violence Policy Center, 2002b). Epidemiologists estimated that in Canada, close to 10% of all homicides are followed by suicides whereas, in the United States, about 33% of all homicides are followed by suicides (Carcach and Grabosky, 1998). Elliot Leyton, a Canadian sociologist and the author of the bestseller *Hunting Humans*, stated in a media interview that murder-suicide is "one of the most common and consistent types of tragedies that has occurred without any particular change in frequency or rate, from the very beginning" (*CBC News*, 2006).

Murder-suicides can be external or internal crimes. External murder-suicides happen when persons who are intent on killing themselves randomly kill innocent bystanders in the suicide act. A driver wants to end her life by driving her vehicle into a truck or bus, killing herself and the other driver or passengers. This form of murder-suicide is hard to prove because it is easily camouflaged as an accident with due causes such as reckless driving. As fate would have it, while innocent people die, the person attempting suicide lives to face the murder charge. The following case illustrates this type of murder-suicide.

Terence Patrick Lynch was driving on the wrong side of the road, aiming his car directly at a vehicle coming towards him. He was travelling 130 to 140 km/h. The woman, upon seeing the oncoming vehicle, braked to avoid the collision. Gouge marks left on the road showed that her car was straddling the edge of the road, veering sharply to the left in an attempt to avoid the crash (Violence Policy Center, 2002). Lynch hit the woman's vehicle head on, somersaulted in the air, and turned 360° before landing on her car. The woman was killed on impact, but Lynch survived with serious injuries. After the crash, Lynch confessed that he had planned to kill himself.

Internal murder-suicides happen when victims know each other. Partners or friends have an informal pact that one partner will help kill the other, after which time the surviving partner takes his own life. It also happens when both partners die under the same circumstances. For example, two friends stoned on drugs smash the car into a tree or are asphyxiated by carbon monoxide. Occasionally, a devoted older couple will commit a murder-suicide. The couple typically has had a lifelong, secure relationship but is now facing serious financial stress or the onslaught of a debilitating disease. In this circumstance, there is considerable planning and forethought, and a quick, painless death for the victims. Because two people have died, it is difficult to determine who instigated the plan.

A common strategy is for asphyxiation through exhaust fumes. There is no consensus on the causes, personalities, or psychiatry involved, or on the behaviours that precede the incidents. In one case, officials noted that a resident of a local nursing home in Connecticut was missing after a visit from her husband. A police officer found the husband's vehicle a few hours later, parked in a secluded area of a nearby store. The husband, aged seventy-nine, and his wife, aged seventy-seven, had died of carbon monoxide poisoning (*WNBC News*, 2006, September 6).

Murder-suicide also happens without the consent of the murder victim. In the following case, the woman was not a willing participant. Names and other identifiable information have been altered for anonymity.

Andy was a thirty-year-old man living in a western British Columbia town. He earned his living by pushing dope. He trafficked locally—mostly Ecstasy, methamphetamines, and amphetamines. He was also a user, popping pills on a regular basis. The local RCMP knew Andy. He had been in and out of jail for crimes like illegal possession of marijuana and drug dealing. In addition, he had collected a variety of speeding tickets.

The RCMP considered Andy to be a danger to himself and others around him. They had issued a warning advising detachments to use caution when dealing with him. Andy was vocal about his plan never to be sent to jail again. He told a close friend about his desire to commit suicide one day by parking on the railway tracks and waiting for the train.

Nicole was a seventeen-year-old girl who was on her way to Vancouver. She stopped in town for a short stay but decided to stay longer after meeting Andy. She had come from a broken home with an abusive father and an alcoholic mother. She had run away but no one in her family had bothered to look for her.

Nicole decided to move in with Andy, even though she knew he dated other women. She was happy to be one of his lovers and to be a recipient of his constant supply of Ecstasy.

One day, after taking a dose of Ecstasy, Andy and Nicole left the house around noon and headed to the diner. There, three men approached Andy and confronted him about a $2000 debt for drugs. Heated words were exchanged and threats were made. Andy became incensed. He grabbed Nicole and the two of them jumped into Andy's pickup truck. They drove out of town through a maze of back roads.

It was now thirteen minutes after the confrontation. Andy stopped the truck about twenty yards before an unmarked railway crossing on a dead-end road, used only by farmers to access their crops. He was highly irritated. He then drove up to the train crossing and parked on the track. Nicole, high on Ecstasy, wasn't paying attention to where they were. She sat with her back to the passenger-side door, which was the side from where the train was coming. Andy watched the train approach.

Andy was talking but became fidgety and scared. Nicole looked out her window and saw the oncoming train. At the last minute, she tried to jump out of the truck, but Andy was holding her leg. The train collided with the truck. Nicole was hurled out and struck her head against the train. She died immediately. Andy also died, his body badly burned. The police closed the file as a murder-suicide.

SERIAL KILLERS

Serial murders are reported over time, as victims are found. Heiner (2002), reviewing U.S. Justice Department figures, suggested that there are about fifty to seventy serial homicides per year, and that there could be over thirty-five serial killers active in the United States at any given time. Serial killers often take a cooling-off period between their crimes. It may be days, months, or even years before they kill again. They make up approximately 1 to 2% of all American homicides (Hickey, 2006).

FBI profilers have studied male serial killers and concluded that the men share a common underlying sexual motivation. They kill to fulfill their entwined sexual and violent fantasies. They typically use motor vehicles to find their prey, engage the victims in violent sexual acts in the vehicle, or drive their victims to an isolated location, raping, torturing, and killing them in fields, forests, isolated houses, or sometimes in the killers' homes. In these cases, the vehicle is the pickup or trolling tool.

A reverse situation can also arise. For example, Aileen "Lee" Wuornos, a serial killer in Florida, was found guilty of killing seven men. She had flagged men down for rides on Florida highways. Once she was in their cars, she offered them sex then shot them (Russel, 2002).

A strategy typically used by serial killers is to cruise the streets in their cars or pickup trucks, searching for prey. Once potential victims are located, they are invited inside, where they are subsequently killed. David Berkowitz, or Son of Sam, one of America's most famous psychotic killers, used to spend his evenings cruising for his next prey. He would carry a gun in a paper bag and hunt for women. He was obeying voices in his head to kill. One night he saw two women sitting and chatting in a parked Oldsmobile. Here's what happened next:

> He parked his car around the corner and strode confidently toward
> the Oldsmobile, determined to make the kill "as a kind of joke." As he
> reached the car window, he opened fire, emptying five cartridges into
> the women in the car. (Leyton, 1987: 158)

Although the vehicle is seldom used in the murder, it is the most important asset the murderer has. As mentioned in an earlier chapter, RCMP characterized a serial murderer near Edmonton as having three important features: drives a reliable, high-mileage truck, van, or SUV; is comfortable driving in rural areas; and may clean his vehicle at odd times of the day (RCMP News Release, 2005, June 17).

IN SUMMARY

We will never know for sure how many traffic crashes are really murder-suicides or how many victims were menaced by a killer's car. But we do know that most of the murders with motor vehicles reflect vengeance, emotional transference, road rage, murder-suicide, or serial killing. The underlying motivations for murder by vehicle are consistent with those of other weapons.

CONCLUSION

You have to show violence the way it is. If you don't show
it realistically, then that's immoral and harmful. If you
don't upset people, then that's obscenity.

— ROMAN POLANSKI

In Canada and the United States, violence on the road is a spill over of cultural attitudes that embrace deviance, criminality, and violence. When a society believes the world is hostile and competitive, the people come to expect scenarios filled with challenges and retaliation. When we examine our society more closely, we can easily catalogue manifestations of violence in people's lives. The increasing turbulence of the world is reflected on the roadway.

Motor vehicles occupy our attention in many ways. They are vandalized, broken into, and stolen. They are weapons and outlets for aggression. They are more than just transportation.

The issues and cases explored in this book illustrate that violence or the antecedent of violence is just beyond the beams pouring from our headlights. The person we may have accidentally or intentionally cut off may be the same person who then blows off steam against another, perhaps more vulnerable, road user. The drivers we pass every day may be ready to explode.

We need to be sensitive to the stimuli around us. The questionable or unfamiliar should be questioned and observed. We need to analyze events in the light of our personal and public safety. It is our duty as drivers to expect the unexpected so that we can anticipate, and take subsequent action.

When we try to understand roadway violence, we find two key elements. First, driving-related violence is not an aberration. It shares the same basic psychological and sociological features as other criminal violence, namely that it is directly attributable to the thoughts, attitudes, and beliefs of the perpetrator. It is not excusable. Like other forms of violence, it is criminal behaviour, punishable under law.

The second element is that much of vehicle violence is intentional, rational, and willful. A number of aspects influence the likelihood that violence will be chosen by the perpetrator as a solution to a perceived problem. The violence is psychologically damaging, anti-social behaviour that rewards the actor and inflicts pain on the victim. The circle widens to the victim's family and friends, who also suffer with sorrow, rage, guilt, or regret.

For the foreseeable future we will continue to live in a society in which violence on the roadway plays a major role. It is incumbent on us, then, for our own sakes and the benefit of the community, that we be aware of the dangers posed by automobility so that we can curb the infringement of violence.

RECOMMENDATIONS FOR PUBLIC POLICY

We begin this discussion with two central tenets. One is that vehicle violence is a criminal act. Yet it is often undetected—buried in research and investigations that are formulated to provide certain information in a timely fashion. For example, police officers, pressured by time, analyze traffic crashes according to pre-defined categories included in a standard traffic accident reporting form. Hence, major or contributing causes such as aggressive driving, revenge, or even road rage seldom appear in the analysis. Furthermore, causes of collisions are usually determined without reference to the driver's mental state, ideological beliefs, or social standing. As a result, officers on site can easily miss the fact that a crash may have been the result of a criminal or intentional act triggered by preceding events in the perpetrator's life.

We propose that more time, personnel, and technology be made available to engage in social and psychological audits and to investigate the circumstances of collisions more thoroughly. In particular, social and psychological audits must reach into antecedent circumstances. We appreciate that such a recommendation is costly and practically impossible to implement. We believe, however, that by announcing a gold standard of investigation, criminology, justice, and traffic safety personnel will discuss the possibility of implementing a silver standard.

The second tenet is that vehicle violence should be a significant component when considering issues of public safety, similar to the use of firearms. Traffic crashes produce one of the highest numbers of casualties and one of the most costly expenditures for the community. We could start by spending considerable time studying vehicular suicide, road rage, and vehicular homicide as key issues in public health.

More research into the social and psychological causes of collisions and traffic safety problems is needed in all sectors: private (e.g., transportation industries); not-for-profit (e.g., lobby groups like Mothers Against Drunk Driving); and public (e.g., departments of transportation, health, or justice). A closer relationship should be established between justice and transportation officials to do a better job of linking criminal involvement in transportation processes.

Rather than focussing entirely on the driver, we should pay more attention to the family, friends, colleagues, lovers, employers, and other relevant individuals linked to potential aggressors—the community of significant others. We need to become more informed about the nuances of victim and victimization so that we can interrupt the processes that may lead to fatality.

Traffic safety professionals must not view crashes as singular issues with analytical characteristics divorced from other social behaviours. Traffic safety is linked to the social context. It is one social problem that is intimately linked to other behaviours, such as family violence, bullying, suicide, sexual misconduct, fanaticism, professional crime, and family breakdown, among others.

Finally, more attention needs to be directed toward the way that the media present violent people and violent action on the roadway. Films, television, video games, and other media glamourize road violence as daredevil and seductive. We must resist making individuals who cause serious hurt through their vehicles, whether fictitious or real, into folk heroes.

POSTSCRIPT

Misery is the river of the world. Row on! Row on!

— TOM WAITS

This book took five years to complete. It started as a concept then moved into research, writing, and rewriting. Recently, the years of penning and creating were eclipsed by a personal tragedy. My life was shattered. The words in the book no longer resonated with me. My son's goal was to become a crime investigator. His mind was always on human hurt. He took his life at the tender age of sixteen, for reasons unspoken to me. As a tribute, I present a short story he wrote in Grade 9, which won him an award for best short story in the school. It is on roadway violence.

GUNS ARE NOT THE ONLY WEAPONS

by NICCO ROTHE

Bye Julie, came a dark, disfigured voice from the shadows beside me. I don't know why but, even though he was my coworker since I got out of the institution 6 months ago, his voice always sent shivers down my spine. It was a raspy voice, a sort of husky whisper. He never spoke louder than a whisper.

The lights turned off in my office block, cloaking it in shadows broken only by the computer monitors.

Bye Rob, I quietly said back to him staring down at my feet. Walking out of the office building, I kept my head hung low, until I knew I was away from Rob. Finally looking up I headed over to my car, a 1988 Pontiac.

Pulling out of the parking lot I drove immediately onto the street. Looking at my watch I yawned. It was. Looking at the road sign I allowed my mind to wander as I drove down the main street, the traffic lights flashing on my windshield. Green, green, green, red.

Damn, swearing to myself. I stopped. I really wanted to get home and I couldn't keep my eyelids from drooping just a little. All of a sudden, a man appeared on the street corner and began to cross. He had on a kangaroo sweatshirt with the hood pulled low over his face, leaving his eyes in total blackness and making deep shadows around his nose. He walked out onto the road and stopped in front of my car. I could feel him staring at me from the cold darkness of his hood. The shadowed lines around his mouth showed him deep in thought. All of a sudden the lines disappeared and he smiled. It wasn't a smile of welcome or thanks, but a sick, twisted smile that I had only seen on one person before, but couldn't remember where. The man ran towards my car. Starting to worry I moved to lock the passenger side door but I wasn't quick enough and he jumped into my car.

Drive! he yelled at me pulling a gun from the pouch in his sweatshirt. I stepped hard on the gas and drove through the light, which had once again turned red.

Wh...where do you want to go? I asked him shakily, trying hard to keep the fear out of my voice but failing. He smiled another grim smile.

You'll see. Just follow my directions, he hissed at me.

The man pulled back his hood exposing lightly tanned skin and deep brown hair. The man was probably about 35, but lines of worry had made him look at least 10 years older. The thing that scared me the most were his eyes. They were black and deep, just like two holes bored into his skull. Inside there was no flicker of life. No flicker of a conscience. No flicker of a soul.

Turn here, he smirked.

I turned the corner and shifted my body slightly to try to get another look at the man. He noticed and pistol-whipped me across the face. The car swerved violently almost crashing into a tree. Finally, after what seemed like forever I regained control. I felt the warm trickle of blood slowly drop from my nose to my lips.

You better behave. He told me, his eyes shining with inner laughter. You won't like what I do to people who don't. He was obviously enjoying every little bit of the pain I was suffering. *What's he going to do to me?* I thought bitterly. *Is he going to kill me? Or rape me? Is there anything that's worse? I wouldn't be able to stand it, I just couldn't. I can't die I just can't. There has to be something I can do, anything. I'm too scared I'm just too scared!* The road straightened and I continued on, when I saw a transport truck pull out onto the road from one of the many winding side roads. *Hey, look at that, a truck.* I continued to think to myself, *it sure is...I wonder what would happen if I accidentally drove right into its path. That would get rid of this guy! That would get rid of him for good!*

I shook my head, trying to clear it of the thought. I felt my sanity slowly breaking, tearing down the seam, being held together only by one last strand of common sense, just what had happened before. The memory of what happened before the institute, before I had become what I had become in my mind ran through my head. I remember vividly a man beating me, falling unconscious then waking up in the hospital, being told I may die, and my mind had broken. *I can't go on...not like this, not like this! The doctor had told me I was all right, I had no more problems. Why would he lie? Why?* I found myself starting to cry but I shook the tears out of my eyes. *Or a bus! Yes, a bus that will take this guy!* I let out a scream of laughter, and then remembering what I was laughing at, I quickly shut my mouth.

Shut up! The man beside me yelled again, if you do that again, you'll wish I had shot you! Although his words had sounded convincing at first, some of the sureness had left his voice, making it sound frail.

Yes, a bus! My sanity was gone, crumbled under the constant fear of being shot, or worse. Yes, a bus! I found myself shouting out loud but not caring. A bus will solve all my problems! I roared out in laughter that was high pitched.

What are you talking about? The man yelled at me, Tell me!

Or a train! A train is even bigger! I yelled out and howled in laughter. I looked into the eyes of my captor and I could now see the beginning of fear and doubt creep into him. *Now he will know, now he will know the fear one has when, whether you are to live or die, is in the head of another human!*

A train! A train! A train! A train! I howled out, shrieking in laughter. The man's gun had begun to waver and shake. He was worried. Now I was able to enjoy his misery.

Stop the car, he yelled out but it turned into a shaking croak. In the background I heard the gentle whistle of an oncoming train.

A train, I barely whispered, but I could see in his eyes he was beginning to understand.

Stop, was all he was able to get out. The whistle sound became louder and louder. I found the train tracks and stopped on there, still laughing shrilly. The man raised the gun and there was a bang. It was not of the gun going off however; it was of the train hitting the car. Now, as I wheel myself around today I realize, guns are not the only weapons.

APPENDIX:
THE INQUIRY PROCESS

I have such a strong desire to help reduce the sum of
unhappiness and of bitterness, which empoisons mankind.

— ALBERT CAMUS

Three theoretical principles informed the accounts included in this book. First, the featured violence is a product of the social context which is, at best, a uniform, patterned, and mundane world. Violence is part of regular patterns of action, which are produced by compliance to a normative order. Many elements of roadway violence are typical features of everyday life. They are taken for granted, understood but overlooked. Other elements of roadway violence stand outside the normative order. They are extreme and demand attention accordingly.

Second, people's behaviours are influenced or moderated by conditions in major social and psychological domains like image, personal gain, power and control, family influence, revenge, greed, anger and aggression, and inequality among others. This range of factors enables full range of influences, impacts, and orientations.

Third, to be forewarned is to be forearmed. There is potential danger of violence when we disapprove of another driver's behaviour and discipline him by raising our middle finger.

BROAD TERMS OF REFERENCE

The terms of reference are the scope and details of the project, specification of thoughts, and the conditions that helped produce the textual descriptions in this book. They reference the definition of violence on the road, circumstances that led to violence taking place, and a list of assumptions that helped guide the thoughts, research, and interpretation of findings.

Traditional data like police reports are a poor source of data, because each police department maintains its own incident report database in its own format and filing system. It is virtually impossible to gather and consolidate such information into a single, meaningful database. Furthermore, many police departments do not include significant pieces of information on their incident reports, such as police pursuits, thus ruling out computer searches.

Professional drivers, such as cabbies, truckers, couriers, and others, contribute to the vagaries of data collection because of their widespread reluctance to report assaults, thefts, and threats. Most of them are not reimbursed for the time they take to make an official report. If the assault is not life-threatening, it likely does not get reported. Hence, it is impossible to quantify some of the acts of crime and violence that appear to be widespread.

DEFINITION OF VIOLENCE

The World Health Organization says violence is the intentional use of physical force or power, threatened or actual, against oneself, another person, or against a group or community that either results in or has a high likelihood of resulting in injury, death, psychological harm, mal-development, or deprivation. Violence on the road is not much different from that definition. However, the emphasis in road violence is more on physical and sexual harm than on psychological abuse or social harm. For the purposes of this book, violence on the road includes the following:

- » physical assault on a road user, or an attack on a vehicle with the intent of hurting a driver and/or passenger
- » transferring experiences from another part of life to the roadway and thereby imposing violence
- » creating genuine fear in another person through or with a motor vehicle
- » targeting a person for sexual assault through or with a motor vehicle
- » inflicting self-harm through the vehicle
- » inflicting harm to others through collective violence imposed by the state or organized political groups through or with a motor vehicle

To clarify the nature of the violence, we considered the mitigating circumstances and situational factors that contributed to the roadway violence. The five considerations are:

- » intent and motive of the perpetrators
- » impact of the action on the recipients
- » situations in which the act was committed
- » factors that contributed to the actions
- » the social context that supported the violence

Linked to these five considerations are four basic assumptions that underscore the definition of violence, scope and details of the project, and our analytic approach. They are the following:

- » The incidents discussed must be an act of violence as defined within this study.
- » The incidents must be motor vehicle-related. The vehicle, owner-driver, and/or passenger must be involved in an active or passive way.
- » The violence can be planned or happen impulsively, arising from premeditated acts or driving-related incidents.
- » The incidents can involve strangers and/or acquaintances, such as spouses, family members, colleagues, or employers.

CONTENT ANALYSIS

In the absence of controlled data collection, we relied on past data collected or reported through official national or regional databases, reporting systems, or surveys, and published by official criminal justice or traffic safety agencies. The reader is cautioned not to make formal comparisons between the data collected from different studies because of different terms of reference, relevant concepts, and data-collection strategies used. For example, self-reported surveys on victimization use different definitions of aggressive driving, as do national and criminal databases. Furthermore, violence reported to the police may not be separately reported and identified in official provincial or national justice databases. For example, carjacking is a category of crime reported in American police databases, but in Alberta it is designated as auto theft with assault.

A review of traffic-related research reports, analyses of formal research studies and relevant literature in criminology, media reports, policy documents, and historical interpretations were used as a form of document analysis. This type of analysis is an insightful and practical qualitative research method to detect the more important structures of textual information. It allowed us to describe and make inferences about the antecedents and characteristics of roadway violence.

THE CASES

The cases described throughout the book were collected from media news reports, court files, medical examiner files, published and unpublished research reports, and Internet articles.

When detailing media news reports, we have included the actual names of the people involved and other specific information. The rationale is that a name made public may be repeated in discourse that reflects the same context. Safety was the rule of caution.

When describing cases drawn from legal files, medical examiner files, personal interviews, or unpublished reports, however, we have changed names and other identifiable information to protect the confidentiality of all involved.

WEB MINING

We extracted and analyzed information from thousands of sources on the Internet and in other unstructured data sources. We used these sources to verify concepts and theories. Some sources provided key linkages to relevant ideas that we had not initially considered.

LITERATURE SEARCH

We used library search vehicles to find and extract research articles that provided valuable input into the book. In all, we collected and reviewed more than 400 research and academic articles over a period of four years.

REVIEW OF THE MASS MEDIA

We completed searches of mass media representations of the concepts discussed in the book. We gave special emphasis to the representation and exemplifications of the concepts in everyday life.

Incidents do emerge in the mass media that are important to the project but rarely is there any degree of consistent reporting. Because most news presses are independent businesses, they are less likely to attend to the mundane crimes or to attend to the official reporting processes. If an assault is not life-threatening, it is not likely to get reported, despite the number of times it happens, or how widespread it is. This situation makes quantifying reports difficult to do.

FINAL FOOTNOTE

A primary source of Canadian and American crime statistics is the Uniform Crime Reporting Survey (UCR) developed by Statistics Canada in 1962. A word of caution is that violent crime as defined by UCR data may change because of changes in reporting practices of citizens and the police.

The information in this book is footnoted by the John Howard Society's consideration that nearly 70% of violent crime goes unreported. No doubt, similar numbers apply to vehicular crime.

REFERENCE LIST

630 CHED (2007, January 4). Photo radar fizzles. Retrieved from http://www.630ched.com/news/news

Abadinsky, H. (1983). *The crime elite: Professional and organized crime.* Westport, CT: Greenwood Press.

Accident Reconstruction Network (undated). *$290 Million verdict against Ford upheld.* Los Angeles.

Affiliated Computer Services [ACS] (undated). Retrieved from http://www.acs-inc.com

Ahira, M., & Ahira, H. (2003). Studies on suicide among Japanese. Retrieved from http://www.medline.ru/public/sudm/a2/art3-1-1.phtml

Alberta Rural Crime Watch (2002, Winter). Fish and wildlife officers rely on assistance from the public. *The Bulletin.*

Alberta Solicitor General (1990). *Motor vehicle pursuit guidelines.* Edmonton, AB: Queens Printer.

Allender, D.M. (2001, December). Gangs in Middle America: Are they a threat? *FBI Law Enforcement Bulletin.*

Alpert, G.P. (1998, August). *Helicopters in pursuit operations.* Washington D.C.: U.S. Department of Justice, National Institute of Justice.

Amalgamated Transit Union Local 113 (2006, May 24). Toronto transit workers' union says operators will no longer risk assaults by enforcing fare payments. *Toronto Transit Workers News.*

Amato, P. R. (2000). "The consequences of divorce for adults and children." *Journal of Marriage and the Family* 62:1269–1287.

American Academy of Child and Adolescent Psychiatry (2004). Children and divorce. *Facts for Families.*

American Academy of Child and Adolescent Psychiatry (1999). Children of alcoholics. *Facts for Families.*

American Automobile Association [AAA] (2008, January 4). 25 000 crashes a year due to vehicle-related road debris, study finds. Press release.

American Public Health Association (2005, Spring). No bullies on board: Putting the brakes on school bus bullying. Newsletter.

Anderson, C.A., & Bushman, B. (2002). The effects of media violence on society. *Science,* 295 (5564): 2377–2379.

APB News (1999). Today's police and crime headlines. Retrieved from http://www.apbnews.com

Arad, Y. (1987). *Belzec, Sobibor, Treblinka.* Bloomington: Indiana University Press.

Associated Press (2007, March 26). Baby critically wounded in drive-by shooting.

Associated Press (2006, December 4). Truck driver convicted in human smuggling case that left 19 illegal immigrants dead.

Associated Press (2004, February 26). Torch guilty in fender bender.

Associated Press (2003, June 27). Timeline of events in the Chante Mallard windshield death case.

Associated Press (2000, February 24). Mother screams in horror as son dragged by car thief.

Associated Press (1998, December 24). Suspect in carjacking, beating of Wyoming man charged.

Bandura, A. (1986). *Social foundations of thought and action: A social cognitive theory.* Englewood Cliffs, NJ: Prentice Hall.

Bandura, A. (1973). *Aggression: A social learning analysis.* Englewood Cliffs, NJ: Prentice Hall.

Barancik, S. (2000, August 11). Ocala lawyer has been fighting tire makers on safety for years. *St. Petersburg Times.*

Barger, S. (2002). *Ridin high, livin free.* New York: HarperCollins Publishers.

Batten, P.J., Penn, D.W., & Bloom, J.D. (2000). A 36-year history of fatal road rage in Marion County, Oregon: 1963–1998. *Journal of Forensic Science,* 45 (2): 397–399.

BBC News (2003, June 18). U.S. Catholic bishop quits.

BBC News (1999, February 14). World: Europe joins Holocaust fund.

B.C. Government Employees' Union (2003, August). The government's plan to close B.C. Liquor Stores is bad for consumers, bad for workers, and bad for communities. *BCGEU Information Report.*

Beautrais, A.L. (2003). Suicide and serious suicide attempts in youth: A multiple-group comparison study. *American Journal of Psychiatry,* 160: 1093–1099.

Beazley, D. (2007, March 15). Red light cameras do work: Chief Boyd. *Edmonton Sun.*

Begona, S.J., Van Oers, H.A., van de Mheen, D., Henke, F., Garretson, L., & Mackenbach, C.H. (2000). Stressors and alcohol consumption. *Alcohol and Alcoholism,* 35 (3): 307–312.

Bell, K. (1999). Leisure is executed after Supreme Court.

Berger, P., & Berger, B. (1975). *Sociology: A biographical approach.* New York: Basic Books.

Berger, P., & Luckmann, T. (1967). *The social construction of reality.* New York: Anchor Books.

Best, S., & Kellner, D. (1999). Rap, black rage and racial difference. *Enculturation,* 2 (2): 12.

Bethesda, L.M. (1997, March). *Aggressive driving.* A report presented to the AAA Foundation for Traffic Safety.

Bloomberg News (2007, March 29). Judge allows lawsuit against Exxon Mobil. *Edmonton Journal.*

Bollen, K.A., & Phillips, D.P. (1981). Suicidal motor vehicle fatalities in Detroit: A replication. *AJS,* 87 (2): 404–412.

Boyd, N. (1991). *High society. Legal and illegal drugs in Canada.* Toronto: Key Porter Books.

Brenneman, R. (2004, May 14). Wozniak seeks changes in parking enforcement. *Berkeley Daily Planet.*

Brochu, S., Cournoyer, L.G., Motiuk, L., & K. Pernaen (1999). Drugs, alcohol and crime: Patterns among Canadian federal inmates. *Bulletin on Narcotics,* LI, (1 and 2).

Broughton, J. (2004). Hit and run accidents, 1999–2002. A report prepared for the British Road Safety Division, Department of Transport.

Brown, H. (1998, May 15). Suicide by cop. *HSC Weekly,* Volume 4 (34): 1–3.

Bruyere, D., Gillet, J., & Foster, K. (2005, May). *National operator assault survey results 2005.* Mississauga, ON: Amalgamated Transit Union Canadian Council.

Buchanan, W., Rubenstein, S., & Wildermouth, J. (2006, August 30). Hit-and-run: Within half an hour, 14 pedestrians picked off one by one on streets of San Francisco. *San Francisco Chronicle.*

Burns, R.G. (1999). Socially constructing an image in the automobile industry. *Crime, Law & Social Change,* 31: 327–346.

Bushman, B., & Huesmann, L. (2000). Effects of televised violence on aggression. In Singer, D.G., & Singer, J.L. (Eds.), *Handbook of Children and the Media.* Newbury Park, CA: Sage.

Bushman, B.J., & Cooper, H.M. (1990). Effects of alcohol on human aggression: Validity of proposed explanations. In Galanter, M. (Ed.), *Recent Developments in Alcoholism: Alcoholism and Violence,* Vol. 13, 227–243. New York: Plenum Press.

Calleja, C.F. (2002, November 5). Cab hold-ups on web. *Toronto Star*.

Canada Safety Council (2004). *Caution: Animal crossing*. Ottawa: Canada Safety Council.

Canada Safety Council (2004). Status of pocket bikes in Canada. Retrieved from http://www.safety-council.org/info/traffic/pocketbikes.html

Canadian Association of Mental Health (2003). One in ten Ontario students contemplate suicide. *CAMH Bulletin Studies*, January/February (18).

Canadian Bomb Data Centre (2007a). *Incidents and bombings in Canada: Statistics for 2006*. Ottawa: Royal Canadian Mounted Police.

Canadian Bomb Data Centre (2007b). *Attempted bombings, hoax devices and recoveries of IEDs in Canada: Statistics for 2006*. Ottawa: Royal Canadian Mounted Police.

Canadian Bomb Data Centre (2002). *Statistical Bulletin*, 1. Ottawa: Royal Canadian Mounted Police.

Canadian Press (2006, January 4). Teen hit by three cars, no one stopped.

Canadian Press (2005, January 5). Winnipeg cops allege teens stealing cars, rig them to crash into buildings.

Canadian Press (2000, November 7). Prostitutes' clients risk cars under bill.

Canadian Security Intelligence Service [CSIS] (2005). Terrorism. Retrieved from http://www.csis-scrs.gc.ca

Cappell, H., & Greeley, J. (1987). Alcohol and tension reduction: An update on research and theory. In Blane, H.T., & Leonard, K.E. (Eds.), *Psychological Theories of Drinking and Alcoholism*. New York: Guilford Press, pp. 15–54.

Carcach, C., & Grabosky, P.N. (1998, March). Murder suicide in Australia. *Twenty-sixth annual report of the Australian Institute of Criminology*. Canberra: Australian Institute of Criminology.

Carrère, S., Yoshimoto, D., Mittmann, A., Woodin, E.M., Tabares, A., Ullman, J., et al. (2005). The roles of marriage and anger dysregulation in biobehavioural stress responses. *Biological Research for Nursing*, 7 (1) 1: 30–43.

Carrigg, D. (2005, December 28). Two men suffering from gunshot wounds refuse to co-operate. *The Province* [final ed.].

Casavant, L., & Collin, C. (2001, October 3). Illegal drug use and crime: A complex relationship. A report prepared for the Senate Special Committee on Illegal Drugs, Ottawa.

Catalano, S.M. (2003). *Criminal victimizations, 2003*. Bureau of Justice Statistics. Washington, D.C.: U.S. Department of Justice, Office of Justice Programs.

CBC News (2008, January 18). Ford ad backfires in Manitoba.

CBC News (2007, December 9). Women still missing from Vancouver amid Pickton convictions.

CBC News (2007, August 3). Black markets in air bags lucrative: York chief.

CBC News (2006, December 5). House arrest for second teen after deadly boulder drop.

CBC News (2006, November 16). N.L. murder-suicide rate stable over time: Crime expert.

CBC News (2006, August 31). Car passenger killed in drive-by shooting.

CBC News (2006, May 6). One arrest in bus driver attack.

CBC News (2006, January 28). Memorial held for cab driver killed in alleged street race.

CBC News (2005, January 4). Police investigate violent carjacking.

CBC News (2004, August 13). Edmonton leads the country in police chases.

CBC Newsworld (1999, August 21).

Centre for Addiction and Mental Health (2004, January). *Retail alcohol monopolies and regulation: Preserving the public interest*. CAMH position paper, University of Toronto.

Center for Disease Control (2002). *Injury fact book*. Atlanta: Department of Health and Human Services.

Center for Disease Control (1994). *Deaths resulting from firearms and motor vehicle related injuries in the United States, 1968–1991*. Atlanta: Center for Disease Control.

Chappell, D., & Di Martino, V. (1998). *Violence at work*. Geneva: International Labour Office.

Charlton, P.K. (2003, July 25). *Increasing violence in human smuggling has resulted in a humanitarian crisis.* Testimony before the United States Senate Committee on the Judiciary Subcommittee on Crime, Corrections and Victims Rights.

Chicago Tribune (2003, May 17). 2000 crime report.

Cialdini, R.B. (1993). *Influence.* Toronto: HarperCollins.

Clarke, R.V., & Goldstein, H. (2003). *Theft from cars in city center parking facilities: A case study.* U.S. Department of Justice, Office of Community Oriented Policing Services.

Clarke, R.V., & Lester, D. (1989). *Suicide: Closing the exits.* New York: Springer-Verlag.

Claxton, M., & Hurt, C. (2000, March 26). Fraud adds $130 to each insurance bill. *Detroit News.*

CNN (2003, June 18). Archbishop arrives to "heal" Phoenix diocese.

CNN (2000, January 12). Supreme Court: Fleeing at sight of police can be cause for search.

CNN (1998, April 27). Supreme court to hear federal carjacking case. Retrieved from http://www.cnn.com/U.S./9804/27/court.carjacking.ruet/

Cohen, L., Miller, T., Sheppard, M.A., Gordon, E., Gantz, T., & Atnafou, R. (2003). Bridging the gap. *Journal of Safety Research,* 34: 473–483.

Colorado Division of Wildlife (2003, November). *Colorado wildlife wardens announce winter range patrols to control poachers.* Denver: Colorado Department of Natural Resources.

Compas Inc. (2007, February 26). Violence and aggression in the workplace. *Financial Post.*

Conger, J., Gaskill, H., Glad, D., Hassel, L., Rainey, R., Sawrey, W., & Turrell, E. (1959). Psychological and physiological factors in motor vehicle accidents. *Journal of the American Medical Association,* 169: 1581–1587.

Conniff, R. (1999, January). Crash, slam, boom! *Smithsonian Magazine.*

Consumer Affairs (2003, December 8). Report alleges massive fraud in auto sales. Retrieved from http://www.consumeraffairs.com/news03/auto_fraud.html

Convention on the Prevention and Punishment of the Crime of Genocide (1948, December 9). United Nations General Assembly.

Cooper, F.J., Pemberton, M.J., Jarvis, A., Hughes, M., & Logan, B.K. (2002). Prevalence of drug use in commercial tractor trailer drivers. *Journal of Forensic Sciences,* 47 (3): 562–567.

Cormier, R. (2005, May 13). Car chase ends in gunfire. *Edmonton Journal,* p. A14.

Corimer, R. (2004, December 29). Joy riders likely at fault for crashing cars into businesses. *Edmonton Journal,* p. B3.

Court News (2006, August 22). AIDS activist convicted in death of cabdriver during dispute over $8 fare. Chicago.

Court of Appeals of Indiana (1999, February 16). Appeal from the Monroe Circuit Court, Division IV. *Morris Lee Burton v. State of Indiana.*

Crank, J.P. (2004). *Understanding police culture.* Cincinnati: Anderson Publishing.

Crashworthiness (2005, March 30). Jury orders Ford to pay surviving spouse $10.2 million for SUV rollover death. Retrieved from http://www.crashworthiness.com/articles/suv-death.html

Crime Reports (2000, March 30). Police seek suspect in carjacking in parking garage. Retrieved from http://crimereports.com/states/va/arlington/Plc_Sk_S.html

Criminal Intelligence Service Canada (2006). *Organized crime in Canada in 2006: Annual report.* Ottawa: Criminal Intelligence Service Canada.

Criminal Intelligence Service Canada (2005, Winter). *2005 Intelligence trends: Aboriginal-based gangs in Saskatchewan.* Ottawa: Criminal Intelligence Service Canada.

Criminal Intelligence Service Canada. (1999). Outlaw motorcycle gangs. Retrieved from http://www.cisc.gc.ca/Cisc99/omg.html

CTV News (2006, March 3). Edmonton man beaten to death on transit bus.

Culley, T. (2001). *The immortal class: Bike messengers and the cult of human power.* New York: Random House.

Daly, M., & Wilson, M. (1988). *Homicide*. New York: Aldine de Gruyter.

DeadlyRoads (undated). Famous victims or infamous drivers. Retrieved from http://www.deadlyroads.com/famous.html

DeBord, K. (2004). *Focus on kids: The effects of divorce on children*. Columbia, MO: University of Missouri-Columbia.

Decker, S. (1996, June). Collective and normative features of gang violence. *Justice Quarterly*, 13 (2), 243–264.

De Leseleuc, S. (2007). Criminal victimization in the workplace. Ottawa: Canadian Centre for Justice Statistics, Statistics Canada.

Dennerlein, J. (2003, Fall). Caution: Work can be hazardous to your health. *Harvard Public Health Review*.

DenverChannel (2002, October 12). Suicide notes examined in former trooper's death.

Dever, P. (1996). Class action lawsuits against Ford seek replacement of ignition switches. The Auto Channel, 10/12.

De Wyze, J. (2005, March 31). Why do they die? *San Diego Reader*.

Dingsdale, P. (1998, December 4). Suicide by cop: Disturbing new trend revealed by usc study of fatal shootings. Retrieved from http://www.usc.edu/hsc/info/pr/1vol4/434/shootings.html

Dirt Wheels Magazine (2004). Hunting with atv's. Retrieved from http://www.dirtwheelsmag.com/detail.asp?id=218

Dobbs, M. (1998, November 30). Ford and GM scrutinized for alleged Nazi collaboration. *Washington Post*, p. A01.

Donnelly, J. (2000, April 26). PA man goes on car crashing spree. *Burlington County Times*.

Drug and Crime Prevention Committee (2005). Inquiry into violence associated with motor vehicle use. Final Report presented to the Parliament of Victoria Session, 2003–2005.

Edmonton Journal (2005, January 11). Editorial section.

Edmonton Journal Staff (2005, January 3). A year of killings. *Edmonton Journal*.

Edmonton Sun (2007, December 16). Sunday comment.

Eikel, R. (2000). Killers for hire, mercenary fighters in car wars. *ADQ*, 8 (4): 1–4.

Eiseland, G.A. (1990, September). Attacks in parking lots, driving home liability of owners. *Trial*, 108–113.

Etiquette Hell (2005). Road rage archive. Retrieved from http://www.etiquettehell.com/content/eh_everyday/roadrage/roadrage2004–1arc.shtml

Evans, S., & Lundman, R. (1987). Newspaper coverage of corporate price-fixing. *Criminology*, 21 (4), 529–541.

Fairstein, L. (1993). *Sexual violence: Our war against rape*. New York: William Morrow.

Farley, M., & Barkan, H. (1998). Prostitution, violence against women, and posttraumatic stress disorder. *Women and Health*, 27 (3): 37–49.

Farley, R. (1999). Defensive driving: Being a cabbie is one of the most dangerous jobs in America. *Dallas Observer*.

Farrell, J. (2006, September 12). Bikini model victim of drive-by. *Edmonton Journal*.

Fatality Analysis Reporting System [FARS] (2006). National Highway Traffic Safety Administration, Washington, D.C.

Fatality Analysis Reporting System [FARS] (2004). National Highway Traffic Safety Administration, Washington, D.C.

Fatality Analysis Reporting System [FARS] (2000). National Highway Traffic Safety Administration, Washington, D.C.

Federal Highway Administration (1995). *Random drug and alcohol pilot program: Final report*. Washington, D.C.: Federal Highway Administration.

Fedorowycz, O. (1998). Homicide in Canada, 1997. *Juristat*. Ottawa: Statistics Canada, Canadian Centre for Justice Statistics, 18(12).

Feinstein, D. (2000, February 16). Senator Feinstein calls for more inspectors, detection technology at U.S. seaports. Press Release.

Field, S.R., Clarke, P., Harris, B. (1991). The Mexican vehicle market and auto theft in border areas of the United States. *Security Journal,* 2(4): 205–210.

Fight Bad Faith Insurance Companies [FBIC] (2005) Group insurers ranking: Payment of claims records. Retrieved from http://www.badfaithinsurance.org

Fishman, M. (1978). Crime waves as ideology. *Social Problems,* 25: 531–543.

Flanagan, G. (2003, June). *Sobering result: The Alberta liquor retailing industry ten years after privatization.* Edmonton: Canadian Centre for Policy Alternatives and Parkland Institute.

Flanagan, N.G., Wootton, D.G., Smith, G., & Goff, D.K. (1978). An unusual case of carbon monoxide poisoning. *Medical Science Law,* 18 (2): 117–119.

Fleenor, P. (2003, February 6). *Cigarette taxes, black markets and crime: Lessons from New York's 50 year losing battle.* Policy Analysis #468.

Fotsch, P.M. (1999). Contesting urban freeway stories: Racial politics and the O.J. chase. *Cultural Studies,* 13 (1): 110–137.

Fox News (2003). Chante Mallard case. Retrieved from http://www.foxnews.com

Frascara, J. (2004). Revisiting communications in traffic safety. In Rothe, J.P. (Ed.), *Driving Lessons: Exploring Systems That Make Traffic Safer.* Edmonton: University of Alberta Press.

Freund, P., & Martin, G. (1993). *The Ecology of the Automobile.* Montreal: Black Rose Books.

Gadd, J. (2000, January 28). Siegles describe horror of abduction to court. *The Globe and Mail.*

Garrett, H. (1968). The tragedy of the commons. *Science,* 162: 1243–1248.

Geranios, N. (2002, October 24). Odometer fraud begs the question: Would you buy a used car from Canada? *Auto Facts.*

Gerber, J., & Fritsch, E. (1993). On the relationship between white collar crime and political sociology: A suggestion and resource for teaching. *Teaching Sociology,* 21: 130–139.

Gerbner, G. (1994). *The killing screens: Media and the culture of violence.* Northampton MA: Media Foundations Education.

Ghosh, P. (2000, May 19). Road rage grips Delhi. *BBC News.*

Gillet, J.M., Hunniford, P., & Bruyere, D. (2003). *Assault survey 2003.* London, ON: London Transit Operators.

Glasbeek, H. (2003). *Wealth by stealth, corporate crime, corporate law, and the perversion of democracy.* Toronto: Between the Lines Publishing.

Glassner, B. (2000). *The culture of fear: Why Americans are afraid of the wrong things.* New York: Basic Books.

Goffman, I. (1959). *The presentation of self in everyday life.* Garden City, NY: Doubleday Anchor Books.

Goldsmith, S.K., Pelmar, T.C., Kleinman, A.M., & Bunney, W.E. (Eds.) (2002). *Reducing suicide: A national imperative.* Washington, D.C.: National Academies Press.

Goldstein, P.J. (1985). The drugs/violence nexus: A tripartite conceptual framework. *Journal of Drug Issues,* 15(4), 493–506.

Gould, M., Greenberg, T., Velting, D., & Shaffer, D. (2003). Youth suicide risk and preventive interventions: A review of the past 10 years. *Journal of the American Academy of Child and Adolescent Psychiatry,* 42(4), 386–405.

Gouras, M. (2004, October 23). Appeals court lets Bridgestone shareholders' lawsuit go ahead. *Detroit News Autos Insider.*

Gray, J. (1998). *False dawn: The delusions of global capitalism.* New York: New Press.

Gregoire, L. (2001, January 26). Beware the car air bag thieves. *Edmonton Journal.*

Grossman, M., Chaloupka, F.J., Saffer, H., & Laixuthai, A. (1994). Effects of alcohol price policy on youth: A summary of economic research. *Journal of Research on Adolescence,* 4: 347–364.

Gruenewald, P., Stockwell, T.R., Beel, A.C., & Dyskin, E.V. (1999). Beverage sales and drinking and driving: The role of on-premise drinking places. *Journal of Studies on Alcohol,* 60 (1): 47–53.

Habib, M. (2003, December 17). Untitled. Canadian Press.

Hagan, J., and Peterson, R. 1995. Criminal inequality in America: Patterns and consequences. In Hagan, J., & Peterson, R. (Eds.), *Crime and Inequality.* Stanford, CA: Stanford University Press, pp. 14–36.

Hamburger, E. (1969, June). Vehicular suicidal ideation. *Military Medicine,* 441–444.

Hamrick, J. (2004, May). Underwriting special risks: Motor vehicle racing. *Transamerica Messenger Newsletter.*

Hankiss, E. (2006). *The Toothpaste of immortality: Self-construction in the consumer age.* Washington, D.C.: Woodrow Wilson Center Press.

Hardin, G. (1968). The tragedy of the commons. *Science,* 182: 1243–1248.

Harding, R. W., Morgan, F. H., Indermaur, D., Ferrante, A., & Blagg, H. (1998). Road rage and the epidemiology of violence. *Studies in Crime and Crime Prevention,* 7, 221–238.

Hartman, D.M., & Golub, A. (1999). The social construction of the crack epidemic in the print media. *Journal of Psychoactive Drugs,* 31(4), October–December: 423–431.

Harvey, I. (2005, December 17). Air bag thefts raise safety flag for repairs: Gangs plundering cars for expensive crash bag systems. *Collision Industry Information Systems.*

Haught, J. (1995, Summer). True believers and utter madness. *Free Inquiry.*

Hazelwood, R.R., Dietz, P.E., & Warren, J. (1992). The criminal sexual sadist. *FBI Law Enforcement Bulletin.* Washington, D.C.

Heafey, S. (2000, September 23). Speech on high speed pursuits. Presented at the Canadian Association of Civilian Oversight of Law Enforcement Conference, Winnipeg, MB.

Health and Safety Alert (2005, February 2). Unsecured load causes fatalities.

Heiner, R. (2002). *Social problems: An introduction to critical constructionism.* New York: Oxford University Press.

Hemenway, D., Vriniotis, M., & Miller, M. (2006) Is an armed society a polite society? Guns and road rage. *Accident Analysis and Prevention,* 38: 687–695.

Hennessy, D.A. (1999). *The interaction of person and situation within the driving environment: Daily hassles, traffic congestion, driver stress, aggression, vengeance and past performance.* Doctoral dissertation. York University, Toronto.

Hennessy, D.A., & Wiesenthal, D. (2002, Fall). Aggression, violence and vengeance among male and female drivers. *Transportation Quarterly,* 56 (4), 65–75.

Henslin, J.M. (1996). *Essentials of sociology.* Englewood Cliffs, NJ: Prentice Hall.

Henslin, J.M. (1994). *Social problems.* Third Edition. Englewood Cliffs, NJ: Prentice Hall.

Herald Journal (1994, November 3). Susan Smith's handwritten confession.

Herzog, L. (2005, February 10). Odometer tampering. *Canadian Drivers Magazine.*

Hickey, E. (2006). *Serial murderers and their victims.* Belmont, CA: Thomson Wadsworth.

Highway Safety Information System [HSIS] (1995). *Investigation of crashes with animals: Summary report.* Washington, D.C.: U.S. Department of Transportation Federal Highway Administration.

Hills, J. (2002, July). High speed police pursuits: Dangers, dynamics, and risk reduction. *FBI Law Enforcement Bulletin.*

Hills, J. (1999). *Police pursuits and the risks to bystanders.* Doctoral program paper presented to Nova Southeastern University, Fort Lauderdale, FL.

Hills, S.L. (1987). *Corporate violence: Injury and death for profit.* Totawa, NJ: Rowman and Littlefield.

Hobbes, T. (1999). *The Leviathan.* Middlesex, England: Penguin Books.

Holl, J. (2006, June 26). High-tech thieves use laptops to steal cars: Transmitters, software crack the code of keyless entry systems. Retrieved from http://www.forbesautos.com

Horowitz, I. (1982). *Taking lives, genocide and state power.* New Brunswick, NJ: Transaction.

Howell, J.C. (1999, April). Youth gang homicides: A literature review. *Crime and Delinquency,* 45 (2), 208–241.

Howell, M. (2004, August 5). Cab company owners question drug sting. *Vancouver Courier.*

Huston, A.C., Danerskin, E., & Fairchild, H. (1992). *Big world, small screen: The role of television in American society.* Omaha: University of Nebraska Press.

Hutson, H.R., Anglin, D., & Eckstein, M. (1996, April). Drive-by shootings by violent street gangs in Los Angeles: A five year review from 1989 to 1993. *Academic Emergency Medicine,* 3 (4): 300–303.

Hutson, H.R., Anglin, D., & Pratts, M.J. (1994, February). Adolescents and children injured or killed in drive-by shootings in Los Angeles. *New England Journal of Medicine,* 333: 324–327.

Hutson, H.R., Anglin, D., Yarbrough, J., Hardaway, K., Russel, M., Stoote, J., Canter, M., & Blum, B. (1998). Suicide by cop. *Annals of Emergency Medicine,* 32 (6): 665–669.

Insurance Bureau of Canada (2006). *Facts of the general insurance industry in Canada.* Toronto: Insurance Bureau of Canada.

Insurance Bureau of Canada (2004). *Impact of auto theft.* Toronto: Insurance Bureau of Canada.

Insurance Canada (2006). IBC hosts 2006 auto theft export summit (June 8–9). Combating Auto Theft, Organized Crime & Terrorism. Ottawa.

Insurance Information Institute (2008, January). Auto theft.

Insurance Information Institute (2006). Things you may not know about hit and run accidents.

Insurance Information Institute (2005, March). Auto theft. Retrieved from http://www.iii.org/media/hottopics/insurance/test4/

Insurance Institute for Highway Safety (2005, January). Human deaths in crashes with animals can be reduced even without reducing collisions. *Status Report,* 40 (1).

Insurance Research Council (2005, January). Fraud and buildup in auto injury insurance claims: 2004 Edition.

Iseek (2004). Career: Parking enforcement officers. Retrieved from http://iseek.org

James, L., & Nahl, D. (2002). Dealing with stress and pressure in the vehicle. In Rothe, J.P. (Ed.), *Driving Lessons: Exploring Systems That Make Traffic Safer.* Edmonton: University of Alberta Press.

James, L., & Nahl, D. (2000). *Road rage and aggressive driving: Steering clear of highway warfare.* Amherst, NY: Prometheus Books.

Jamieson, L. (2002, July 24). Violence in sports reflects society says Indiana University professor. *Indiana University Media Relations.*

Janeshewski, L. (2004). Highway robbery. *MoneySense.* Retrieved from http://www.moneysense.ca/autohighway robbery.htm

Jet (2002, August 26). Chicago fatal van crash: Deadly vigilantism draws national attention.

Jha, B. (2001). *Taxicab safety issues.* An independent report presented to the Minister of Transportation and Government Services, Winnipeg, MB.

Johnson, V., & Pandina, R.J. (1993). A longitudinal examination of the relationships among stress, coping strategies, and problems associated with alcohol use. *Alcoholism: Clinical and Experimental Research,* 17: 696–702.

Jones, D.A. (2005, May 25). Supply-chain theft: A new LP challenge. *Loss Prevention Magazine.*

Joyner, J. (2004, July 24). Car bomb in Nashville. *Outside the Beltway.* Retrieved from http://www.outsidethebeltway.com/archive/2004/07

Juergensmeyer, M. (2000). Terror in the mind of God. *Comparative Studies in Religion and Society,* 13.

Jung, C.G. (1957). *The undiscovered self (present and future).* New York: American Library.

Juristat: Canadian Crime Statistics (2003). *Crime Statistics,* 24 (6).

KABC TV (2004, February 17). Murder-suicide: Woman decapitated, ex-lover steps in front of tractor trailer.

Kabrick, B. (2004). Keynote speech. NIOSH Conference on Workplace Violence, Kansas City, April 30–May 7.

Kabrick, B. (2001a). *Criminal intent: Workplace violence.* Paper presented at the Conference on Violence as a Workplace Risk. Montreal, November 29–30.

Kabrick, B. (2001b, June). How safe is taxi driving for women? *Journal of Dial-a-Cab.*

Karmen, A. (1994). *Crime victims.* Pacific Grove, CA: Brooks/Cole Publishing.

Katz, J. (1995). What makes crime news? In Erierson, R. (Ed.), *Crime and the Media.* Brookfield, VT: Dartmouth Publishing.

Kay, J.H. (1999). *Asphalt nation: How the automobile took over America and how we can take it back.* Berkley: University of California Press.

Keller, S.R. (1996). The value of life: Biological diversity and human society. In Hoage, R.J. (Ed.), *Perceptions of Animals in America.* Washington, D.C.: Smithsonian Institution Press.

Kelling, G.L., & Cole, K. (1996). *Fixing broken windows.* New York: Free Press.

Kelly and Associates (2000, August 23). Retired tire builders testify against manufacturer. *Chicago Sun-Times.*

Kessler, R.C., Berglund, P., Guilherme B., Nock, M., & P. Wang (2005). Trends in suicide ideation, plans, gestures, and attempts in the United States, 1990–1992 to 2001–2003. *Journal of the American Medical Association,* 293:2487–2495.

Key, S. & Popkin, S.J. (1998). Integrating ethics into the strategic management process. *Management Decision,* 36: 331–338.

KFMB TV (2005, January 19). Man held for threatening D.C. car bombing.

Kiecolt-Glaser, J.K., Bane, C., Glaser, R., & Malarkey, W.B. (2003). Love, marriage, and divorce: Newlyweds' stress hormones foreshadow relationship changes. *Journal of Consulting and Clinical Psychology,* 71:176–188.

Kiley, D. (2003, January 22). Lawsuits give Ford publicity problem. *USA Today.*

Klein, M. (1971). *Street gangs and street workers.* Englewood Cliffs, NJ: Prentice Hall.

Klein, M., & Maxson, C. (1989). Street gang violence. In Wolfgang, M.E., & Weiner, N.A. (Eds.), *Violent Crime, Violent Criminals.* Newbury Park, CA: Sage.

Koch, A. (2000, August 30). Mom tells of carjacking terror. *Seattle Times.*

Kogon, E., Langbein, H., & Ruecker, A. (1993). *Nazi mass murder: A Documentary history of the use of poison gas.* New Haven, CT: Yale University Press.

Koss, M.P., & Dinero, T.E. (1988). Predictors of sexual aggression among a national sample of male college students. *Academic Sciences,* 528: 133–147.

Koss, M.P., Dinero, T., Seibel, C., & Cox, S. (1988). Stranger and acquaintance rape: Are there differences in the victim's experience? *Psychology of Women Quarterly,* 12, 1–24.

Kostyniuk, L.P., Streff, F.M., & Zakrajsek, J. (2002). Identifying unsafe driver actions that lead to fatal car-truck crashes. Report for the American Automobile Association Foundation for Traffic Safety. Washington, D.C.

Krause, N. (1991) Stress, religiosity, and abstinence from alcohol. *Psychology and Aging,* 6: 134–144.

Krug, E.G., Dahlberg, L.L., Mercy, J.A., Zwi, A.B., & Lozano, R. (Eds) *World report on violence and health.* Geneva: World Health Organization.

Kupchinsky, R. (2003, February 23). Organized crime and terrorism watch. *Report on Crime, Corruption and Terrorism in the Former USSR, Eastern Europe and the Middle East.* Radio Free Europe.

Lam, D. (1999, November). Parenting stress and anger: The Hong Kong experience. *Child and Family Social Work,* 4 (4): 337–346.

Lam, L., Norton, R., Connor, J., & Ameratunga, S. (2004). Suicidal ideation, antidepressive medication and car crash injury. *Accident Analysis and Prevention,* 37(2): 335–339.

LaMar, W.J., Gerberich, S.G., Lohman, W.H., & Zaidman, B. (1998). Work-related physical assault. *Journal of Occupational and Environmental Medicine,* 40 (4), 317–324.

Lavan, M. (2005, January 22). Grand jury charges man with car arson. *Rochester Democrat and Chronicle News*.

Law Reform Commission of Victoria (1991). *Death caused by dangerous driving*. Discussion Paper 21, Law Reform Commission of Victoria, Melbourne, Australia.

Lay, B. (2004, November 14). Road rage turns ugly: Shots fired during S.W. traffic spat. *Calgary Sun*.

Legal Notices (2003). Joyriding and youth: Communicating the facts. Retrieved from http://www.stopautotheft.ca/carrecovery.htm

Leger Marketing (2001). *A study on road rage*. Montreal: Canadian Press.

Leiss, W. (1972). *The domination of nature*. New York: George Braziller.

Lesage, A.D., & McPhil M.D. (2005). Can psychiatrists prevent suicide? Yes, in collaboration. *Canadian Journal of Psychiatry*, 50: 507–508.

Lester, D. (1994). Car ownership and suicide by car exhaust in nations of the world. *Perceptual and Motor Skills*, 79: 898.

Lester, D. (1990). Suicide rates around the world. *Crisis*, 11: 82–84.

Lester, D., & Abe, K (1989). Car availability, exhaust toxicity, and suicide. *Annals of Clinical Psychiatry*, 1: 247–250.

Leyton, E. (1987). *Hunting humans: The rise of the modern multiple murderer*. Toronto: Seal Books.

Lichter, S.L., & Rothman, S. (1994). *Prime time: How TV portrays American culture*. Washington, D.C.: Regnery.

Liebson, R. (2003, June 5). Car-theft ring busted. *The Journal News*.

Liska, A.E. & Baccaglini, W. (1990). Feeling safe by comparison: Crime in the newspapers. *Social Problems*, 37: 360–374.

Lopiano-Misdom, J. (1997). *Street trends*. Toronto: HarperCollins Canada.

Los Angeles News (2007, June 5). 86 arrested in auto insurance fraud bust.

Los Angeles Times (2001a, December 21). Murder-suicide culminates in freeway traffic jam. Los Angeles Police Department Press Release.

Los Angeles Times (2001b, January 27). Driver's intent for running through day-care baffling.

Loyie, F. (2006, August 28). Deadly argument started at red light. *Edmonton Journal*, p. A3.

Magner, C. (2000b, October). Insider job. *Commercial Carrier Journal (CCJ)*, 1–3.

Mann, R. (2004, April). Alcohol consumption and problems among road rage victims and perpetrators. *Journal of Studies on Alcohol*.

Marsh, P., & Collett, P. (1986). *Driving passion: The psychology of the car*. London: Johnathan Cape.

Matheson, A. (undated). Rape. *Green Left Weekly*. Retrieved from http://www.greenleft.org

Mathews, F. (1995). *Making the decision to care: Guys and sexual assault*. Ottawa: National Clearinghouse on Family Violence, Healthy Communities Division, Centre for Healthy Human Development, Health Canada.

Matza, D., & Sykes, G.M. (1961, October). Juvenile delinquency and subterranean values. *American Sociological Review*, XXVI: 712–719.

Maxson, M., Gordon, M.A., & Klein, M.W. (1985). Differences between gang and nongang homicides. *Criminology*, 23: 209–222.

Mayron, A. (2003, March 15). Minneapolis man charged with one in a string of sex assaults. *Pioneer Press*.

McCain, J. Personal letter, February 10, 2004.

McComas, J., McKay, M., & Pivik, J. (2002). Effectiveness of virtual reality for teaching pedestrian safety. *CyberPsychology and Behavior*, 5(2): 185–191.

McCord, J., Widom, C.S., & Crowell, N.A. (2001). *Juvenile crime; Juvenile justice*. Panel on Juvenile Crime: Prevention, Treatment, and Control. Washington, D.C.: National Academy Press.

McDiarmid, M. (2002, February 20). Who killed Mary? *CBC: The National*.

McGoey, C. (2002). Parking lots, security tips. Retrieved from
http://www.crimedoctor.com

McGoey, C.E. (2001). *Auto theft facts*. San Francisco: McGoey Security Consulting.

McGoey, C.E. (2000a). Top 25 stolen cars. Retrieved from
http://www.crimedoctor.com/autotheft2.htm

McGoey, C.E. (2000b). *Auto theft facts*. San Francisco: McGoey Security Consulting.

McLean, A. (2005, January 29). No jail time for man who drove car and wife into phone
pole. *Edmonton Journal*.

McLeod, R., Stockwell, T., Rooney, R., Stevens, M., Phillips, M., & Jellinek, G. (2003). The
influence of extrinsic and intrinsic risk factors on the probability of sustaining an
injury. *Accident Analysis and Prevention*, 35: 71–80.

McLoughlin, E., & Fennell, J. (2000, September). The power of survivor advocacy: Making
car trunks escapable. *Injury Prevention* 6 (3): 167–170.

Mello, T.B. (2002). Gray area: What you need to know about Canadian cars in the U.S.
Retrieved from http://www.edmonds.com

Menninger, K.A. (1935). Purposive accidents as an expression of self destructive
tendencies. *International Journal of Psychoanalysis*, 17: 6–16.

Merritt, B. (2007, December 10). Teen in custody after cabby's throat slashed. *Edmonton
Sun*.

Miceli, M.J. (2002). *Fatalities and injuries as a result of stolen motor vehicles (1999–2001)*.
A report submitted for Project 6116. Montreal: Transport Canada.

Miller, M.V. (1987). Vehicle theft along the Texas-Mexico border. *Journal of Borderland
Studies*, 2:12–32.

Miller, W.B. (1982). *Crime by youth gangs and groups in the United States*. Washington
D.C.: U.S. Department of Justice, Office of Juvenile Justice and Delinquency
Prevention.

Mills, C.W. (1951). *White collar*. New York: Oxford University Press.

Mittleman, F., & Mittelman, T. (2002). *What do we learn from murder-by-car case?*
Chicago: Conscious Choice. Retrieved from http://www.consciouschoice.com

Moir, L. (2001). What do we mean by corporate social responsibility? *Corporate
Governance*, 1 (2): 16–22.

Mokhiber, R. (1994). The ten worst corporations of 1994. *Multinational Monitor's
Corporate Rap Sheet*. Retrieved from
http://wwww.essential.org/monitor/mm1294.htm1#topten

Mokhiber, R., Gozan, J., & Knaus, H. (1992). Multinational monitor's corporate rap sheet.
Multinational Monitor. Retrieved from http://www.ratical.org/corporations

Monday, M., & Stubblefield, G. (1997). Protecting against the car bomb. A report of the
POINTS Project on Insurgency, Terrorism and Security, San Francisco.

Moorhouse, M.D. (1983). American automobiles and workers' dreams. *Sociological Review*,
31: 403–426.

Morgan, C. (2002, April). *Preliminary report: The incidence rate of odometer fraud*.
Washington, D.C.: National Highway Traffic Safety Administration (NHTSA).

Morton, P. (2006). *How to drift: The art of oversteer*. Detroit: S-A Design.

Moyle Information Services for Law Enforcement (undated). Special types of suicide.
Retrieved from http://dmmoyle.com/sikinds.htm

MSNBC (2007, January 15). Video game sales post a record: Sales of games, game
consoles and accessories top $12.5B in 2006.

Myer, J. (2006). Road terror. *The Harvest*, 6 (2): 1–2.

Nathans Centre for the Study of Organized Crime (2003). *Organized crime in Canada: A
quarterly summary, January to March 2003*. Toronto: Osgoode Hall Law School.

Nation (2004, February 4). 30 arrested in Long Island gangs sweep. Retrieved from
http://www.usatoday.com/news/nation

National Adolescent Health Information Center (2007). *2006 fact sheet on suicide:
Adolescents and young adults*. San Francisco: University of California.

National Center for Health Statistics (2004). Births, marriages, divorces and deaths: Provisional data for November 2003. *National Vital Statistics Report,* 52 (20).

National Committee to Reduce Auto Theft (2002). *A report on fatalities and injuries as a result of motor vehicle theft collisions (1999–2001).*

National Crime Research Center (undated). Bombs and arson crimes among American gang members: A behavioural science profile. Retrieved from http://www.ngcrc.com/bombarso.html

National Highway Traffic Safety Administration [NHTSA] (2007, September). *Motor vehicle traffic crash fatality counts and estimates of people injured in 2006.* Washington, D.C.: U.S. Department of Transportation.

National Highway Traffic Safety Administration [NHTSA] (2002). *Fatality Analysis Reporting Systems: Annual Report.* Washington, D.C.

National Highway Traffic Safety Administration [NHTSA] (2000). *Fatality Analysis Reporting Systems: Fatalities in crashes involving law enforcement in pursuit, 1998.* Washington, D.C.

National Hot Rod Association [NHRA] (2003). Race the strip, not the street: Illegal racing stats. Retrieved from http://www.nhra.com/streetlegal/stats

National Institute on Drug Abuse (2005). *Monitoring the future 2005.* Washington, D.C.: National Institutes of Health, U.S. Department of Health and Human Services.

National Institute for Health Care Research (1998). Divorce: The forgotten injury. *Colorado Chiropractic Journal,* 2 (6).

National Institute for Occupational Safety and Health [NIOSH] (1995). Preventing homicide in the workplace: Workers in certain industries and occupations are at increased risk of homicide. *NIOSH Alert,* publication #93–109. Atlanta: NIOSH.

National Insurance Crime Bureau (2005). Motorcycle theft statistics. Washington, D.C.

National Insurance Crime Bureau (2003). Airbag theft & fraud: Deflating a growing crime trend. Washington, D.C.

National Post (2001, September 6). Editorial section

National Post (2000, November 22). Don't kill the messenger.

National Safe Kids (2004). *Children at risk fact sheet.* Washington, D.C.

Nationalsozialistische Massentotungen (undated). 84–86.

NBC 5 News (1996, October 13). Ford-TFI class action.

NBC News (2006, January 10). Judge sentences former Dallas Cowboy Dwayne Goodrich.

Neiderhoffer, A. (1967). *Behind the shield.* Garden City, NY: Anchor Books.

Neil, D. (1999, January). Heats up, no bust on asphalt. *Car and Driver,* 146–159.

Nettler, G. (1989). *Criminology lessons.* Cincinnati: Anderson Pub. Co.

Nettler, G. (1989). *Explaining crime.* New York: McGraw-Hill.

New Hampshire Department of Justice (2001, November 8). *Consumer alerts.*

News 3 (2006, March 10). Gangsta rap and violence against police officers.

News 10 ABC (2004, June 25). Surgeon sentenced for vandalism against former colleague.

Newsday (2006, July 19). Arrest in drive-by shooting of 11-year-old girl.

New York Governor's Traffic Safety Committee (2000, January 3). Aggressive driving. New York Department of Motor Vehicles Report.

New York Times (1997, November 16). Officers kill 19-year-old said to be suicidal.

New York Times (1993, October 19). Imitating a stunt from "The Program."

Norman, A. (2004). *The case against Wal-Mart.* Atlantic City, NJ: Raphel Marketing.

Novaco, R.W. (1991). Aggression on roadways. In Baenninger, R. (Ed.), *Targets of Violence and Aggression.* North Holland: Elsevier.

Novaco, R.W., Stokols, D.S., & Milanesi, L. (1990). Objective and subjective dimensions of travel impedance as determinants of commuting stress. *American Journal of Community Psychology,* 18: 231–257.

NPD (2003). Video game sales break $7 billion in 2003. *Funworld.*

Nussbaum, M. (1999). Equity and mercy. In *Sex and Social Justice.* New York: Oxford University Press.

O'Connor, N. (2004, August 5). Meter madness. *Vancouver Courier*.

Office of the Attorney General, State of Louisiana (2004). Insurance fraud. In *Programs and Services: Crime*. Baton Rouge: Office of the Louisiana Attorney General.

Office of the United States Attorney, District of Arizona (2007, January 29). Sacaton man sentenced to 10 years for voluntary manslaughter.

Ohberg, A., Lonnqvist, J., Sarna, S., & Pentilla, A. (1995). Trends and availability of suicide methods in Finland. Proposals for restrictive measures. *British Journal of Psychiatry*, 166 (1): 35–43.

O'Keefe, C. (2002, April 17). Joyriding could spark vigilantism. *Irish Examiner*. Dublin, Ireland.

Olson, N.K. (1994). Workplace violence: Theories of causation and prevention strategies. *AAOHN Journal*, 42 (10): 477–482.

Ontario Women's Directorate [OWD] (1995). *Facts to consider about sexual assault*. Toronto: OWD.

Outdoor Central News Network (2003, February 6). Deer decoy effective on West Bay W.M.A. Retrieved from http://www.outdoorcentral.com/mc/pr/03/02/07a6.asp

Overdrive (2001, October). Auto theft facts: U.S.A.

Parker, R.N., & Auerhahn, K. (1998). Alcohol, drugs and violence. *American Journal of Sociology*, 24: 291–311.

Parker, R.N., & Rebhun, L.-A. (1995). *Alcohol and homicide: A deadly combination of two American traditions*. New York: State University of New York Press.

Parks, M (2002). Identification of youth theft occurrences for the City of Toronto. A report prepared for Transport Canada.

Parks, R.E., & Burgess, E.W. (1925). *The city*. Chicago: University of Chicago Press.

Peak, K., & Glensor, R.W. (2004). *Street racing*. Office of Community Oriented Policing Services, U.S. Department of Justice Report #28.

Peck, D., & Warner, K. (1995, Summer). Accident or suicide? Single-vehicle car accidents and the intent hypothesis. *Adolescence*.

Pelkonen, M., & Marttunen, M. (2003). Child and adolescent suicide: Epidemiology, risk actors, and approaches to prevention. *Pediatric Drugs*, 5 (4): 243–265.

Pergament, R. (1999). *Susan Smith: Child murderer or victim?* South Carolina: Dark Horse Multimedia.

Pfeffer, C.R. (1989). Studies of suicidal preadolescent and adolescent inpatients: A critique of research methods. *Suicide and Life-Threatening Behaviour*, 19 (1): 58–77.

Phillips, D.P. (1979). Suicide, motor vehicle fatalities and the mass media: Evidence towards a theory of suggestion. *American Journal of Sociology*, 84: 1150–1179.

Poachers On-line (undated). Wyoming. Retrieved from http://gf.state.wy.us/wildlife/enforcement/index.asp

Professional Research Consultants (2005). *National health assessment: Ten years of monitoring the health status, risk and needs of Americans*. Omaha, NE: Professional Research Consultants Inc.

Public Safety Canada (2003, March 24). The Honourable Wayne Easter, Solicitor General of Canada, Youth and Auto Theft. Archive.

Raleigh News & Observer (2003, October 10). Radio host infuriates cyclists.

Ramos, D. (1998). *The gang guidebook*. Columbus, Ohio: The Office of Criminal Justice Services.

Ramos, R. (1998). Anatomy of a drive by: What we can learn from an unexpected death. *Sociological Quarterly*, 39 (2), 271–288.

Ramstedt, M. (2002). *Are suicide rates in Canada related to changes in alcohol consumption? A time series analysis of the postwar period*. Paper presented at the Canadian Alcohol Experiences and Nordic Perspectives seminar, December 12–13, Oslo, Norway.

RCMP (2004, July). *Drug situation in Canada: 2003*. Ottawa: Criminal Intelligence Directorate.

RCMP, K Division (2005, June 17). Project KARE offers reward for information on sex trade worker homicides. News Release. Edmonton.

Regina Police Service (2007, March 9). Crime Stoppers.

Reich, W. (Ed.) (1990). *Origins of terrorism: Psychologies, ideologies, states of mind.* New York: Cambridge University Press.

Reinmer, J. (1998). *The rich get richer and the poor get prison.* Boston: Allyson & Bacon.

Rice, H. (2005, January 3). Death penalty at center in smuggling case. *Houston Chronicle.*

Richards, C. (2003, January 15). Cowboys DB Dwayne Goodrich charged with manslaughter in fatal hit and run. *Yahoo Canada Sports.*

Rideout, V.J., Vandewater, E.A., & Wartella, E.A. (2003). *Zero to six: Electronic media in the lives of infants, toddlers and preschoolers.* Washington, D.C.: Henry J. Kaiser Foundation.

Roadragers (2004, January 5). Results: Analyze your driving style comparison of country data. Retrieved from http://www.roadragers.com

Rondeau, B., & Graf, A. (1996). *Research on vandalism.* Vancouver, BC: CPTED.

Rossow, I. (2002). *Alcohol consumption and homicides in Canada 1950–1999.* Paper presented at the Canadian Alcohol Experiences and Nordic Perspectives seminar. December 12–13, Oslo, Norway.

Rothe, J.P. (2000). *Undertaking qualitative research.* Edmonton: University of Alberta Press.

Rothe, J.P. (1995). Unpublished personal interviews with truckers and dispatchers, Vancouver and Toronto.

Rothe, J.P. (1990). *The trucker's world of risk, safety and mobility.* New Brunswick, NJ: Transaction Publishers.

Rothe, J.P. (1979). *Existential phenomenology and evaluation.* Doctoral thesis. University of Alberta, Edmonton.

Rousseau, J. (1987). *The basic political writings.* Donald A. Cress (Trans.). New York: Hackett Publishing Company.

Routley, V. (1998). Motor vehicle exhaust gassing suicides in Australia: Epidemiology and prevention. Monash University Accident Research Centre, Report #139.

Royal Commission on Aboriginal Peoples (1995). *Choosing life: Special report on suicide among Aboriginal people.* Ottawa: Canada Communication Group Publishing.

Rupert, J. (2005, January 19). "It just felt like trouble," victim's widow tells court. *Ottawa Citizen.*

Russel, C. (2007, March 16). Phoenix trip among alleged perks. *Edmonton Journal.*

Russel, S. (2002, October). Serial killer Aileen Wuornos chooses execution. *Sunday Express Review.*

Russell, M., & Weissman, R. (2003). Multiple corporate personality disorder. *The 10 Worst Corporations of 2003,* December 24 (12).

Rutenberg, J. (2002, December 13). Media: Audience for cable news grows. *New York Times.*

Saksida, S. (2006, September 11). Facts about insurance fraud. *The Epoch Times.*

Sakuta, T. (1995). A study of murder followed by suicide. *Medicine and Law,* 14 (1–2): 141–153.

Sanders, W. (1994). *Gangbangs and drive-bys: Grounded culture and juvenile gang violence.* New York: Aldine de Gruyter.

Saskatoon StarPhoenix (1999, May 5). Cadillac crashes into school yard, killing two toddlers; Driver tells police he wanted to "execute" innocent children.

Schimmel, S. (1997). *The seven deadly sins.* New York: Oxford University Press.

Schneidman, D. (1968). Orientation toward cessation: A reexamination of current modes of death. *Journal of Forensic Science,* 33: 1–4.

Schudson, M. (1995). *The power of news.* Chicago: University of Chicago Press.

Schuman, M. (2004, June 28). Mitsubishi's shame: A string of safety scandals has left a Japanese carmaker facing the scrap heap. *University of London Magazine.*

Schutz, A. (1970). *On phenomenology and social relations.* Chicago: University of Chicago Press.

Scott, H. (2003). Stranger danger: Explaining women's fear of crime. *Western Criminology Review*, 4 (3).

Selzer, M.L., & Payne, C.E. (1962). Automobile accidents, suicide and unconscious motivation. *Journal of Psychiatry*, 119: 237–240.

Selzer, M.L., Rogers, J.E., & Kern, S. (1968). Fatal accidents: The role of psychopathology, social stress, and acute disturbance. *American Journal of Psychiatry*, 124: 1028–1036.

Serafin, R. (1995, October 2). Ginzu campaigns. *Automotive News Insight*, 101, 111.

Sex Professionals of Canada [SPOC] (2006). Bad client list. Retrieved from http://www.spoc.ca/bad.html

Shankar, U. (2003). *Pedestrian roadway fatalities.* DOT HS809–456 Technical Report. Washington, D.C.: U.S. Department of Transportation.

Shearing, C. & Ericson, R.V. (1991). Culture as figurative action. *British Journal of Sociology*, 42: 481–506.

Shepherd, R.L. (1994). *New York plans for a numbered stamping system.* In Proceedings of the 64th Annual Meeting of the National Tobacco Tax Association. Chicago: Federation of Tax Administrators.

Simons, P. (2007, March 10). Meter ticking on parking costs. *Edmonton Journal.*

Skolnick, J. (1982). Deception by the police. *Criminal Justice Ethics*, 1: 40–54.

Slagle, J. (2006, July 30). Border narcotics smuggling, stolen vehicles, illegal aliens and politics. Retrieved from http://www.newswithviews.com

Smart, R.G., Butters, J., Mann, R.E. (2004), Alcohol, drug use and psychiatric problems among frequent road ragers. *The International Council on Addiction, Drugs and Traffic Safety Reporter.*

Smart, R.G., & Mann, R. (2002, October). Deaths and injuries from road rage: Cases in Canadian newspapers. *Canadian Medical Association Journal*, 167 (7): 761–762.

Smart, R., Mann, R.E., Zhao, J., & Stoduto, G. (2005). Is road rage increasing? Results of a repeated survey. *Journal of Safety Research*, 36 (2): 195–201.

Smith, M.J. (2005, March). *Robbery of taxi drivers.* Report submitted to the Office of Community Oriented Policing Services (COPS). Washington, D.C.: U.S. Department of Justice.

Solomon, L. (2007, March 1). Supreme Court cuts to the chase. *Tennessee Journalist*, University of Tennessee.

Sommer, R. (1969). *Personal space: The behavioral basis of design.* Englewood Cliffs, N.J.: Prentice Hall.

Song, V. (2006, September 1). Siege ties up city core: ETF fire tear gas into cab, subdue suspect after bomb scare over alleged unpaid fare. *Toronto Sun.*

Stancu, I. (2005, August 10). An "unbelievable" loss: Families try to cope with gun slayings of two young men. *Toronto Star.*

Standard & Poor's Rating Services (2000). *The auto theft industry: The cost to Canadians.* A report prepared for the Insurance Bureau of Canada.

Stanzler, J.J. (2003, December 29). Bad faith insurance litigation coverage disputes and the public nature of insurance; Understanding the recovery tools available to policyholders. Retrieved from http://www.inscobadfaith.net

State Farm Insurance (undated). Auto theft has new faces, but old crime still trouble. Retrieved from http://www.statefarm.com/about/media/backgrounder/theft.asp

Statistics Canada (2007, July 18). Crime statistics. *The Daily.*

Statistics Canada (2007, February 16). Study: Criminal victimization in the workplace. *The Daily.*

Statistics Canada (2006, October 2). Violence against women: Statistical trends. *The Daily.*

Statistics Canada (2006, July 20). Crime statistics. *The Daily.*

Statistics Canada (2006). Rate of violent crimes in Canada by provinces, 1976–2004.
Statistics Canada (2005). Exploring the involvement of organized crime in motor vehicle theft.
Statistics Canada (2004). Motor vehicle crimes.
Statistics Canada (2004). Revised uniform crime reporting survey.
Statistics Canada (2003a, March). Crime statistics.
Statistics Canada (2003b, December 18). Crime comparisons between Canada and the United States. *The Daily*.
Statistics Canada (2003c). The people: Break up.
Statistics Canada (2001, December 18). Crime comparisons between Canada and the United States. *The Daily*.
Statistics Canada (2000, July 18). Crime statistics, 1999. *The Daily*.
Sternheimer, K. (2007, February 28). "Killer" video games do not produce killer kids. *ASA News*.
Stewart, W. (2005, December 10). Unchecked moose hunt concerns Mi'kmaq. *Cape Breton Post*.
Stillwell, N. (2004, March 12). *Canadian murder hotspots*. Discovery Channel.
Strobel, L.P. (1980). *Reckless homicide? Ford's Pinto trial*. South Bend, ID: And Books.
Su, H.T. (2002, November 12). *Liquor license density and domestic violence in Baltimore County, Maryland*. The 130 Meeting of the American Public Health Association.
Suicide Prevention Center (2003). Canadian statistics: Causes of death 2003(1).
Surette, R. (1994, July). Media, violence, youth and society. *Crime, Media, Culture,* Volume 9.
Surface Transportation Policy Project (2003). Improving traffic safety. Policy and Practice #10. Washington, D.C.
Sutherland, E.H. (1949). *White collar crime*. New York: Dryden Press.
Thompson, J. (2005). Police pursuits: Are no-pursuit policies the answer? Presented at Criminal Justice Institute, School of Law Enforcement Supervision, Bentonville, Arkansas.
Times News On Line (undated). Trucking firm facing heavy fines. Retrieved from http://www.carteretnewstimes.com
Toronto Police Service (2005, January 12). Assault of parking enforcement officer. News release.
Toronto Police Service (2000). 2000 environmental scan. Report.
Tsunenari, S., Kanda, M., Yonemitsu, K. & Yoshida, S. (1985). Suicidal carbon monoxide inhalation of exhaust fumes. *American Journal of Forensic Medicine and Pathology,* 6 (3): 233–239.
U.S. Bureau of Alcohol, Tobacco, Firearms and Explosives [ATF] (2004). *Explosive incident reports for bombing periods January 2003 to December 2003*. U.S. Bomb Data Center.
U.S. Bureau of Alcohol, Tobacco, Firearms and Explosives [ATF] & Federal Bureau of Investigation (2004). *Arson and explosives intelligence databases: Audit report*.
U.S. Department of Health and Human Services (undated). One in four children exposed to family alcohol abuse or alcoholism. *NIH News*.
U.S. Department of Justice (2007, September). *Crime in the United States*. Washington, D.C.: Federal Bureau of Investigation.
U.S. Department of Justice (2006). *Crime characteristics*. Washington, D.C.: Bureau of Justice Statistics.
U.S. Department of Justice (2006). *Criminal victimization in the United States, 2005*. Washington, D.C.: Bureau of Justice Statistics.
U.S. Department of Justice (2006, September 18). *FBI releases its 2005 crime statistics: Crime in the United States*. Washington, D.C.: Bureau of Justice Statistics.
U.S. Department of Justice (2006). *United States preliminary semiannual uniform crime report, January through June*. Criminal Information Services Division. Retrieved from http://www.fbi.gov/ucr/prelim06/table3.htm

U.S. Department of Justice, Federal Bureau of Investigation (2005). *Motor vehicle theft: Crime in the U.S. 2005.* Washington, D.C.: Government Printing Office.

U.S. Department of Justice (2004). Law enforcement officers killed and assaulted. Retrieved from http://www.fbi.gov/ucr/killed/2004/section2.htm

U.S. Department of Justice (1999, March 7). Carjacking in the United States, 1992–96. News release.

U.S. Department of Justice (1997). *National crime victimization survey.* Washington, D.C.: Bureau of Statistics.

U.S. Department of Justice, Federal Bureau of Investigation (1989). *White collar crime: A report to the public.* Washington, D.C.: Government Printing Office.

U.S. Department of Labor (2007). *National census of fatal occupational injuries in 2006.* Washington, D.C.: Bureau of Labor Statistics.

U.S. Department of Labor (2000). *Risk factors and protective measures for taxi and livery drivers.* Washington, D.C.: OSHA.

U.S. Government Accountability Office (2005, May 5). *Combating alien smuggling: Opportunities exist to improve the federal response.* Report to the Chairman, Subcommittee on Immigration, Border Security and Claims.

U.S. Office of Juvenile Justice and Delinquency Prevention (1999, November). Reporting crimes against juveniles. *Juvenile Justice Bulletin.*

U.S. Senate Committee on Banking, Housing and Urban Affairs (2003 October 4). Eleventh report.

Valero, R., Sawyer, G., & Schiraldi, G. (2000, Summer). Violence and post traumatic stress disorder in a sample of inner city street prostitutes. *American Journal of Health Studies.*

Valiquet, D. (2006, July 4). Bill C-19: An act to amend the criminal code (street racing) and to make a consequential amendment to the *Corrections and Conditional Release Act.* Canada Law and Government Division.

Van Blaricom, C. (1998). He flees—To pursue or not to pursue: That is the question. *Police,* 22 (11): 11.

Verhoek-Oftedahl, W., Pearlman, D.N., & Babcock, J.C. (2000). Improving surveillance of intimate partner violence by use of multiple data sources. *American Journal of Preventative Medicine,* 19: 308–315.

Vertanian, D. (2006). Hit and run pedestrian crashes on the increase. Michigan: Office of Highway Safety Planning.

Victorian Community Council against Violence (1999). *Aggression and/or violence associated with motor vehicle use.* Melbourne, Australia: Victorian Community Council against Violence.

Violence Policy Center (2007). Drive-by America. Washington D.C.: Violence Policy Center.

Violence Policy Center (2002a). When men murder women. Washington, D.C.: Violence Policy Center.

Violence Policy Center (2002b). American roulette: Murder-suicide in the United States. Washington, D.C.: Violence Policy Center.

Voas, R.B. (1971, Fall). Vehicle violence: An American tragedy. *MRI Quarterly*: 4–11.

Voehl, F. (2000, August 10). Deja vu at Firestone; Deming electronic network. *Washington Post.* Retrieved from http://www.baldrigeplus.com/firestone.html

Wagner, D. (2003, June 20). Bishop's car yields human tissue. *Arizona Republic.*

Wakefield, Rebecca (1998, February 8). Most vehicle break-ins are rental cars. *Naples News.*

Warr, M. (2000). Fear of crime in the United States: Avenues for research and policies. *Criminal Justice,* 4: 453–489.

Wasserman, D., Cheng, Q., & Jiang, G. (2005, June 4). Global suicide rates among young people aged 15–19. *World Psychiatry,* (2): 114.

Weber, B. (2003, October 9). Edmonton police growing more cautious as suspects aim vehicles at them. *CNNEWS*.

Weber, M. (1947). *The theory of social and economic organization.* New York: Oxford University Press.

Weissman, M.M., Bland, R.C., Canino, G.J., Greenwald, S., Hwu, H.G., Karam, E.G., et al. (1995). Drinking, problem drinking and life stressors in the elderly general population. *Journal of Studies on Alcohol,* 56: 67–73.

Welte, J.W. and Mirand, A.L. (1995) Drinking, problem drinking and life stressors in the elderly general population. *Journal of Studies on Alcohol,* 56, 67–73.

White, J. (2005). State farm and punitive damages: Call the jury back. *JHTL,* 5 (1), Lambert Tort Law Conference Symposium.

White, J. (1999, July 26). Ford offers settlement to block lawsuits over Michigan plant explosion. *World Socialist.*

Wilson, J.Q., & Hermstein, R.J. (1985). *Crime and human nature.* New York: Simon and Shuster.

WNBC News (2006, September 6). Editorial.

Wolfgang, M., & Ferracuti, F. (1967). *The subculture of violence: Towards an integrated theory in criminology.* London: Tavistock.

Worker's Health and Safety Centre (1997). *Health and safety training solutions that fit: ATU workplace violence.* Participant's Manual. Toronto.

WorldNet Daily Exclusive (2006, September 10). More illegal aliens tried in gang rapes. Retrieved from http://www.worldnetdaily.com

World Tribune (2005, February 3). New non-lethal weapon lets troops dispel hostile crowds.

Yablonsky, L. (1962). *The violent gang.* Toronto: Macmillan.

Zickefoose, S. (2005). Carjackers dump handicapped driver. *Edmonton Journal.*

Zimbardo, P.G., (1969). The human choice: Individuation, reason, and order versus deindividuation, impulse, and chaos. *Nebraska Symposium on Motivation,* 17: 237–307.

Zimring, F. (2003). *The contradictions of American capital punishment.* New York: Oxford University Press.

INDEX

men. *See* gender
mental illness
    and accident reports, 206
    children, 24, 25, 182–83
    family breakup, 25
    family violence, 24
    motivating violence, 173
    serial killers, 204
    suicide, 180, 182–83
Midnight Club: Street Racing, 41
military, 52, 67–71
militia, 42, 189–90
mini-vans, 37, 82
minority groups 92, 99–100, 147. *See also*
    ethnicity; First Nations; immigrants
Mitsubishi Motors, 54, 163
modified vehicles, 41, 42, 44, 163
Montreal, 144, 160, 162, 164, 187
motorcycles
    competition with other vehicles, 43
    drive-by shootings, 163–64
    drug abuse, 30
    gangs, 30, 91, 162, 163–64, 187, 192
    image, 12
    pocket, 48
    racing, 18, 19
    theft of, 91
    See also gangs
movies
    marketing of vehicles, 89
    street racing, 20, 21
    suicide, 176
    vehicular violence, 39–40, 207
    See also individual movie titles
moving-vehicle vandalism, 14–15
music. *See* hip hop music; rap music

names, vehicle, 13
narcotics. *See* drug abuse
NASCAR racing, 18
National Committee to Reduce Auto
    Theft, 83
National Highway Traffic Safety
    Administration
    hit and runs, 152
    odometer fraud, 56
    overpass vandalism, 15
    police pursuits, 143, 144
    street racing, 20, 21
    substance abuse, 26–27
National Hot Rod Association, 20
National Institute for Health Care
    Research, 25
National Insurance Crime Bureau, 88

National Safe Kids, 34
nature, dominance over, 5. *See also*
    animals; hunting
Nazis, 52, 68–70
news, 36–37, 39, 42–43, 49
NHTSA. *See* National Highway Traffic
    Safety Administration
Nova Scotia, 48, 136

occupational violence. *See* workplace
odometer fraud, 55–56
Office of Juvenile Justice and
    Delinquency Prevention, 24
oil companies. *See* fuels
Ontario, 102, 144. *See also* Toronto
organized crime, 192–193. *See also* gangs
Outlaws, 163, 192, 193
overpasses, 15

parking
    and bombs, 189
    disputes causing road rage, 113, 119,
      124, 125
    drive-by shootings, 159
    enforcement, 112–14
    illegal, resulting in police pursuits, 141
    See also parking garages and lots
parking garages and lots
    carjackings, 166
    characteristics of, 15–18
    design, 17
    sexual assault, 132, 135
    stress, 17–18
    theft of vehicle contents, 90–91
    torchings, 93
    truck stops, 109
    See also parking
partners, 201, 202
parts, 50–54, 88–91
pedestrians
    children, 34
    in collisions, 34
    competition with vehicles, 33, 43
    hit and runs, 152, 154
    homicide, 198
    suicide, 183–184
    tweaking drug users, 30
personal space, 14, 32
pets, 155
pickup trucks
    advertising, 12, 36–37
    serial killers, 204
    sexual assault, 134, 139
    theft rate, 82